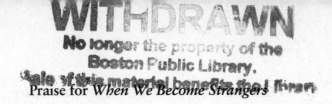
Praise for *When We Become Strangers*

'I loved this book. An invaluable roadmap for envisioning a new society that builds connection back into community. It calls us to slow down, to rethink the frenzied pace, and reignite the power of the human spirit.' **Aimee Davies, Author of** *Imperfect*

'Maggie has again, done what she does best, placed a microscope over modern society and looked closely at who, what and how we are. Her wisdom, research and interviews uncover the complex realities of life in the 2020s. But rather than being a tale of despair, Maggie's reflections and myriad strategies create a vision of hope.' *When We Become Strangers* is a book every person should read.' **Andrew Lines, Creator/Director, The Rite Journey.**

'*When We Become Strangers* encapsulates the workings of our modern world. It's an intuitive read, examining issues of our time, consumerism, loneliness, social media fixation, greed and the rule of technology on our kids. It prompts the reader to behold the future with eyes wide open, enjoying a sense of wisdom and faith.' **Lisa Friedlander, Sales and Leadership Coach**

Praise for *What Men Don't Talk About*

'Hamilton achieves what she sets out to achieve – to give men a voice.' *Sunday Telegraph*

'This book is one every parent of boys should read. It's a no-nonsense astute book about boys and men.' *New Idea*, **New Zealand**

'It's amazing, when you talk about men, I felt you were talking just to me.' **Peter**

'Not a day goes past that I don't think of some aspect of your book.' **Sue**

'[Your book] is full of insight, it's encouraging, it's really very valuable. Thank you on behalf of us blokes.' **Simon**

'I wish this book had been written 20 years ago. It would have saved a lot of misunderstandings and heartache. The best book I have ever read.' **Linda**

Praise for *What's Happening to Our Girls?*

'I found myself so engrossed that for two days running I nearly missed my tram stop ... A definite must-read for parents with daughters, for teachers and for other people dealing with girls. In fact, everyone should read this book.' **Australian Bookseller and Publisher**

'A crucial tool for greater understanding.' *Sunday Mail*

'*What's Happening to Our Girls?* moves parenting into the twenty-first century by highlighting the power of outside forces in shaping the personalities, morality and ultimate wellbeing of our daughters ... This work is a must-read for both parents and young adults attempting to understand and bridge the generation gap.' **Bill O'Hehir, senior psychologist**

'Having worked with men and boys for twenty years, I was amazed, fascinated and quite horrified to read such a succinct and well-documented account of all the issues facing girls today.' **Dr Arne Rubinstein (MBBS, FRACGP) CEO, Pathways Foundation**

'I found this book to be very interesting ... [it] helped me to understand why girls like myself are behaving the way they are ... Thank you.' **Amanda, teenager**

'Just wanted to say thank you. Thank you for raising the awareness level of (in particular) parents and caregivers about what is going on in their children's world.' **Moira, mother of two teenage girls**

'As a grandmother of two small girls, I have found your book on girls invaluable.' **Marianne, grandmother of two young girls**

Praise for *What's Happening to Our Boys?*

'*What's Happening to Our Boys?* is a must-read book for all parents with boys. Full of great ideas and practical solutions.' **Warwick Marsh, Dads4Kids Fatherhood Foundation**

'It's impossible to argue with this author's pungent advice.' *Australian Women's Weekly*

'In an immensely readable way, she [Maggie] provides practical tips for parents on many of the big issues facing adolescent boys – drugs, drinking, sexualisation, bullying and more.' **Barbara Biggins OAM, Australian Council on Children and the Media**

'This book will open the eyes of parents and other adults. In addition to the bad and the ugly, it provides a lot of very good ideas on how to raise well-adjusted and resilient boys and young men.' **Gary Bryant, Executive Officer, Men's Advisory Network**

'Thank you, Maggie, for exposing the undercurrent in our society that is playing havoc with not only our children's wellbeing but also our own.' **Rick Wilson, Vice President, NSW Parents' Council**

'Maggie Hamilton's book, *What's Happening to Our Boys?*, is informative and readable. Perhaps most importantly, this book takes a positive view of boys: it sets out to build on what is good about being a boy and to strengthen that side. It also looks at the pitfalls facing boys in today's world.' **Professor John J. Macdonald, Foundation Chair in Primary Health Care, Co-Director Men's Health Information and Resource Centre, Western Sydney University**

When We
Become Strangers

When We Become Strangers

HOW LONELINESS LEAKS
INTO OUR LIVES,
AND WHAT WE CAN
DO ABOUT IT

Maggie Hamilton

murdoch books

Sydney | London

Published in 2021 by Murdoch Books, an imprint of Allen & Unwin

Murdoch Books Australia
83 Alexander Street, Crows Nest NSW 2065
Phone: +61 (0)2 8425 0100
murdochbooks.com.au
info@murdochbooks.com.au

Murdoch Books UK
Ormond House, 26–27 Boswell Street, London WC1N 3JZ
Phone: +44 (0) 20 8785 5995
murdochbooks.co.uk
info@murdochbooks.co.uk

 A catalogue record for this
book is available from the
National Library of Australia

A catalogue record for this book is available from the National Library of Australia
A catalogue record for this book is available from the British Library

ISBN 9 781 92235 119 7 Australia
ISBN 9 781 91166 806 0 UK

Cover design by Josh Durham
Text design by Josh Durham

Typeset by Midland Typesetters
Printed and bound in Australia by Griffin Press

Every reasonable effort has been made to trace the owners of copyright materials
in this book, but in some instances this has proven impossible. The author(s)
and publisher will be glad to receive information leading to more complete
acknowledgements in subsequent printings of the book and in the meantime extend
their apologies for any omissions.

10 9 8 7 6 5 4 3 2 1

 MIX
Paper from
responsible sources
FSC   FSC® C009448
www.fsc.org

The paper in this book is FSC® certified.
FSC® promotes environmentally responsible,
socially beneficial and economically viable
management of the world's forests.

Contents

Introduction   1

1. Our Brave New World   9

2. iGen Kids   17
   Why This Generation Is Different   18
   Starved of Touch   20
   Mustn't Get Messy!   23
   The Importance of Stories   26
   Effective Ways to Engage with iGen   28

3. Parenting Right Now   31
   Raising the Next Generation   32
   The Rise in Maternal Depression   40
   The Pitfalls of 'Sharenting'   44
   Looking After Yourself as a Parent   52

4. Hyper-connectivity   53
   How Connected Are We?   54
   Why 'Likes' and Speed Matter   60
   Dipping in the Popularity Stakes?   67
   Reclaiming Precious Time Lost on Devices   77

5. Looking for Love   **79**
   Why the Love Stakes Are Higher Now   80
   Instant Attraction   89
   Everyone Lies a Little   97
   How to Avoid Dating Disasters   104

6. When Love and Reality TV Collide   **107**
   Train-wreck TV   108
   The Impact on Viewers   115
   Is it Time for a Reality TV Detox?   125

7. Home Alone   **127**
   Living Alone   128
   Ordering In   129
   Binge-watching   132
   Powerful Ways Back to Connection   138

8. A Curated Life   **141**
   Who Gets to Choose?   142
   When Perfect Is too Perfect   148
   Reclaim Your Unique Self   153

9. Narcissism Rules   **155**
   And Now, Back to Me   156
   Living in a Narcissistic World   165
   How to Handle Narcissism   168

10. The Empathy Deficit   **169**
    Doesn't Anyone Care Anymore?   170
    I Feel Your Pain   175
    Invite More Empathy into Your Life   178

11. Brain Fatigue   **179**
    Who's Messing with Our Brains?   180
    What's Happened to Our Memories?   183
    Time for a Brain Reset?   191

12. Working Life Doesn't Appear to Be Working   193
    Why Is Everyone so Stressed?   194
    Vocation Frustration   202
    Lost in Self-absorption and Spin   208
    Workplace Solutions   214

13. Understanding Our Current Work Ethos   217
    The MBA Workplace   218
    When Greed Became Good   230
    Generosity Mindset   244
    Humanising the Workplace   245

14. Workspace Challenges   247
    Time to Be More Open   248
    Working from Home   255
    Hot-desking   260
    Lonely at Work   266

15. Opportunities for More Benign Design   275
    Connecting with Nature   276
    Socially Led Design   279

16. Transforming Our Cities   285
    Changing Cityscapes   286
    What Do Hipsters Have to Offer?   297

17. Belonging   307
    What it Takes to Belong   308
    Finding Our Way Back   317

18. A Vision for the Future   323

References   334

Appreciation   336

For wild nature,
which never fails to feed the soul,
and for all those who work tirelessly
to draw others into the quiet joy
that comes with genuine belonging

Introduction

There's a lot of talk in the media and in our own conversations about our growing sense of disconnection. We hear accounts of incidents that annoy or trouble us, and more so since COVID-19. But what does estrangement look like right now? What is the impact of the constant, rapid changes in technology? How are we meant to cope with the intensifying sense of isolation felt in our communities and workplaces as we come to terms with our new normal? What do we do with our desperation at the worsening plight of the environment? And who doesn't feel a little overwhelmed living in a world that feels as though it's perpetually in crisis? *When We Become Strangers* offers an intimate window into how and where we're coming adrift, and what you and I can do about it.

Few would doubt that we're in the middle of a seismic shift – more so since the pandemic. We sense it in our homes and families, in our neighbourhoods and beyond. In spite of the glittering choices presented to us over decades, there's an underlying sense of unease. Life is increasingly less stable. Our relationships, even close relationships, are more competitive, more transactional and more mediated, and our workplaces are ever more inhospitable.

While we are facing huge challenges, we're not alone in this. Our forebears had their struggles, too. Living during the bubonic plague or a world war must have felt impossible. And yet, each challenge offers the possibility of new ways of coping and relating, of embracing the best of what is before us. However, unless we're clear about where we're vulnerable, it's hard to step confidently into the future. History doesn't serve those well who bury their heads in the sand. It's essential that we question where we are. When we stop questioning, we lose momentum. We fail to find new ways forward. We stagnate.

One of our biggest challenges in finding a path out of the fog is to deal with our distraction, so we can see where this constant need to be connected is taking us. If we hope to turn things around, we need clear heads. That's the only way we can come up with effective solutions to the issues we face. The difficulty is that we're all so frantic right now – busily scrolling and skimming through mountains of details, reducing our capacity to comprehend information, let alone recall the salient points. Over three decades ago, the iconic American educator Neil Postman warned in his classic work, *Amusing Ourselves to Death*, that 'People will come to adore the technologies that undo their capacities to think.'[1] This is one of several uncomfortable realities that we now face.

The social fabric is fragile right now. Too many are feeling isolated from those around them. We've become strangers, exiled from people and situations that are meaningful to us. And, with the many pressures and expectations we face, increasingly we're becoming estranged from ourselves, leaving us wondering whether we're being led by our own impulses or persuaded into thinking this is who and how we should be.

There's nothing new about feelings of estrangement. Cycles of dislocation have occurred throughout history. Our current growing sense of dislocation has been intensifying for some decades now. And a body of research has been growing along with it. In the early nineties, renowned psychologist and social researcher Hugh Mackay talked of 'the last straw syndrome' in *Reinventing Australia*. This syndrome is a trend marked by a weariness with constant change and a loss of faith in government, banking and other institutions.[2] In his landmark work *Bowling Alone*, American political scientist Robert Putnam nailed our burgeoning sense of isolation. Touching on a range of areas from a decline in volunteering to changes in technology, Putnam charts this intensifying isolation, including 'individualising entertainment', thus making it possible for people to go bowling alone, instead of in groups as they had always done.[3]

London psychotherapist Dr Jay Watts sees our growing sense of isolation as due, in part, to a growing hard-edged individualism that's so focused on personal success, it has little regard for 'soft relationships' – those bedrock relationships we can rely on, which help nurture and bind us to each other, and which are increasingly being 'sacrificed to the god of efficiency and performance'.[4]

Our current sense of estrangement is a complex beast, sparking a range of emotions – from intense sadness to indifference or quiet rage. This feeling of being a stranger is not just a symptom of age, culture or colour, although it is more acute for those living on the fringes. Estrangement is something we all grapple with. In his book *Loneliness*, Professor John Cacioppo highlights how disconnected some of us have become, with an astonishing 25 per cent of people having no-one to confide in. Can you imagine that? No-one to share moments of doubt, frustration or unhappiness. No-one to help you through the fog of despair. Imagine the pain. And it's important to recognise that there is a tangible pain that comes with loneliness, and that social pain is real, activating the same area of the brain as physical pain.[5]

It's essential that we wake up to this deepening sense of dislocation, that we get clear about what this looks and feels like, because loneliness is contagious. One long-term study found that people were 52 per cent more likely to feel lonely if they had a direct connection to someone else who was lonely.[6] What's more, this sense of dislocation is growing. In less than two decades, the number of Americans admitting they don't have a single person to confide in has tripled.[7] Responding to British statistics around loneliness, the government appointed their first ever Minister for Loneliness.

Our brains, we are told, are wired for pleasure. So where, when we're feeling isolated, do we turn? As the lines between our real and virtual lives blur, it's getting harder for many to face the complexities of real life – to deal with one-on-one encounters, to make the effort to go out. And with the accessibility of gaming, Netflix and Uber Eats, there's even less incentive to leave home. Increasingly, we're turning to cyberspace for comfort, to seek out those of like mind. Glued to our devices, we trawl the net looking for love; for someone to tell us we're clever, daring or beautiful; for a kitchen makeover or wall art; for a summer coat or casual sex. In a recent e-bulletin, Los Angeles influencer agency Mediakix reported that four out of ten millennials believe their favourite online influencer 'understands them better than their real-life friends'.[8]

When we come adrift from the social fabric, we become strangers to each other and, just as critically, to ourselves, until we have no sense of who we are beyond our fraying connection to our world. For decades now, most of us have lived in relative affluence, and have become used to having our needs swiftly met. In our desire to gain as much of this largesse as we can, we've set about renovating our homes, buffing and botoxing our bodies, and losing ourselves in passive entertainment and shopping, only to see depression, anxiety and related disorders soar. Affluence hasn't served us well. We can't buy or talk our way out of loneliness and its resulting sense of despair.

Belonging isn't just about a sense of connection. It's about shared values and dreams, and about feeling useful and understood. To be understood we need to have others around us who are willing to listen closely and sympathetically. Belonging also requires a healthy dose of self-awareness. Yet where in these distracted times do we, and our children, go to be heard?

In a few short years, kids have become isolated, spending worrying amounts of time on devices and at home. Too often they lack one-on-one attention and touch, creative and spontaneous real-life play, and they have little or no connection with nature. Our children are also losing connection to their family and cultural stories, drowned out by wall-to-wall entertainment and endless mind-numbing details of the vacuous lives of celebrities, leaving them with little to hold onto.

Parents are also feeling the cruel pinch of isolation. Increasingly, stay-at-home mums struggle with their loneliness, sharing more and more of their children's lives online as a way of being heard and connecting with friends, until they're mining their lives to entertain others – their way of ensuring they haven't slipped from sight.

As we step into the Fourth Industrial Revolution, a world of artificial intelligence, biotechnology, robotics, nanotechnology and more, the very notion of what it means to be human is being challenged. In a climate obsessed with efficiency, and where financial considerations rule, one of our greatest challenges is how to preserve and enhance our humanity, amid a growing desire to hand over our lives to technology. As tech advances speed up, there's also a sense for many of no longer being in charge of the process, a fear of being left behind. The world can feel so big and complex, leaving those who are fragile feeling small to the point of insignificance. And the domination of mega tech corporations reinforces this feeling, along with creating a sense of powerlessness when it comes to issues of surveillance and privacy.

Several years ago I came across the work of Danish architect Jan Gehl, and was immediately struck by his work. Renowned for making cities people-friendly, Gehl stresses the importance of 'human scale' when designing buildings and cityscapes. The human scale is a measurable scale, where people feel comfortable – where all of us, young and old, can thrive. The many insights surrounding Gehl's human-scale approach lingered, reframing the way I observed our current way of life. I began to see how we've lost sight of human scale in so many aspects of our lives – how we've let go of those qualities that meaningfully connect us to each other, and that enhance our wellbeing. As I began to think about how to apply human scale in wider contexts, I started to see how powerfully relevant it is to numerous areas of life.

Part of Gehl's genius is that he's not trying to turn back the clock, so much as accommodate our very real human needs amid rapidly changing urban landscapes, with their towering edifices and ever-expanding populations. So, as we contemplate our biting sense of estrangement, where is the human scale to be found in our homes, workplaces and communities? This is a profoundly liberating question, and one that has the capacity to free us in all kinds of ways.

This book has been brewing for several years, and is a result of much time spent in chat rooms and delving into research on a variety of subjects, immersing myself in the news and social media, interviewing a wide range of people, and listening more closely to the conversations around me. Estrangement is such a big topic, it's impossible to comprehensively cover the whole subject. I've chosen to look at a range of issues – little snapshots – which I hope will help give you a better, more panoramic sense of our current landscape, and how we might best move forward.

As always, I try to bring an intimacy to my observations, threading the trends explored here with the voices of everyday people, along with those of experts, so we can each see how our lives mirror, or are in contrast with, the topics we explore together.

Dozens of voices and opinions are captured here from my own interviews, along with those gleaned from numerous chat rooms – Reddit, Quora, Ask MetaFilter and others. While occasional comments have been edited for clarity, or to correct typos and misspellings, every attempt has been made to preserve the original intention of that quote.

'Civilisation, the orderly world in which we live, is frail.
We are skating on thin ice.
There is a fear of a collective disaster.'
Sociologist Zygmunt Bauman[9]

1

Our Brave New World

On a chilly January morning in 2007, a violinist made his way to L'Enfant Plaza Metro station in Washington, D.C. to play a number of classical pieces during rush hour. In less than an hour, just over a thousand people hurried past. A handful stopped to listen for more than a minute. A few small children wanted to enjoy the music, but were nudged on by the adults with them. The violinist was internationally renowned Joshua Bell. No stranger to sell-out concerts, Bell was playing a Stradivarius worth in excess of US$3 million.[1]

Our growing inability to see what's in front of us – good, bad or indifferent – is played out in a thousand different ways every day on our streets, in our homes and workplaces, and while catching up with friends. Until COVID-19 we were all so ridiculously busy, and constantly plugged into our devices, that there was little time or space to be 'in the moment'. The pandemic has given us the opportunity for a reset. As we emerge from self-isolation we have the chance to do things differently, or to choose more of the same.

American photographer Eric Pickersgill recently attempted to capture the resulting sense of isolation that comes from our chronic distraction, when he shot a series of photos of people staring at their hands, as if their devices were invisible to everyone but themselves. His images of people staring at their empty palms are poignant and a little strange. The subjects have almost no awareness of those close to them, even when cuddled up in bed, sitting around the dinner table, or out and about with friends.[2]

The more estranged our society becomes, the more the personal skills that previous generations took for granted are slipping away. Experts report that we're losing our ability to strike up a conversation with a stranger, or even to flirt. This is happening at a time when increasing numbers of young people struggle to sustain an adult conversation and to be confident in face-to-face encounters, especially those laced with conflict, choosing to turn to the comfort of their phones instead. Yet, notes professor of sociology Sherry Turkle, 'conversation is the most human and humanizing thing that we do. It's where empathy is born, where intimacy is born – because of eye contact, because we can hear the tones of another person's voice, sense their body movements, sense their presence.'[3] When we communicate with others, we come to know and understand them, and also understand more of ourselves. Now, though, we're so busy and exhausted, it's often easier just to zone out.

Living in a Liquid World

Having pondered our growing restlessness, sociologist Zygmunt Bauman describes us as 'liquid moderns' – individuals who are 'forever at work, forever replacing quality of relationship with quantity – always panicking about being left behind' or becoming out of date. It's not easy to be a liquid modern, as there's little let-up. Driven by a relentless need to keep pushing forward, we're forever trading plans, relationships and careers, and freeing ourselves up from anything that feels remotely restrictive. Going about our lives like nomads or tourists, we rush through our days with little or no reflection. 'We must keep on the move,' observed journalist Stuart Jeffries after an interview with Bauman, 'reinventing ourselves if we are to triumph over our fears of becoming obsolete at work, friendless, unloved.'[4]

With almost every aspect of our lives shifting, some days it feels like we're trapped on a rapidly melting icefloe. And with so much momentum in our lives, what is there to hold onto? Who can we trust? As we struggle to get on with our post-pandemic lives, we do so against an all-too-familiar backdrop of war and threats of war, faltering economies, the mass migration of displaced peoples, and the inability of many leaders to deliver effective leadership, leaving us with little faith in the future. It's not just our surviving institutions and workplaces that have us worried. Everywhere we look, we see signs of fear and anxiety. Relationships, even close relationships, are struggling. Where does this climate of escalating impermanence leave us?

When Loneliness Bites

Those most vulnerable right now, it seems, are our young. In its *The Lonely Society?* report, Britain's Mental Health Foundation reported that loneliness is now more prevalent in those aged 18 to 34 than in those aged over 55.[5] Today's young people have good reason to be worried. Who wouldn't be anxious living in a highly competitive performance culture, while facing shaky work prospects and ever-worsening tales of environmental degradation? It's uncomfortable living in a society where the social fabric is coming apart at the seams. In the world's largest survey on loneliness, undertaken by BBC Four, two out of five 16- to 24-year-olds admitted to feeling lonely 'often' or 'very often', while less than 30 per cent of people aged 65 to 74 said they felt lonely.[6]

These findings may come as a surprise, until we look more closely at what's happening. You don't have to hang out for long in chat rooms before you see the length of the threads on loneliness, and just how desperate many feel. 'I'm very afraid of making friendships,' Sheree confesses. 'I'm forcing myself to go to a bowling night with my mom and her coworkers. Sometimes finding small activities works, going by yourself can seem nerve-racking.' Hamish tells of crying himself to sleep at night, believing he doesn't matter to anyone. 'I have no friends and my family relationships are practically nonexistent,' he confesses. 'We're all more like strangers who tolerate each other's presence than a family. Anyways, problem solved. When I wake up, I'll be too groggy to remember anything I was thinking about from before. Rinse and repeat until I find something else to occupy myself with.'

> **'We started realizing about 15 years ago that loneliness is actually a pretty serious risk for health problems. It's as serious of a risk as smoking, obesity or eating a high-fat diet with lack of exercise.'**
> Chris Segrin, head of University of Arizona Department of Communication[7]

One landmark study on loneliness included several hundred people aged 18 to 91. The University of Arizona study tested social skills, stress and loneliness, along with physical and mental health, finding a strong link between those with poor communication skills and those who felt more stressed and lonely. Good communication skills don't just help us in casual conversations. They assist us to be more assertive, to have the confidence to make an off-the-cuff comment that may lead to a lifelong friendship. Being able to connect helps us 'get' those around us, and to respond to them accordingly – to respect everyone's boundaries, including our own. Yet now, with communication often so impersonal, reaching out in real-life situations is harder. 'Everything is so condensed and parsed out in sound bites, and that's not the way that human beings for thousands of years have communicated,' reflects behavioural scientist Chris Segrin, who headed up the study. 'It makes young people more timid when they're face-to-face with others, and they're not sure what to say or what to do. There's no social interaction, and I fear that's really hurting young people.'[8]

Drowning Out the World

Many young people are retreating from the real world – a habit established early in childhood, since parents have become too busy to sit and listen, and to engage. Retreat becomes a habit, a way of life that follows young kids into adulthood. 'I have constant noise,' Sam explains, when asked about how he deals with loneliness. 'YouTube videos, Netflix, TV shows, music. I kind of don't like that it's what I subconsciously feel like doing (I didn't realise that I'd started doing it at first), but it's better than constant silence in the house.' Paulo, a graduate student who's lived alone for two years, admits to 'rarely' going out. 'I work most of the day on research and writing,' he explains. 'Then, if I have a free night (I do almost every night I don't take my work home with me), I draw, paint, practise music, read, listen to music, podcasts, or the news, or watch a critically acclaimed film. To be honest, I smoke too much weed though, to compensate for the dull ache of loneliness that hits at night.'

The hours hang heavily on too many of our young people, yet this snapshot of their lives is not seen in the endless galleries of smiling faces on social media. All we see there are the kind of people we're meant to be – the ideal selves we project onto the world. Still, with many more means of communication now, does it really matter if we're losing the ability to engage in casual conversations – to pass up the chance of a momentary exchange with someone about the weather, or the fact that our bus is late?

Too Busy Accumulating Stuff

Living in a world that offers so much choice, and the promise that we can have it all, has left us constantly on the go, and determined to grab as much as we can. We're constantly encouraged to buy more and do more, until we end up exhausted, and often in debt. Yet, as psychology professor Suniya Luthar points out, there's a mental price to affluence. We're seeing that American teens from upper-middle-class families are now up to two-and-a-half times more likely to suffer from anxiety and depression, and to be involved in substance abuse, than any other group of teens. Why is this? Partly because of the crushing pressure to achieve that these kids feel. When your sense of self is purely about accumulating the 'right' stuff and getting runs on the board, you can easily become fearful about 'making the grade'. These challenges tend to hit around age 13, when young teenagers start to think about who they are and where they're heading. And, with no-one helping them find a way out of their fears, these teens are taking their cues from peers and their parents, and self-medicating on drugs and alcohol.[9]

Age of Anger

The more we retreat from the real world – from connection and from a quiet belief in ourselves – the less we have to hang on to. It's then that the world starts to feel like a hostile place. With this growing sense of estrangement, we're seeing a rise in angry, out-of-control behaviour. After witnessing staff being verbally abused, punched or spat at, hospitals are now forced to employ increasing numbers of security guards, and to train staff in how to help defuse potentially explosive incidents. No-one should have to face such issues at work, but hundreds of thousands do. 'It is very disconcerting to have well-meaning people who dedicated their lives and their careers being put in harm's way by trying to help others,' admits Dr Tom Mihaljevic, who heads up the Cleveland Clinic.[10]

One 2017 Australian survey of over 6000 staff revealed that over 80 per cent of people working in retail and related industries have been abused by customers. One in four told of dealing with some form of verbal abuse every week. Over a third had been threatened in the last year, while 14 per cent had suffered some form of physical abuse. Participants told of being punched, spat on and sworn at, dragged over the counter and having food thrown at them.[11] We witnessed this abuse in supermarkets on the nightly news during the early days of the pandemic, seeing how much harder work had become for those on the frontline.

What's behind this growth in out-of-control anger that's being seen in our workplaces as well as in our homes? 'In my own clinical experience, anger is almost never a primary emotion in that even when anger seems like an instantaneous, knee-jerk reaction to provocation, there's always some other feeling that gave rise to it,' notes clinical psychologist Leon Seltzer. These feelings, experts tell, are often indicative of hurt, fear or helplessness. Basically, anger helps mask vulnerable emotions, allowing people to feel more in control.[12]

With more people getting antsy or worse, is this something to be concerned about? Global strategists suggest that it is. 'Emotionally, people are quite lonely. We're seeing in many societies a kind of breakdown of family, or connection with family . . . That can create all sorts of emotions of fear and frustration, and in some cases that frustration can get expressed as anger,' reflects John Scott, head of sustainability risk at Zurich Insurance Group. 'Individual psychological and emotional problems can become collective concerns when loneliness and frustration meet populist and identity politics – an emerging reality in what is becoming known as the "age of anger". According to the *Global Risks Report*, these trends may pose a significant threat to geopolitical stability.'[13] Given this growth in loneliness, fear, hurt and helplessness, where is it manifesting and what can we do about it?

2

iGen Kids

Why This Generation Is Different

Starved of Touch

Mustn't Get Messy!

The Importance of Stories

Effective Ways to Engage with iGen

WHY THIS GENERATION IS DIFFERENT

Born between 1995 and 2012, how are Generation Z (affectionately known as 'iGen') travelling? Their Generation X parents, whose own mothers were the first wave of women to enter the workforce since the Second World War, learned self-reliance early as latchkey kids. Growing up with political and economic uncertainty – the Cold War; the Enron, WorldCom and One.Tel disasters; stock market fluctuations and decreased job security – Gen X parents know the importance of saving, and have modest expectations for their lives, which they've passed on to their iGen kids.

Living in homes hit by the global financial crisis, the iGen have also watched their parents working hard to claw their way back, so they're more risk averse than millennials.[1] 'We differ from the Millennials on many levels,' tells iGen-er Stacey. 'For one, we grew up with technology advancing every day and with a smartphone which allows us to communicate, be more accepting, and increase our knowledge. On the not so bright side, we grew up with terrorism, school shootings, and a fear that it could happen to us. All those aspects played a role in how we are who we are today.'[2] This generation understands the importance of hard work, and are willing to put in the effort to get where they need to be. Stability is essential, too. Maturing more slowly, the iGen are not in as much of a rush to take their place in the world as millennials.

American professor of psychology Jean Twenge sums up the iGen as 'more tolerant, less happy – and completely unprepared for adulthood'.[3] Concerned with physical and emotional safety, this generation is less optimistic about their job prospects. They seek reassurance, whereas millennials tend to be in search of praise.[4] 'This generation is VERY smart,' insists Amie, when reflecting on her iGen daughter, 'hard-working, aware of what's going on in the wider world, ambitious, PRACTICAL, and demanding.'[5]

Happy to stay home and connect through their phones, iGen kids live in their bedrooms, leaving them less confident in face-to-face interactions. 'I have also noticed large numbers [of the iGen] utilizing our mental health facility,' tells Harvey, an American graduate teacher. 'While that is not bad, the high numbers are surprising and lead me to question why today's students feel so much more stress. That is a troubling trend.'[6] This observation isn't a total surprise since, as discussed, the iGen are reporting the highest levels of loneliness amongst all age groups, and we have yet to see how this will play out in adulthood.

Electronic Screen Syndrome

With devices now central to children's lives, what effect are they having? Psychiatrist Victoria Dunckley, an expert on the impact of screen time on the developing brain, tells of how many of the children she sees suffer from 'sensory overload, lack of restorative sleep, and a hyperaroused nervous system'.[7] This is a concern, as electronic screen media, she warns, is 'unnaturally intense'. Overstimulating a child's nervous system means it is hard for a child to calm down or enjoy a deep sleep.

Whenever a child uses their device, the 'rewards' of new information stimulate that child, and yet more dopamine is released. Huge waves of information follow, tiring the brain. At the same time, the blue light emitted from devices plays havoc with a child's body clock and stores of melatonin, further stressing the child. Blood flow then moves away from the parts of the brain responsible for a child's attention levels, creativity and social behaviour to the more primitive areas of the brain, making it hard for a child to concentrate and settle. If this pattern of overload continues, the child's brain literally shrinks.[8]

STARVED OF TOUCH

Even a brief snapshot of iGen kids suggests that childhood is experiencing its own seismic shifts. This is a generation growing up never knowing what it's like to live without devices, or without the adults in their lives constantly busy and distracted. As they watch others endlessly scrolling through their smartphones during meals, when out with friends or family, or while going for a walk, this becomes their template. Who is there with the time to listen to our young – to listen deeply to this new generation, to ensure they feel heard and understood? How can we create an *engaged* village of adults to support these young lives, when we're all so ridiculously busy?

'We have come to think of ourselves and our children more like machines than living creatures – keep the tank full, keep the body clean and shiny, rest it overnight, get it back to work in the morning,' suggests psychology professor Darcia Narvaez of the University of Notre Dame.[9] Yet we're not machines, we're individuals with very human needs. And, like animals, children need a warm caring nest, 'until 18 months of age or so, and so [kids] need to experience an "external womb" of calming, affectionate care in order to grow their body and brain systems properly, all of which influence their psychological and social and moral development,' Narvaez adds.

> 'Kids want to be hugged and touched, they don't want to be texted. There's a basic need to fill that social bond.'
> *Marc Brackett, director of Yale University's Center for Emotional Intelligence*[10]

Our stressed-out, constantly busy way of life is also poor soil for empathy to thrive in. And if children don't experience warmth and understanding, there's little reason for them to be empathetic – to read or respond well to the ever-changing emotional landscape they'll encounter at home and school, and later in relationships and at work. Where there's a lack of empathy, entitlement and narcissism creep in. To understand others, first a child needs to experience the joy and relief of being listened to and understood, then he or she is motivated to reach out to others.

Can I Have a Hug?

With all this distraction has come an increasing lack of touch – too many kids are missing out on abundant hugs and the joy of being held close. This is creating what developmental psychologist Tiffany Field calls 'paediatric pain symptoms', where little ones are suffering such symptoms as irritable bowel syndrome and fibromyalgia (widespread pain in the body and a heightened sensitivity to light, cold, heat or smell), conditions previously associated with adults. According to Field, the director of Miami's Touch Research Institute, this trend is due to children feeling stressed and lacking touch.[11]

Touch brings many gifts, helping lower a child's heart rate and blood pressure, and reduce stress. When a child is touched kindly, their feel-good neurotransmitter, serotonin, gets a boost, helping keep the doldrums at bay. Dopamine is also released, allowing a tiny burst of pleasure to flood their system. Spending time in Romania's notorious orphanages, Field saw the devastating impact on children who had received minimal interaction, noting how the kids no longer smiled, made eye contact or even talked. Mentally and physically stunted, these children behaved like those with 'severe autism' and this, Field concluded, was partly due to an absence of touch.[12]

In another piece of Field's research, instead of leaving premature babies in their incubators, a number of these babies were massaged for 15 minutes, three times daily. The result? The nervous system of the massaged babies matured faster than the babies left on their own. The massaged babies were also more responsive to their immediate environment and, while they didn't eat more than the other babies, they gained weight 47 per cent faster than the premature babies left alone in their incubators. 'The weight gain,' Field states, 'seems due to the effect of contact on their metabolism.'[13]

> '... if you want empathetic children – and an empathetic culture – touch and be touched.'
> *Maia Szalavitz,* Psychology Today[14]

If we want to help nurture this generation of kids, we need to put aside our smartphones and hold them close. Children are wired for the full range of sensory experiences, including the stimulation of 'a parent's voice, music, touch and eventually play', affirms parenting expert Denise Daniels,[15] and it's essential that all the senses are brought into play.

Get Those Fingers Working

Childhood is the best time for sensory exploration, but with kids now spending so much time on devices, their sensory experiences are minimal and their fine motor skills are taking a hit. Some children are starting school with fingers that aren't strong enough to hold a pencil. The muscles in a child's wrists, hands and fingers, and in their feet and toes, need to be put to work if that child is to button their cardigan, tie their shoelaces, or use cutlery and scissors.

Starved of sensation, too many of our kids spend their early years in rooms full of plastic games and soft toys, missing out on the joy, adventure and excitement of a world of touch, and the delight that differing textures bring. Our children need more arts and crafts play at home, and messy play inside or outside. They need a healthy dose of playdough and puzzles, practice using small scissors, playing with building blocks, and getting outside to play in the mud, water and sand, if they are to thrive.

MUSTN'T GET MESSY!

Influenced by relentlessly powerful marketing campaigns, many iGen parents are keen for their kids to appear 'cool' at all times. Dressing their kids in trendy clothes, parents are then reluctant to see these clothes get messy or dirty.[16] COVID-19 aside, there's also the worry amongst many parents about germs, even though experts stress the importance of germs and a bit of dirt, in helping keep allergies and asthma at bay.[17] We now know that messy play also helps children be more creative. Then, as they grow, children can harness this creativity to think up new ideas and approaches to issues they're facing, and to better handle difficult people and situations.

Experts tell of how working with different unrelated materials and textures, and experimenting with stray objects found at home or out in nature, helps bring kids' senses to life. It's also a great opportunity for them to learn about shared play, and how to get on with other children. Losing themselves in sand and mud and puddles, kids get to immerse themselves in a host of sensory experiences. It's the difference between a child going to the beach and spending happy hours playing in the sand and waves, and sitting at home staring at a beach scene on their computer.

The more we engage with the world through our senses, the richer life is. In a recent exchange with Melinda Tankard Reist, Australia's tireless campaigner against the sexualisation of young people, Reist recalled her own childhood in the country, where she was constantly outdoors. 'I wonder,' she reflected, 'if some of our kids aren't drawn into risky sexual and other behaviours, because they've never experienced sensory richness as a child.'

It's a comment I've pondered often. It seems particularly pertinent, given the amount of time kids now spend in their rooms and, increasingly, using devices as their go-to for comfort. Yet, experts insist, children need a solid emotional connection to others to thrive – to help them understand and deal with their own emotions, read the emotions of others, and know how best to respond. When kids fail to get what they need from their family, their attention is funnelled into spaces that are always and instantly available. That's when children tumble into sitcoms, gaming and social media to fill the gap. Later, when they flee the family nest, they feel isolated and unsure of themselves as they struggle to forge strong connections with others in the real world.

Nature Nurture

Time out in nature, even a short amount of time, also feeds a child's senses. In his groundbreaking book *Last Child in the Woods* child advocacy expert Richard Louv talks of our growing 'nature-deficit disorder', where few children have any real connection with the outdoors. With more than half of the planet now living in cities, ready access to nature can be tricky. Yet it's well worth making the effort. One recent UK study found that adult prisoners spent more time outside than the average British child. Perhaps the most disturbing finding was that one in five of these children *never* played outside.[18]

The less time a child spends in nature, the more they come to fear it, and be terrified of insects and other creatures. In earlier research I undertook, I was stunned at how knowledgeable children as young as seven were about brands and the lives of celebrities.[19] Yet how many seven-year-olds know or care as much about plants and trees? Our connection to nature is first formed by our family and our own childhood experiences in nature, helping us to get to know and appreciate different natural environments. Aside from the opportunity for physical exercise, the natural world helps settle a child's emotions and clear their head, helping them learn.

Nature Enhances Learning

Over four years, Britain's Natural Connections Project promoted outdoor learning in an effort to demonstrate how much nature helps kids learn. One child reported, 'You kind of tend to work better outside because you are more relaxed . . . you are not stuck in the same place, you are able to move around, you are able to experience different things using your senses.' The teachers involved in this project were equally impressed. 'Every single subject in the curriculum has been delivered outside,' one assistant head told. 'The benefits are massive in terms of student motivation, student behaviour and teacher motivation.'[20]

> 'You do not have to swim with dolphins, a short walk outside will do. Insects, worms, soil, leaves, bark, stones all serve as an interest for children.'
> *Judy*[21]

It's curious that our children know the planet is facing huge environmental issues – we're quick to teach them about that. Yet most know little of the joy of being in nature – of exploring and discovering, and being inspired. Too many spend their days inside, glued to their devices, which often contributes to weight, sight and breathing issues, and other health problems.[22] Time in nature provides kids with plenty of adventure, helping them build confidence, self-esteem and useful life skills.[23] There are also the added benefits of helping reduce anxiety and anger, while sharpening their attention, and feeding the child's spirit.[24] When children learn to embrace the natural world around them, they enjoy an intimate sense of belonging to the web of life, and all the inspiration and reassurance that brings.

THE IMPORTANCE OF STORIES

Stories matter, too. So much of a family's story is often held in a handful of old buttons, a chair or old china, in forgotten books and letters, or in a battered shoebox of postcards, medals or photos. Family stories help kids work out who they are and where they've come from. They speak to a child's innate worries and dreams. But today's kids are facing a loss of their family story, with many objects that hold keys to the past disappearing from the home. As life becomes ever more uncertain, parents turn their attention inwards, to renovating their nest – ditching all the possessions that no longer 'fit' the neatly packaged lives they aspire to. Precious items, which have been in families for decades, are sent off to second-hand stores or are sold in garage sales, or end up as landfill, making the threads of a family's past much harder to access.

With breakthroughs in neuroscience and psychology, we're beginning to see how much we process the world around us through the stories we tell of ourselves and others. It's not that story has ceased to exist. There are plenty of new stories emerging. Sadly, most are stories of celebrities, laced with mind-numbing details of their self-indulgent lives. All this is a world away from previous generations, who grew up immersed in the stories of the Great Depression and two world wars – stories that told of how sometimes we have to dig deep, to sacrifice more than we dare imagine, and how hope against all odds can win out. It's interesting that during the pandemic, so many people took comfort from the stories of grandparents and great grandparents, who had found their way through stretching times.

The stories kids identify with shape their lives in unexpected ways, giving meaning to the present and helping shape the future. Freud stated that we're never free until we know our own story. So what of our current stories? While we live in a time of relative plenty, hope is in short supply. It's not just the tales of the empty lives of celebrities that are cause for concern, so too is the explosion of violent apocalyptic tales found in young adult books, movies and video games, offering this new generation little hope or life wisdom. Stories underpin and nurture a child's imagination and sense of self. And the stories we, as a society, tell are the stories our children become. What impact is this crop of stories likely to have on our children?

The need for kids to connect with their backstory is all the more important for the children of First Nation and migrant peoples. It's a richer world when we encourage these stories to be told, when we value such stories and use them to help us understand, be saddened and/or inspired by those whose life experiences are similar or very different from our own. We need also to be brave enough to tell the stories we'd prefer to keep silent about. Germany is a great exemplar in this regard, with reminders in its towns and cities of what took place in the

Holocaust. Story is powerful and has the capacity to convey so much – to inspire and to caution us about the past, and to offer a sense of what we've emerged from as we step into the future. Stories also connect us powerfully to each other, sometimes in unexpected ways. They help us see the bigger picture, and teach us that we're not alone. When kids understand their backstory, they hold a more realistic, nuanced sense of what life offers – the good moments and those that challenge – along with powerful cues as to how best to move forward. What better way to step into the future?

Effective Ways to Engage with iGen

As the future beckons, it promises lots of change. With all the distraction and overstimulation that devices bring, neuroscientist Maryanne Wolf is concerned children are not building up useful 'reservoirs of knowledge' they can draw on in coming years.[25] Thinking, reflection and creativity are essential life skills but, she and other experts warn, these skills are under threat, so here are some ways through.

First up, don't let iGen's legendary independence fool you. iGen kids still need strong, focused adults to help them become highly skilled, face-to-face communicators – and to be resilient, practical, creative and flexible individuals. The activities below will assist in creating experiences that are richly layered, helping iGen kids build a life of shared talk and experiences, of creativity and community. The more iGen kids communicate, learning to listen as well as to express themselves, and the more time they spend in real life, the more able they will be to navigate difficult people and tricky situations, and to make the best use of life's easy and more challenging choices.

- **Take a Fresh Look at Your 'Village'**
  What does your immediate 'village' look like? Are your kids exposed to a mix of differing people and ages, or do you need to work on this? Take time to explain the characteristics of each individual in your group, and the specific needs this person has to make them feel comfortable. These cues help kids understand that everyone has their own way of being in the world, and the importance of accommodating others alongside their own needs.

- **Build Strong Social Skills**
  iGen kids need help to develop strong emotional intelligence – to 'read' how others are feeling, and to respond in a way that's helpful. Prepare them on how best to handle new people they're about to meet. If there's a visitor, encourage them to do something to welcome that guest. Assist them in getting to know your neighbours and local shopkeepers, and teach them to greet these and other individuals in your 'village' whenever they meet. These steps help develop the skills your kids need to build their own community as adults.

- **Work Actively on Hospitality Skills**
  When you have guests over for a meal, weave your kids into the preparations by getting them to bake a cake or put up lights – something they can be proud of – along with more routine chores. Brief them to look after a couple of guests, and establish a range of activities they can do with guests their own age. Encourage them to help offer food around, as it's a brilliant icebreaker. Then reflect on the gathering afterwards, sharing funny and difficult moments. How many people's names did they remember? What worked well, and what could you all do better? Teaching them these skills helps them learn how to bring people together.

- **Keep Communicating**
  Create an environment that allows for lots of discussion – at meal-times, on the way to school or out walking the dog. This helps keep the family vibe healthy, and teaches iGen essential life skills. Model positive ways to reach out to others with considerate gestures – let others go first and hold doors open. On public transport, stand for elderly or pregnant passengers, don't put bags on spare seats while others are standing, and don't put your feet on the seats.

- **Teach Your Family Story**
  Help your kids build a rich life and identity through your family story. Take them to visit family graves. Get out old family photos and introduce each of the characters, explaining how they fit together. Create a family tree and talk about family likenesses. Tell the stories behind old family objects. Be proud of your cultural heritage, and don't hesitate to celebrate with special foods and festivals.

- **Shared Screen Time**
  Make time for a regular shared family movie or TV show. While everyone has their own favourite programs, it's important that iGen kids learn the quiet joy of *shared* experiences. Get into the habit of discussing what you've watched so that your viewing is less passive.

- **Think About What You Post About Your Kids**
  Ditch the nude and other embarrassing photos, and only share material with those you personally know and trust. Make sure your location is switched off when taking photos. And never reveal your child's full name and other identity details.

- **Take a Close Look at Your Family Habits**
  Think about what is and isn't working. Value the simple togetherness of shared meals around the table. Carve out device-free time during meals and when having precious one-on-one time, for starters. Establish a handful of little weekly rituals – a shared favourite family dish midweek; the chance to play ball or other outside games without interruption; watching a family-friendly movie together, snuggled up close; or taking the dog for long walks over the weekend somewhere interesting. Such moments build closeness and memories that linger, creating a warm space for everyone.

- **Everyone Needs Jobs to Do**
  Involve your kids in *daily* tasks at home, helping teach them responsibility along with a growing range of practical skills. These jobs should be seen as a privilege and not a chore – that they're old enough to be trusted with essential jobs. Tasks can be anything from stacking the dishwasher and putting away groceries, to helping in the garden. Ensure jobs vary and increase in complexity as your children mature.

- **Make and Mend**
  When you create a 'make and mend' culture at home, your kids learn how things work and how to fix things when they go wrong. These skills could include how to sew on a button and mend a tear, put together half-a-dozen meals, use a screwdriver and hammer a nail, and effectively clean up different spills.

- **Safety First**
  If you live in an area prone to drought, flood, bushfire or earthquake, what essentials do your kids need to know, should something happen while you're not around? If they only had a short time to evacuate, what should they take, and what should they secure? Work together to prepare a plan everyone can follow.

- **Holidays**
  During road trips, ditch individual screen time in favour of shared audio books that the whole family can listen to and then discuss the nuances of the story. Encourage the kids to create a scrapbook or photo essay of their holiday, and to send postcards to older family members.

3
Parenting Right Now

Raising the Next Generation

The Rise in Maternal Depression

The Pitfalls of 'Sharenting'

Looking After Yourself as a Parent

RAISING THE NEXT GENERATION

Given the very real challenges small children face, what's it like to be a parent right now? Few doubt that parenting is hard, doubly so as today's parents are treading new ground, with a shaky job market, new technologies and social media. This change of direction places new and different pressures on parents, as does the fact that many parents live a long way from extended family. And, with most mothers working, the early years of parenting can be stretching. With the rise in real estate prices, those lucky enough to buy a home often have substantial mortgages to service, while others have hefty rents to pay.

Many mothers struggle to be effective at home and at work, while stay-at-home mums (SAHM) wrestle with what is often a keen sense of isolation, given that many communities now empty during the working week. It doesn't help that motherhood is also devalued, explains senior social worker and social innovator Kristen Burriel. 'With so much talk around whether you can afford to have a child,' she reflects, 'having a child is now seen as a liability as far as mortgages are concerned.'

> 'It's very hard to love being a parent when you're in the moment. I only know I love being a parent when my MIL [mother-in-law] will take the kids occasionally and I immediately miss them and reflect on the fun we had throughout the week.'
> *Adrian*

Chat rooms are full of impassioned discussions about the challenges of motherhood and, in particular, how it feels to be a stay-at-home mum or dad. 'Currently SAHM right now,' one young mother tells. 'Sent my friend a text this morning, "I hate being a SAHM, all I do is spend money and be sad".' 'Being a stay at home mom has been tough for me,' another admits. 'I feel isolated and like my house is a mess and no-one knows what it's like to be me. I get no outside help and my husband works a lot . . . I get no time off . . . I'm exhausted all the time.'

Inundated with expert advice, and often working long hours at home and work, there's little chance for parents to slow down and simply enjoy 'moments' together with the family. Added to this were the huge challenges faced during COVID-19, with one or both parents working from home, or struggling to meet family responsibilities while battling on the frontline. And now, parents are adjusting yet again to this, our new normal.

Parenting used to be about food on the table, a roof over a child's head and a good education. With so many boxes now needing to be ticked, parenthood is far less about the joyful messiness of mayhem and mud, looking for worms and getting covered in soil. Right now, parents often feel that bringing up kids is more like an exam to be passed. 'Nowadays, parents are told that they are responsible for fostering their children's success in a wide range of areas: academic, social, musical, athletic, spiritual, artistic, etc.,' reflects clinical psychologist Dr Eileen Kennedy-Moore. 'Many parents are afraid to do anything less than everything possible to ensure their children's success.'[1]

Gotta Keep Them Happy!

Being a good parent now also means paying close attention to your child's emotional wellbeing, leading to a constant monitoring of a child's feelings to ensure the child is always in a good headspace. This places parents in a complicated place of trying to work out when to be genuinely concerned, and when to let what may prove to be a momentary upset pass. Most do a great job, but could our current obsession with happiness be impacting parents as well, leaving them anxious whenever they see their children unhappy? Does this need to constantly 'check in' with their kids subtly change the dynamic? Are parents focusing more on keeping their kids happy and entertained than on creating and reinforcing boundaries, working on enhancing communication skills, and allowing children to fail and learn from their mistakes?

The World's a Scary Place

It's also tricky rearing children against a growing backdrop of fear. With so much emphasis on online and real-life predators, there's a heightened need for today's parents to hold their children close and keep them safe 24/7, which makes it harder to be spontaneous and allow unsupervised play outside. 'Every day I hear something on the news or any media type that young children are being abducted, abused and killed by strangers,' tells Danika. 'I feel that nowhere is safe anymore and you can't even trust having your kids walk home safely without hearing someone was following them.'

City living has certainly changed parenting. Previous generations of parents were often based in smaller, tight-knit communities, where children were allowed to roam for long spells during the day, giving everyone a break. Now children are almost always in sight, unless they're at school or a friend's place, or in their bedroom, which also means little downtime for mums and dads.

Aside from the daily awfulness portrayed on the news, we've seen an explosion of violent movies and TV shows, video clips and online games, which can so easily lead parents to take a very dark view of the world. 'Children show no independence due to their parents' overriding fears that something will happen to them,' reflects Ella, a mother and grandmother. 'New parents don't help,' she adds, 'by overindulging a child's every whim, not allowing children outdoor activities and independence, by influencing children at times with their own narcissistic attitudes.' Ella's concerns are echoed by many. 'There only seems to be one style – hover like a helicopter, smother them no matter how old they are,' says David.

> 'I love both my children but I'm still waiting to love motherhood. I think I truly will be in mourning forever for my pre-parent life.'
> *Joni*

When we step back a little, we see how the world is becoming an ever more dizzying place and how these pressures are rubbing off on parents. 'In previous generations literally a "village" would help raise a child as there was always help at hand from extended family and grandparents,' notes psychologist and bestselling author, Dr Michael Carr-Gregg, adding, 'Today's parents are often doing it alone and it has become "unbelievably hard".'[2]

As the climate of fear grows, parents have become ever more vigilant, wanting to hold on to their children. When children are small, they do need to experience a close attachment to their parents, to feel safe and validated. But as they grow, kids need to push out from mum and dad, and discover who they are as individuals – their strengths and passions, and their weaknesses, too. The difficulty, notes London psychoanalyst Pat MacDonald, is that parents now see their kids 'as extensions of themselves – they want to be mates, the boundaries aren't set – the child gets very confused'.[3]

Perfect Parenting, Please

With the advent of social media and the huge amount of parenting literature now available, increasingly parents feel under constant scrutiny, and that they need to get everything right. 'There is so much pressure to have the best sleeper, the earliest toilet trained, the smartest kid, the cutest kid,' states Diane Wagenhals, director of the UK's Parenting Resource and Education Network. 'I think this results in parents rushing to make bad parenting decisions and feeling guilt over not being able to do everything perfectly.'[4] Clinical psychologist Eileen Kennedy-Moore agrees, believing the 'concerted cultivation' of kids is unhealthy, creating a competitiveness that doesn't help children, and leaves parents feeling 'anxious' and 'inadequate'.[5]

> 'Let's stage a social revolution. Let's use technology to celebrate how imperfect and human we all are.'
> *Jennifer Rabin, Jennifer + Rabin*[6]

Perhaps, as Pat MacDonald suggests, we're not great or terrific – 'maybe we need to know we're just ordinary'. This is sage advice, except that being ordinary isn't likely to appeal to parents under constant pressure in our performance culture. More and more of what we do online and offline is to ensure we're seen as anything but ordinary, and this need to be seen as amazing 24/7 rubs off on our children. Yet it's exhausting and absurd to assume that everything we do is special. This places far too much weight on ourselves and on our kids.

The need to compete is the last thing parents should have to face, but competition is rife, fuelled again by our toxic performance culture. The end result is a string of unhealthy family dynamics and bittersweet friendships, which writer Liane Moriarty captures brilliantly in her bestselling novels, including the multi-award-winning book and TV series *Big Little Lies*, which exposes the fault lines in a seemingly perfect little primary school community by the sea. Where do such friendships leave families? How do you find a way through? 'I am a new parent myself,' Noah admits. 'Do you know how comforting it would be for me to pick on other parents for their personal flaws or their bad parenting habits? It would make me feel less bad about the mountain of bad parenting habits and personal flaws that I myself have.' In summing up his thoughts, Noah adds, 'No, parents should never bully other parents. We all have it hard enough as it is.'

Competition Undermines Friendships Amongst Parents

When parents compete, there's no room for closeness or genuine support – for parents to laugh and cry with each other, or to share all the richly joyous, confusing and stretching moments in between. Again, our performance culture doesn't do parents any favours, with a constant emphasis on the need to be perfect at all times. No-one wins in the resulting 'mummy wars'. Too often parents are drawn into less than helpful scenarios, without wanting to be. 'One of the things that has been really getting to me is not being able to figure out how to handle the ridiculous competitiveness that some parents feel the need to display,' Nikki confesses. 'I find that sort of rank competitiveness extremely distasteful, especially when it's about infants and we're all obviously trying to do the best job we can . . . As a person who already suffers from anxiety, I don't need strangers, or worse, *friends*, adding to it.' Jonah agrees: 'I've found that parents who are like this are usually behaving that way because they're insecure about some other aspect of their lives, and bragging about their kid is helping to compensate for that.'

Often a sense of humour is the best defence when faced with rabidly competitive parents. 'We started fostering our son when he was two and he was so far behind in everything that the competitive bragging by parents really seemed almost cruel,' Fiona reflects. 'I finally landed on "We're following the Finnish model of child development/education" as a way to stop such conversations and send other parents scurrying to their computers to see what was up in Finland. Worked like a charm.'

Gotta Stay in the Game

Competition amongst parents leaks into family life, souring friendships and leaving people feeling 'less than', or under pressure to keep up. In one *Good Housekeeping* article, Kitty Dimbleby talks of a mermaid-themed birthday party she organised for her five-year-old daughter. While she tried to keep costs down, Kitty tells how the party ended up costing 'a rather terrifying £450'. However, Kitty is quick to point out, her friends spend 'the same, if not more, every year' on their children's birthday parties and, in the previous six months, her daughter had been to 'parties with three real princesses holding court, a horse-riding party where every child got to ride a pony, a pizza party where they all cooked'. By contrast, when Kitty was small, her mum served sandwiches and cake, handed out balloons, and oversaw such games as pass the parcel.[7]

Competition creates huge amounts of stress for parents, and doesn't allow for the fact that most kids fail at one or more aspects of life. If only everyone could be more honest, the energy could be funnelled into parents being more supportive of each other, and helping their kids over the inevitable hurdles. Sooner or later, every child will fall short in some way. It's far better they experience failure while young, at home. Here they can be nurtured and taught to bounce back. It's far better that they trip up in a supportive atmosphere than when they've just landed their dream job and/or are living with new flatmates in another city. We support our kids best when we help them understand the value of failure and of being generous when faced with someone else's success. Instead of pretending they're perfect, assist them to find the best way to apologise and make amends, as well as how to accept an apology and move forward.

It's helpful to know that, even years later, most parents beat themselves up about some aspect of their parenting they didn't get right. 'I didn't let her [my grown-up daughter] fail enough. She's a very anxious adult,' Daphne tells. 'She was a super-anxious child, and I felt terrible any time something went really wrong for her, so I tried to teach her strategies to avoid having things go wrong. Now, as an adult, there are times when no amount of "strategy/backup plan/double checking" etc. will prevent something from going wrong, and she just goes to pieces very much the way she did when she was three . . . she's slowly and painfully learning that failure is not the end of the world, and that you can pick yourself up, dust yourself off and start over. But I have a feeling that lesson would be easier and less painful to learn at three than in your twenties.'

Different Parenting Styles Enrich

It's fascinating to look at the diverse parenting styles mums and dads bring, as both are valuable. Sometimes mothers try to shut dads out or direct their behaviour. While done for the best of reasons, this can create a real sense of isolation in that relationship. The fact is that, developmentally, kids benefit from this diversity. Exuberant spontaneous play that fathers tend to display is exciting for small children. Often the kids end up squealing and laughing and getting more than a little hyped up, with mums left feeling anxious and trying to calm things down. It's natural for mothers to want to 'contain' their kids, to hold them close. Yet both sets of experiences help grow a child's sense of their world. From dad they learn there's a bigger world 'out there', and from mum they come to realise she's their secure base to return to when they've had enough adventurous play. These dynamics can play out in a variety of ways in other kinds of parenting situations, but a breadth of experiences is essential.

The burden of parenting does tend to rest with mothers, and this can weigh heavily on some women. In a recent study, Dr Elisabeth Duursma, a senior lecturer in early childhood literacy at Wollongong University, looked at how mothers and fathers read to their kids. 'What I found was that mums see it as a teaching exercise,' Duursma tells. She also found that mothers tended to sit 'straight-backed on a chair' when reading to their kids, while dads were happy to lie on the floor and, if their child didn't want to read, they were more than willing to go along with that.

What emerged from this study was that women place much more pressure on themselves during the parenting years, seeing their role more as a job.[8] Through time, mothers have shouldered the burden of child rearing (and still do, even though dads do a great deal more than they once did), and this can't help but grind many mothers down, making it much harder to be a fully engaged parent, unless a mother is well supported.

THE RISE IN MATERNAL DEPRESSION

Given all this pressure, what is life like for mothers right now? The World Health Organization has indicated that more than ten per cent of mothers currently experience some form of mental health issue, especially depression, after childbirth. In addition, eight out of ten mothers suffer 'baby blues' around three to five days after giving birth, feeling teary, anxious or overwhelmed, and experiencing rapid changes in mood. As in adolescence, a mother's body is flooded with hormones, which can leave her feeling completely out of control. For most, these symptoms only last a few days, but for others the journey back is much harder.[9]

It helps to hear mothers tell of their struggles. Tara, who describes herself as a 'happy-go-lucky person', shares how she felt when her baby daughter arrived:

> When I saw her I was happy but didn't feel that magical ecstatic bond which I had heard many mothers rave about all along my pregnancy. I thought that was okay it might be because of the exhaustion so I just let that feeling slip away. It was not long before the postpartum blues slipped in. One day, after having a bath I was looking at my three-week postpartum body and started crying. My legs were not shaved, my tummy was loose and there was a weird big line right in the middle ... I have never in my life felt so down and low in confidence.

When the Blues Linger

After giving birth, depression can continue, as seen in just over ten per cent of mothers with little ones over six months old. The rate is almost twice as high for women in difficult circumstances. It's hard to bond with your child when you're depressed – to get involved in play, to sing and dance and read to a child, and be consistent in the way you deal with them – when you're barely coping. If not treated, depression can create tension. When a mother's needs are unmet, this can so easily spark conflict and distance between her and her children as they grow.[10] 'There's a tremendous pressure on mothers to cope, with little appreciation that birth is traumatic, and that birth trauma can trigger previous life traumas,' states relationship therapist and social innovator Kristen Burriel. 'When we give birth to baby, we give birth to a mother, who's suddenly responsible for another life, keeping that baby alive and well.' This, she insists, is a huge amount for anyone to take on.

Alexa tells of her descent into depression, dogged by shame at feeling down and a fear that she'd be judged a 'madwoman' if she were to admit to not coping:

> One day my daughter would not stop crying so I put her in the car thinking she may fall asleep in the car ride. She did not stop. I started to sing to her, but that didn't work either. I started to cry and kept driving with her screaming in the back. I felt everything closing in on me ... I phoned my husband at work in tears and told him that I didn't think I could make it through the day ... He told me to drop the baby off at his mother's and to drive to the emergency room. I did so and they put me in a room with a bed and told me that it was going to be a while before someone could come and assess me. I was actually grateful for that because I slept for about 7 hours during that time. Two of my nurse friends happened to be working at the time ... I was so ashamed when I realised that they would know why I was there. But they both reached out and offered unconditional support, both mothers themselves, and both who had also experienced PPD [postpartum depression]. They told me after the fact that they were heartbroken I felt ashamed of myself in that situation.

As we begin to appreciate how many of our new mothers are feeling, we need to ensure these women are getting the support they need. Kristen Burriel points to a 2010 national survey, which found that more than 80 per cent of Australian mothers received no additional support after giving birth to their baby, despite the fact that over half were suffering some form of depression.[11] 'The reality is that it can be very hard for mothers to get dressed and showered,' states Burriel. 'They feel so shut down, overwhelmed and worthless at the expectations of being a mum. Some mums work, and then don't have those networks once at home to fall back on. Or because of past mental health issues they've been off their meds, then their meds have to be re-introduced and managed.'

Aware of the many gaps in support for mothers, especially those suffering from mental health issues, POPPY playgroups (Parents' Opportunity to Participate in Play with the Young) have been set up in New South Wales, offering holistic support for parents and their children through play, positive support and education. Given that one in three Australian parents suffer from a mental illness (and almost 20 per cent of those have bipolar issues) and with over 27,000 children impacted by parents suffering psychosis, we get a sense of why organisations such as POPPY are so important for parents and their little ones. 'It isn't enough to see the doctor ... you need all sorts of help when you are depressed,' one mother tells of her POPPY experience. 'I think the doctors are too quick to prescribe medication,' another admits, adding, 'what helped me after I had the baby was when the services started to come to me and not long after I stopped taking medication and went to counselling.'[12]

Whether it's baby blues or full-blown depression, these issues can be addressed and treated. Often, though, mothers need practical help. Having someone share a cup of coffee, or do the shopping or jobs around the house can be a lifesaver, as can minding the baby for a little while. With over three decades of experience and her own research, Burriel knows this landscape intimately, believing that 'social support is as important, if not more so, than medication' in many cases, given that what most mothers need is tangible reassurance, care and backup to pull through. 'Some mothers feel so low they're not able to look themselves in the mirror, and just getting out of the house is an achievement in itself,' Burriel reflects. 'They tell themselves, "I'm not a good enough mother", putting themselves last. But what we help them learn is to make self-care a high priority.'

As we seek to push back against our growing sense of estrangement, helping to encourage and support parents and their children is a good place to start. Sometimes all that's needed is a restorative coffee or homemade meal, along with the chance to be truly heard. It's evident that many mothers need far more support than they're getting. Even a brief visit to keep an eye on the baby while a mother has a shower helps to relieve the pressure. Mothers also need to be listened to and affirmed. And when taking care of the baby is at its most intense, blogger Heather Dessinger suggests setting up a 'meal train' – a series of friends taking turns to make meals, delivered to the door.[13]

THE PITFALLS OF 'SHARENTING'

With all the pressure, fear and uncertainty swirling around, it's little wonder that parents, especially mums, feel a bit overwhelmed and, in the absence of wider support, turn to social media for their cues. In an attempt to reach out to other mums, many are drawn into sharenting – posting regular, often intimate details of their children's daily lives. Also dipping into mummy blogs, many mums are constantly searching for information and confirmation that they're on the right track. There are hundreds of such blogs, from Scary Mommy and Mamavation, to Tech Savvy Mama and The Mommyhood Chronicles. Some are packed full of great advice, others offer a much-needed laugh.

With a ready-made audience, mummy blogs have become big business. One of the top US mummy blogs, Real Mom Recs, is run by Caitlin, an adoptive and biological mother. It offers pregnancy planners and posts on parenting, pregnancy and breastfeeding, alongside Disney ads and posts, product reviews and giveaways. The power of this and other mummy influencers is such that a number of agencies have sprung up purely to connect companies with top mummy influencers in the hope that they'll endorse their products.

Kidfluencers Rule

As the social media multiverse keeps growing, it's now shining light on the lives of very young children, whose every move comes under close scrutiny. A growing number of mothers are eager to make their mark by placing their kids in the social media spotlight. Previous generations of children had a much gentler, more private introduction to the world than many of today's kids. After leaving her job, Martha Krejci, a self-described 'mom and empire-builder', started posting about her daughter Norah, and now earns around US$10,000 a month, which she's putting away for Norah's future. Inspired by this success, Martha now has a spin-off business, generating an additional US$4500 a month. Whenever there's a live stream, Norah 'will jump in on it', Martha tells. 'She knows there are people on the other side of the camera ... I'm helping her understand what this life is about and what she's doing and the part she's playing in it.'[14]

With these and other success stories, we're now seeing a new phenomenon: 'kidfluencers'. While these kids and their antics are winsome, where is the line between parenting, and creating a business based on your child's noteworthy moments?

Some kidfluencers have hundreds of thousands of followers, causing doors to open and serious money to follow. One of the hottest child influencers is Sparkle, who shot to fame at five years old. Sparkle's New Jersey manager and mum, Simone Gittens, is firmly at the wheel, taking up to 20 per cent of Sparkle's monthly earnings. 'She's paying me now as her employee,' Gittens explains in a *Fast Company* piece. 'I'm her stylist. Instead of paying somebody to do that, she's paying me; she's paying me to creative direct her shoots. I look at it as: She's my child but she's the boss.'[15] Now also a child model, Sparkle can be seen in faux fur and heart-shaped sunglasses, and her very own shiny gold Sparkle pants. Managed by Abrams Artists Agency, Sparkle, we're reliably informed, 'remains humble', often donating 'portions of her income to her church's charitable causes'.[16]

Then there's Japan's eight-year-old fashionista Zooey Miyoshi, with 143k Instagram followers, described by her mother as 'Tokyo's #1 party girl'. Commuting between Tokyo and Los Angeles, with talent agency God and Beauty looking out for her, Zooey is on the fast track, and managed by her mum, who oversees her account and acts as her stylist. Other kids, such as Australia's Pixie Curtis, with just under 100k followers, sells her own brand of hair accessories, including Pixie's Bows, which have already been seen on 'some of the most stylish international celeb tots including Suri Cruise, Coco and Ice T's daughter Chanel, Sarah Jessica Parker's twins Tabitha and Marion, Jessica Alba's daughter Haven, Fifi Box's little girl Trixie Belle and Kate Waterhouse's daughters Sophia and Grace'.[17]

Whose Choice Is it?

With parents constantly posting about their children, filling their Facebook and Instagram feeds with photos and anecdotes, we're facing a new knotty social media issue: how to balance a parent's need to connect with their friends, and a child's right to privacy. For some parents, sharing their child with the world has proved therapeutic. But it's one thing to share your life with the world, and quite another to put your child's life out there. As we seek to strike a balance, it's essential that we fully understand this scenario from a child's view. How would it feel, as a six- or seven-year-old child, to find hundreds of photos and snippets of your life online, and see people's reactions to what you've done, what you were wearing and looked like on any given day?

It's not just parents who are guilty of sharing kids' photos and personal information – schools, dance classes, sports groups and other organisations involved with young people are also busily posting kids' photos and achievements. Such is the posting frenzy, it's now estimated that around a quarter of children have an online presence that began with their prenatal scan.[18] A huge amount of information and images follow – childhood drawings and dress-ups, end-of-year concerts, mischief and mishaps, family holidays and backyard fun. One 2016 study found that by the time a British child is five, almost 1500 photos of them have been posted – a figure that was 54 per cent higher than the previous year.[19]

No-one Asked Me!

How do kids feel when faced with a substantial online footprint they knew nothing about? Some kids love their online presence. Others are scared to think that strangers know all about them, and are left feeling stripped bare. In a survey of 1001 tweens, more than a quarter admitted to feeling embarrassed, anxious or worried about having their parents post pictures of them.[20]

So what should our response be to this trend? 'We need to stop and think about what this means for children's lives now and how it may impact on their future lives as adults,' cautions Anne Longfield, Children's Commissioner for England, in the report *Who Knows What About Me?*. 'We simply do not know what the consequences of all this information about our children will be,' she warns.[21]

One of the reasons parents share as much as they do is that families are now widely dispersed. 'I've built up a cyber village of (beloved) strangers across the globe who've been cheering me on for the majority of my adult life ... providing affirmation, emotional support, encouragement, and a place to talk about my child at length,' admits New York writer Jamilah Lemieux, who has more than 180k Twitter followers. '#MiniMilah became part of the personal "brand" of mine.'[22]

> '#MiniMilah healed my broken heart and brought me something I needed so desperately at the time.'
> *Jamilah Lemieux*[23]

What Have You Done?

What is the potential fallout from this generation of children being 'datafied' so young? Experts warn that this level of sharing leaves a detailed digital footprint. Years later, the fact that a child may have struggled at school or when interacting with friends, could come back to bite when they apply for a job or health insurance, or put together their university application. And, even if kids are comfortable about posting online, they're too young to understand the ramifications of doing so. Don, who works in IT, agrees. 'You might not realise that you are creating a digital footprint/identity of your child – history they will inherit without choice. This history is a huge amount of data, which is stored, backed up and shared over a period of time. So where is that data exactly? Who has shared it? Who has saved it? Who has sold it? Nobody will ever know.'

Parenting has broadened, notes mother and law professor Stacey Steinberg from the University of Florida Levin College of Law, to parents being 'gatekeepers of their children's personal information' and 'narrators of their children's personal stories'. However, this dual parenting role gives children little protection as their online identity evolves. With every post, Steinberg warns, 'a bit of the child's life story is no longer left for the child to tell under her own terms ... a child has the right to tell her own story, or to choose to remain silent.'[24]

It's My Story, Too!

So where does this leave parents? Chicago-based lawyer and mother Christie Tate spent almost a decade writing on motherhood before her young daughter realised she'd been the subject of much of this writing, and asked her mother to stop. In one *Washington Post* piece, Tate was adamant she couldn't agree to her daughter's request. 'Promising not to write about her anymore would mean shutting down a vital part of myself, which isn't necessarily good for me or her,' stated Tate, who's decided on a 'middle course'. 'This will entail hard conversations and compromises,' Tate admits. 'But I prefer the hard work of charting the middle course to giving up altogether – an impulse that comes, in part, from the cultural pressure for mothers to be endlessly self-sacrificing on behalf of their children.'[25] Tate's article sparked a huge backlash. Henry wrote, 'If your child doesn't want you to post about her personal life on the internet, you need to stop. This isn't rocket science. If you need to write about motherhood, write in a journal, don't publish it for the whole world to see.'[26]

What are mummy bloggers and writers focusing on the childhood years meant to do? Like Tate, Charlotte Philby, the English editor of the online parenting magazine *Motherland*, had to come to terms with her own mixed feelings about continuing to write about her growing family. Philby talks of her changing behaviour at home, from being the occasional photographer, to 'obsessively spamming' her Twitter, Facebook and Instagram feeds with 'fragments' of her life as a mother. Over time, Philby saw how her 'tolerance for sharing' aspects of her life grew, until she ended up 'emotionally incontinent'. Seeing the deadening effect of capturing every moment was having on her interactions with her kids, Philby decided to exit social media for a year, to reclaim her 'real life' and family privacy.[27]

Other parents are following suit. 'My husband and I have made this decision [not to share] together because we came of age during a time when social media was *juuuust* starting to become a thing,' tells Erica. 'I got to choose how much private information of myself should go online and who should see it. My seven-month-old son doesn't have that luxury ... I'm less concerned about identity theft as I am about him going online one day only to realise that his entire life has been broadcast on social media.'

Is *Anything* Private?

The difficulty for many parents is that sharing pictures of their kids has become an essential part of connecting with friends and community. 'To shut off this process,' Noel complains, 'is to wall every parent in a blanket of silence that impacts their connection with those they know.' Sharenting does help some parents deal with the isolation and demands of their role. No-one doubts that parenting can be intense, or that being able to share your ups and downs can be comforting. Yet, notes law professor Stacey Steinberg, 'Children who grow up with a sense of privacy, coupled with supportive and less controlling parents, fare better in life. Studies report these children have a greater sense of overall well-being and report greater life satisfaction than children who enter adulthood having experienced less autonomy in childhood.'[28] Social worker Angela Oswalt Morelli agrees. 'Children's need for privacy is something very much linked to the development of this sense of self as separate from others … as children grow and increasingly do appreciate that other people exist, so too grows their need to be able to keep things secret from those other people.'[29]

Childhood Still Matters

It's crucial that we protect the precious childhood years. When we behave in ways that treat our children as anything other than small children in need of nurture and protection, and instead mine their lives for social media, dress them as mini adults, and allow them to spend their lives on devices, our children become strangers to us. This is a lonely place for them, and us, to be.

Looking After Yourself as a Parent

Parenting is challenging, which means that all parents need good support. Too often when we're stressed we drift away from people and situations that feed us, only to end up in a less than ideal personal space.

- **Work on Your Network**
  All parents need a reliable network of people. Gather friends of differing ages around you, as each generation has gifts to offer – peers have the advantage of shared experiences, while older friends are often more reflective and relaxed, helping with fresh insights, humour and reassurance. Create a vibrant community around you – get to know your neighbours and local shopkeepers. Take pleasure in the everyday interactions your community offers.

- **Recognise You'll Make Mistakes**
  Don't be afraid to call or catch up with a trusted friend or family member to talk through any issues or dilemmas. Sometimes when we're stressed or feeling down, all we need is someone to listen to us. Being heard is reassuring and it can help you regain perspective.

- **Make Time for One Passion**
  Everyone needs to stay connected to that one thing they love beyond their role as a parent, whether it's fixing cars, baking cupcakes or playing the ukulele. Encourage your partner to make time with friends to explore a passion or to create their own group of enthusiasts, and ensure you do the same.

- **Chill-out Time**
  As downtime is precious, make the most of it – learn to meditate; switch off the TV and savour some space between your thoughts; take a walk in the park with the kids. Keep your interactions simple and doable. Meet regularly with those who inspire you. And remember that good friends will enjoy your company just as much, if not more, over a coffee or simple meal, savouring in-depth conversation, than while you're staging a full-on dinner party.

- **Avoid Over-scheduling**
  Coaching sessions for kids are valuable, but so too is family time. Don't over-complicate things – add a little spontaneity to your week by heading out with the kids to the local park and letting nature do the rest. Time out in green space calms and inspires. Camp out in the backyard. Grow your own veggies. Nature time is nurture time, encouraging free play and helping you de-stress.

4

Hyper-connectivity

How Connected Are We?

Why 'Likes' and Speed Matter

Dipping in the Popularity Stakes?

Reclaiming Precious Time Lost on Devices

HOW CONNECTED ARE WE?

Social media delivers us many gifts, but it also brings some hefty challenges. It's getting harder to carve out meaningful time with those we care about. In its 2016 media report, Common Sense Media, America's leading not-for-profit voice for families, found that half of their teen participants were 'addicted' to their mobile phones. The parents and teenagers in the study all spoke of their concern at how this was impacting their daily lives, with around a third of parents and teens admitting devices are a source of daily conflict. 'Mobile devices are fundamentally changing how families go about day-to-day lives, be it doing homework, driving, or having dinner together,' said James Steyer, founder and CEO of Common Sense.[1]

However, it's not just kids who are addicted to their devices. 'My mother yells at me when I even glance at my phone when we're watching a movie at home,' tells Tina, 'but I've caught her many times on her phone for 90 per cent of a movie.' Nessa agrees. 'I'm a parent of small kids,' she tells. 'My grandma is enraged by how much time "kids these days spend on their phones". But when I'm over to visit, she spends 80 per cent of her time (or more) on Facebook on her iPad.'

It's essential that kids get into good habits around their devices, the Common Sense report found, as switching 'between multiple screens or between screens and people … impairs their ability to lay down memories, to learn, and to work effectively. Additionally, problematic media use can harm face-to-face conversation and undermine the development of empathy.'[2]

> 'I worry that it [Instagram] provides only a veneer of engagement, while forever hovering on the precipice of impossibly perfect breakfasts eaten by impossibly perfect people.'
> Alex Hern, The Guardian[3]

Real Life Is Receding

It's not just parents and children who are feeling estranged right now. Our growing love affair with our devices is impacting our wider relationships, and 'real-life' moments are diminishing, too. It's hard to gauge just how powerful the digital world is in our lives, and how immersive leading platforms are.

Current statistics help us get a better sense of the situation right now, with upwards of 250 billion emails and 5 million blog pages produced daily, and 5000 domain names registered every single hour. Right now, Facebook has more than 2 billion users, and 500 million tweets are sent each day.[4] All our posting, uploading of photos and tweeting takes increasing amounts of our time. And our kids are now following our lead, posting an average of 26 times daily, totalling a staggering 70,000 posts by the time they're 18.[5] Add to this the time spent online during the pandemic lockdown, whether for schooling, work or just reaching out, and an increasingly unhealthy relationship with our devices is evident.

By one calculation, suggests neuroscientist professor Daniel Levitin, 'we've created more information in the past few years than in all of human history'.[6] With technology so all-pervasive, it is now a necessity in many ways. Yet as startup professional Steven Rosenbaum points out, digital abundance 'needs to be harnessed to make *your life* better, otherwise it threatens to turn us into hamsters in a wheel of information'.[7]

The Digital Divide

So what is life like for those who don't have easy access to devices? In one survey, sociologist associate professor Laura Robinson examined the social media access enjoyed by teenagers attending two rural Californian schools. She found that those from well-off homes had the leisure and devices to put serious work into their social media profiles, and to respond quickly to peers online – two key attributes of successful social media operators. This group was also well placed to swiftly remove posts that failed to hit the mark, thus avoiding social embarrassment.

The kids with moderate internet access – from homes with little additional resources – had less leisure time, as they needed to help out their family and work part-time. Here, devices were shared amongst family members. This meant these teens often relied on school computers to connect with peers, choosing to miss out on lunch, real-life socialising and teacher assistance in order to remain 'connected'. Out of school, these teens stayed up late to get uninterrupted access to a device. This way they could check in with what their peers were doing – except that by the time they got online, most of the day's interactions were over. There was a definite anxiety felt amongst these teens at not being up to date with their peers, and thus judged a 'loser'.

The final group of teens with low internet access lacked permanent homes, and their parents did not have permanent work. These kids had almost no free time. Out of school they were tied up with home chores, and working to help keep their fragile families afloat. As vulnerable teens, they relied on free school lunches, but would often forgo lunch to connect with peers through a school computer. In spite of their valiant efforts, these kids were so far behind the rapid-fire exchanges of their peers that they often felt invisible. With almost no online validation, and little chance of keeping up, all they could do was sit on the sidelines. In this world, which Robinson describes as one of 'longing, shame and stigmatisation', these kids were clearly missing out.

Poignantly documenting the lengths that this latter group of teens went to in order to pretend their isolation didn't matter, Robinson was concerned that by working so hard to put on a good front, the very real life struggles of these teens went largely unnoticed.[8] In this highly connected world, digital resources can enhance a young person's life chances, status and wellbeing. Yet those who are unlucky enough to sit outside the social media game face all the challenges of exile – isolation, feeling invisible and being ignored.

When Social Media Sucks

Access to social media at school is a fraught issue, as teachers wrestle with their students' determination to remain 'connected' 24/7. Aside from creating heightened social anxiety, and compromising a student's ability to concentrate in class, the presence of devices makes it harder for kids to remember what they're learning. There's also the challenge of dealing with the devastating effects of ramped-up peer pressure, as seen in sexting and online bullying. In an effort to claw back some space for students to reconnect in the real world, and refocus on their studies, an increasing number of schools are banning phones.

Some regard this move as a kneejerk reaction, yet there's solid research to back up this decision. One London School of Economics study examined the distraction levels that devices cause, and their resulting impact on academic performance, finding that overall 'student performance in high stakes exams significantly increases' once mobile phones are banned. While mobile phone bans had little effect on high achievers, who seem able to focus 'regardless of the mobile phone policy', this study indicated that the gains from mobile phone bans for low achievers were significant.[9]

'I'm tired of constantly asking students to put their phone in their bags, it wastes so much time, and time is something we don't have enough of to get through the full curriculum at the moment.'
Frieda

Phones and Learning Don't Mix

Another US study looked into the impact of mobile phones during a university lecture, finding that those who put aside their phones took almost two-thirds more notes than those who didn't. The notes and recall of the students focusing on the lecture proved to be more extensive. This group also achieved a full letter-and-a-half grade more than those accessing their phones during the lecture.[10] In this age of information overload, it is becoming ever clearer that our brains have a limited capacity to process and recall information. The more distracted we are, the lower our ability to process and retain information, and the less we're able to engage with a subject and learn, and connect with each other and the wider world.

Until recently, computing and communication devices had limited use. Then we got smartphones, and the whole landscape changed. One study found that our proximity to our smart-phone, even if we're not using it, adversely affects our working memory – the part of the brain that gathers and processes useful information. Added to this, our 'fluid intelligence' – our ability to reason and sort out new problems – is also impacted. In this study, those most dependent on their devices experienced the greatest 'brain drain'. According to the authors of this research, there's 'at least one simple solution': separate yourself from your phone if you want to concentrate on a task.[11]

In July 2018, France banned mobile phones in schools, and others are following suit. Tara Anglican School for Girls in

Sydney is one of a growing number of Australian schools to ban mobile phones. The move was introduced first and foremost 'to assist the girls in developing their relationships with each other', explains Principal Susan Middlebrook. This program, now in its third year, still enables girls to 'move in and out of the use of technology for their learning' at school.

Middlebrook spearheaded this move after seeing girls sitting in groups at recess and lunch, more engaged with their phones than each other. 'I wanted them to really look at each other, engage in discussion, laugh and learn about each other,' Middlebrook explains, adding, 'I wanted them to be so invested in each other that they could have disagreements and work it all out, because they knew how each would react.'

While the girls were initially less than impressed to have to place their phones in their lockers from 8.20 am until 3.20 pm, parents and teachers were supportive of the phone ban. But now, Middlebrook explains, the girls also support the ban:

> The result is a happy and delightfully noisy school at recess and lunch. We have had to arrange more activities at lunch, and buy more equipment for games. The range of clubs at lunchtimes has expanded and are fully subscribed. The feedback from the students has been overwhelmingly positive. They describe themselves as having more freedom without their mobiles during the day and there is no push from the students to allow them access in the future.

What a powerful pushback against possible loneliness in the future these girls are experiencing.

When kids aren't encouraged to connect in real life, it's much harder for them to be well rounded and to recognise the choices they have. And without choices, kids can so easily end up on the fringes, living isolated lives at best. That's why engagement is crucial during teenage years. Being encouraged and supported to connect helps grow a teen's social confidence and emotional intelligence, their ability to read social cues and practise conflict resolution – essential life skills in an increasingly complex world.

WHY 'LIKES' AND SPEED MATTER

Social media is seductive – and not just for kids. Have you noticed how 'likes' that start as pings of delight soon create anxiety, causing us to chase acceptance and prove ourselves online? 'Your Instagram account is like your cool CV,' suggests Rachel Smith, grants manager at the Mental Health Foundation. 'There's a pressure to impress,' she adds.[12] But what happens when we have few or no 'likes'? Suddenly we're left with the uneasy feeling that we exist only as long as people out there can 'see' us. And to be seen we need to work harder at being funnier, more attractive, witty and intriguing, if we've any chance of people taking notice. This requires a lot of effort. Where is all this work taking us?

One Australian study recently looked at the relationship between social media usage and eating issues, finding that photo-based sites were of greatest concern, as they prompted users to constantly assess themselves the way others see them, putting those using sites such as Instagram at greater risk of body shame and eating disorders.[13]

> 'In front of the lens, I am at the same time: the one I think I am, the one I want others to think I am, the one the photographer thinks I am.'
> *Philosopher Roland Barthes,* Camera Lucida[14]

When we start living outside ourselves, ignoring our own feelings and ways of doing things, and even our dreams, we lose sight of who we are, until we're only able to see ourselves from the outside. What room does that leave for a rich inner life? With the number of 'likes' disappearing from sight on many platforms, hopefully the pressure will decrease. That said, as we're still able to see how successful one of our own photos or posts has been, it may well mean we're still trapped in the comparison cycle.

> **'... there is a sense in which we are being humiliated by it [social media]. And betrayed. Betrayed by corporations, data sets, statistical analyses and the algorithms that would presume to know us. But betrayed, too, by ourselves – by our willingness, what can often seem our eagerness, to make ourselves smaller.'**
> *Sebastian Smee,* Net Loss: The Inner Life in the Digital Age[16]

No Chance to Slow Down

We're also living with an escalating sense of urgency. The more effective the delivery of information, the faster data flies in and out of our lives. This raises the biting question of when does fast become too fast, given there's already little or no time to pause or reflect? When we communicate with others, if we haven't heard back within hours, we assume something's wrong. Are they annoyed? Has something awful happened?

'In the old days,' reflects Toronto linguist Heather Lotherington, 'we had letters. Now we have conversations in nanoseconds.'[15] Letters gave previous generations the chance to take a deep breath – to think about how to respond, to fine-tune their thoughts and the words they chose. With speed now essential, and an avalanche of communications to deal with daily, increasingly we're relying on acronyms and emoticons to get our meaning across. While these new forms provide great shortcuts, they're no substitute for more nuanced communication.

Body Language Is Rich in Nuance

A staggering 93 per cent of the way we communicate still comes down to our body language. The cues we pick up from someone's posture and eye contact, the micro-emotions flitting across their face, their tone and how quickly they speak, tell us a great deal more beyond the words a person chooses. How close we stand to someone indicates how comfortable we are around them. Even the subtle scents we emit, including our pheromones, have a story to tell. Take these threads away, and we're left with only a fraction of what's communicated.[17] Texting and emailing flattens communications, which are becoming ever briefer, as do acronyms and emoticons.

Emojis are fun. They do offer a speedy way to respond. But there's not a great range of emoticons on offer, with few hints of a lingering sense of sadness or doubt, of the pain that spears the heart as tears fall. Yet it's these very nuances that help make us human, that help us feel heard and understood. Without this, all we are left with are shallow exchanges.

One autumn afternoon several years ago, Sharon exchanged texts with her college-age daughter. As they 'chatted', Sharon asked her daughter about the usual things. Her daughter responded with hearts and happy emoticons, then a few hours later attempted suicide.[18] Emoticons are useful, but they can short-change us. Texting is how we now tend to communicate. Yet had Sharon been able to sit down with her daughter, or talk on the phone, she may have been able to pick up on how her daughter was actually feeling.

When We Lose Sight of Those Around Us

As we become increasingly self-focused, slowly but surely we're isolating ourselves from others, and from endless possibilities for stimulation and joy, not to mention numerous enriching experiences. In a comprehensive study into the use and impact of selfies, the authors concluded that selfie-taking is fuelled by a need to *prove* we're living a full life, rather than getting on and living one. They described the act of taking selfies as 'a kind of performance, a staging that doesn't allow anyone to oversee and depict the real state of a human soul', and concluded, 'There are no real feelings in such photos.'[19]

So where does this leave us? When talking of workplace trends, LinkedIn's former CEO, Jeff Weiner, said that the biggest skill gap millennials currently face in the US is strong communications/interpersonal skills.[20] This is hardly surprising. With less and less face-to-face interaction, there's a discomfort now in communicating with others in person, especially with strangers. Millennials, it's recognised, often arrive in the workplace with a dazzling array of skills. Yet what they're lacking, according to Mike Fenlon, the global talent leader for PricewaterhouseCoopers, is 'the ability to express complex ideas with clarity and simplicity, to communicate one-on-one, within small groups and to larger groups, all in an engaging and accessible way.' Real-life communication skills remain essential to successfully navigating the world of work but, according to Fenlon, 'these skills are not common' these days.[21] Without such skills, individuals can so easily feel isolated at work. And with no sense of how to remedy this, it's a very lonely place to be.

'I would say that I am way more precise in texting and it just sounds better because I have the time to think about the perfect answer.'
Fenella

With millennials now making up approximately half the workforce, where are work cultures heading, given this generation prefers instant messaging or emailing, to talking with someone in person? Where does this discomfort leave us in one-on-one work situations? 'Overall, I'm better at texting because it's easier for me to pick and choose my words – less risk of getting into an awkward situation, easier to break off from the conversation, etc.,' Angus confesses. 'I'm way better at phrasing what I want to say when I get time to think about it and word it as well as better confidence to say difficult stuff than face to face,' Danny agrees. 'It's so much easier to type a thought out,' says Kaz, 're-read it, go back and change it, and only send it if I'm sure that it's worded the way I want it. I'm not good at talking about emotions.' With less comfort around face-to-face communications, aside from the isolation factor, is it possible millennials may also be more susceptible to manipulation by those who are practised at one-on-one and group dynamics, within and beyond their workplace?

Nature Nurture

It's essential that we're able to pick up on cues from those around us. How else can we read the ways others are reacting, and respond appropriately? These abilities are essential to how well we navigate the world. Fortunately, the solution needn't be that complex. One US study into 11- and 12-year-olds, spending on average four-and-a-half hours a day on their devices, posed an interesting question. Could five days at a nature camp positively impact a tween's ability to read visual emotional cues?

First, participants were shown images and silent video footage of people's faces. Half the group spent five days at nature camp, interacting with each other in nature without any TV or devices. The remaining kids continued as usual, with ready access to their devices and TV. After five days, all of the participants were shown more images and video footage of people expressing varied emotions. The tweens returning from nature camp proved significantly better at recognising non-verbal emotional cues than they had previously, while the control group of tweens stayed the same.[22]

> 'Technology has its own set of values and is transforming the very nature of being human as it impacts the way we think about ourselves.'
> Anita L. Cloete, 'Living in a Digital Culture'[23]

Mental Health Matters

Often we turn to social media as an escape from real life – when we're depressed, tired or bored. To avoid this loop, we first need to recognise when we're most likely to fall into this pattern, and how it manifests. Marcia tells of her experience:

> I am completely addicted to my phone. Instead of reading, meditating, cleaning, working out – basically anything productive, I've been lying in bed browsing through Reddit, texting, even just playing solitaire. I know I'm avoiding life by doing this … but I honestly don't know how to stop. I have downloaded apps that track your phone usage, and help you with staying off your phone. I've tried keeping it plugged in away from my bed at night. I just can't get off it.

Having recognised our behaviour, we have to decide how we want to show up in the world, and in virtual worlds. With the current rise in depression, anxiety and isolation, it's important that we're aware of what triggers these states. Do the social media platforms we use deliver tangible moments of joy? Do they enhance who we are, or chip away at us? In one key UK study into the mental health of young people, teenage participants admitted to struggling to use their devices less, and asked for help in doing so. They suggested that pop-ups appear, warning them of heavy usage, and being automatically logged out of their devices when they reached a certain level of viewing.[24]

iGen Doing Things Differently

If we're honest, we could probably all benefit from more time spent in the real world, especially in our new 'normal' lives, where self-isolation is now a choice. The good news is that there may be a change coming, sparked by our emerging iGen. In a study by Boston-based market researchers Origin, a third of iGen participants told of how they'd deleted their social media accounts in the past year. A fifth of respondents told of being unable to cope with the pressure to get online attention, saying they wanted more privacy. The most common reason for shutting down accounts was the amount of time wasted on different platforms. Just over 40 per cent of participants found their online experiences 'too negative'. A third were unable to engage with the content. At the top of the list of the platforms these young adults were most likely to let go of were Facebook, Instagram, Snapchat and Twitter.[25]

There's a growing tension between our real and virtual lives. As we ponder this disconnect, it's interesting to reflect on the responses of a generation that has never known anything other than constant connection, who is now stepping back and reclaiming more time and space for real life. It's interesting that iGen-ers seem more acutely aware of the time wasted and the need for more privacy than the rest of us, who are increasingly losing ourselves in cyberspace, seduced by the ease of the often questionable connectedness it offers. Perhaps the way forward is to take a good look at the platforms we use, only retaining those that genuinely enhance our real selves and lives.

At the same time, this new level connectivity does enhance our daily lives. Where would we have been without Zoom during the pandemic? And what's not to enjoy about our access to Facebook groups that share our passions – be it pop culture, music and art, or community news and issues? And where would we be without bloggers, who delight us with details of their new recipes and off-the-beaten-track travel, with mindfulness practices, zany fashion choices and insights into everyday challenges? However, let's not forget amid all these often-delicious distractions, that ultimately the best and most nuanced connections happen in real life.

DIPPING IN THE POPULARITY STAKES?

As social media demands ever more of our time, there's a growing pressure to source more and more engaging content and amazing photos. Yet taking perfect wedding photos, amongst other shots, has become a whole lot harder, according to internationally award-winning photographer Corey Ann, who tells of how guests are constantly spoiling what promised to be a beautiful photo. 'My heart literally breaks when a guest ruins an otherwise lovely image or jumps in front of me when I'm capturing a key moment from the day,' she tells. 'It's also been sad to watch the progression from seeing smiling, encouraging and happy faces as the bride is escorted up the aisle to faces hidden behind the backs of cameras and cell phones that line the aisle.' One of Ann's friends, also a bride-to-be, was so sick of this scenario that she asked guests to put down their cameras and turn off their phones before the service. 'The photographer will capture how this moment looks,' she explained. 'I encourage you all to capture how it feels with your hearts.'[26]

This approach, however, is all too rare as we witness what happens at special events and holiday locations, and during our most intimate moments. Following the lead of Facebook and Insta 'it people', with their daily diet of gossip, lurid confessions, never-ending purchases and fashion shots, many of us have been drawn into parading the minutiae of our lives. The problem is that once we enter the social media stratosphere, it's hard to pull back. We're so busy capturing our every moment, and the lives of those close to us, to keep up our 'profile', that perfect strangers know almost as much about us as close friends. We're now living, warns New York actor and filmmaker India Ennenga, in an era of unfolding 'digital self-harm'.[27]

What does this self-harm look like, given that we're wired to connect? Connection on social media platforms is often more about the 'highlight reels' of our days than real life, suggests behavioural scientist Clarissa Silva.[28] This takes us back to the burning question: do we do what we do because it's what we want or are inspired to do, or because it's what online friends and followers expect of us? And what happens then to our unique take on life? Does social media help us connect with others, or lose ourselves in their expectations?

> **'Social media is like kerosene poured on the flame of social comparison.'**
> *Rebecca Webber,* Psychology Today [29]

With all the detail we post comes a lot of scrutiny – from friends and acquaintances, and from perfect strangers – a process aptly described by Miley Cyrus in one *Vanity Fair* piece as 'the weight of a million eyeballs'.[30] We're so busy texting and tweeting, and uploading to Instagram, TikTok and other platforms, that when we do finally have a few spare moments, often a sudden aching emptiness creeps in. All at once we're fearful that some part of us is receding, leaving us with a lingering worry that we may just 'vanish' completely if we don't make our presence felt online. Without realising it, we're on the cusp of that restless kind of loneliness that overuse of new media delivers.

What Do You Want to Be?

Being fully engaged in social media can leave us vulnerable to the attitudes and values of others, prompting us to change our focus, to continually monitor and modify our online persona. If we're not careful, our authentic selves not only take a back seat, they disappear out the window. And in the process we become ever more vulnerable to the demands of others, to a deepening, almost desperate loneliness. When 'interfacing digitally', notes behavioural scientist Clarissa Silva, 'it is much easier to emotionally manipulate others because they are reliant on what I call "vanity validation"'.[31]

So how does this dynamic work? In an inspired moment we post something we regard amazing or amusing, in the hope of sharing our discovery with the world. Yet should we get little to no response to our post, the moment sours. All at once our post becomes a shameful thing – something to bury. How many hundreds of thousands of people experience this downward cycle daily? What does it do to their sense of self as, all at once, they feel separate from the herd? How does it skew their view of the world?

With some platforms now removing likes for others to see, we're taking a step in the right direction. Yet it still doesn't fully address our anxiety around how others respond to us, or our 24/7 access to other people's seemingly perfect lives.

'We compare ourselves to others, get lost in their idealized lives, and forget to enjoy our own.'
Social scientist Emma Seppälä, Stanford University[32]

Of all the platforms, Instagram is currently one of the most popular, as our way of communicating moves rapidly from text to visuals. Launched in late 2010 as a photo app, Instagram now has 1 billion monthly users, with a staggering 500 million uploading daily to their 'Insta stories'. Amid the rush to provide content, new challenges have emerged, and with photos now a key part of our identity, Instagram has become a powerful means for establishing and increasing our online profile. But what of our ache to belong?

Comparisons Deliver Little Joy

A recent Royal Society for Public Health report, #StatusOfMind, noted that of all the leading social media platforms, Instagram was the most detrimental to the health and wellbeing of those aged 14 to 24 years. There were a range of concerns, including how we can so easily get lost in comparisons with others. Descending into a 'compare and despair' cycle can then impact our sleep and intensify our fear of missing out (FOMO).[33] 'Whenever I use Instagram I always feel a little worse after leaving the app, even if it's minor,' admits Cecile. 'I can feel my happiness decrease. The problem is – looking at others' "lifestyles" and peeking at what someone else does for a living or lives like *excites* us because we are curious creatures. Except the minute we do so we go back to the comparison cycle.'

In that 'down' moment, as comparisons kick in, we forget that what we're looking at is a highly edited version of someone's day. 'You're only seeing the best of the best [on social media],' Mikhail reflects. 'You're not seeing the days that they're stuck inside on a gorgeous day doing laundry, or the fact that the picture-perfect concert that they went to was actually overcrowded, the guy behind them spilled a beer all over their new jacket and the band didn't even sound that good.'

Comparing ourselves to someone who is more 'together' than we are may inspire us to push harder to bridge the gap. But by the same token, suggests Rebecca Webber, writing for *Psychology Today*, if the gap feels too great, those comparisons can easily eat away at our sense of self. The same holds true if we see a similarity between ourselves and someone we regard as 'less than', as once more our negative feelings about ourselves are reinforced.[34]

'Funny how we always compare up,' Odette reflects. 'You don't look at the friend that has less and be thankful. You look at the one that has more and become jealous.' Emily agrees. 'I have a few friends on Facebook (not many, as I only add people I actually know), and I find myself getting jealous of them quite often,' she confesses. 'I feel like a terrible person because I feel like I'm begrudging people their successes (when I really just want that same success for myself).' It's intriguing that envy tends to arise around those closest to us, who lead similar lives, with only a few differences between us. In recognising this, we can be more aware of this dynamic.

What a Smile Can Conceal

With the constant depiction of perfect people and parties, holidays, drinks venues and wardrobes, it's no surprise that social media is creating what's been dubbed 'smiling depression', where those who are depressed work hard to appear anything but.

Social media carries an expectation that we'll only project our positive selves. The question is, who's showing up each day – the real us, or the person others expect us to be? And what happens to us in the critical space in between?

> 'I actually had a friend get mad at me for not being on FB [Facebook] any longer because I was missing out on seeing the pictures she posts from her vacations.'
> Lydia

The more time people spend on Instagram, the more likely they are to be anxious and depressed. Those who live by their Insta feed can so easily become imprisoned inside a narrow, often false, image of themselves. All too frequently they're unable to break this cycle, as their social media feed is always demanding more of them. Currently one in ten people suffer from depression, tells Olivia Remes, a Cambridge PhD candidate specialising in anxiety disorders, with 15 to 40 per cent of these individuals struggling with 'smiling depression'.[35]

For those who are already feeling wobbly, social media isn't necessarily good news. As journalist Rebecca Webber points out, social media has the unnerving knack of knowing how 'to kick us in our Achilles heel'.[36] 'I often feel anxious (so, so anxious) or bereft or lost,' Xandra tells. 'On most nights I have trouble sleeping and sometimes, on bad days, I get up in the morning with a sense that nothing is in its place. I don't portray this on social media because I want to highlight the good in my life. It's the internet equivalent of smiling for the camera: you're not being hypocritical,' she insists. 'You want the photo to represent the moment in a way you'd want to remember it.' This all takes a lot of time and energy. What, we need to ask ourselves, is the cost?

Is BoPo the Way to Go?

All negatives aside, social media has the ability to deliver great good. There's a new push online to turn around the 'compare and despair' body image cycle by promoting realistic bodies. Some body positive (BoPo) Instagram accounts, which celebrate a wide variety of shapes and sizes, already have over a million followers. Yet how effective are they? One study into young women aged 18 to 30 found that BoPo Instagram accounts can help create more positive body image, inspiring followers to be more grateful for the 'healthy workings' of their body. Yet even this more realistic landscape can be problematic. This study also indicated that those accessing BoPo accounts tend to focus more on their appearance at the expense of other personal attributes.[37]

In spite of this, Rachel Smith, grants manager with the UK's Mental Health Foundation, insists that we can't ignore social media's ability to connect those who are feeling vulnerable. In one 2018 study, a quarter of teens said social media made them feel less lonely, while almost half of the most vulnerable found social media 'very important' for their mental health. 'Having the ability to speak online is sometimes liberating for people who struggle to communicate face to face,' Smith reflects. She tells how, as a shy 14-year-old, she struggled to play her guitar in front of others at school, yet happily recorded herself playing from the comfort of her living room, then posted her video on Instagram.[38]

How Many People Can You Truly Connect with?

The need to be constantly connected is making ever-increasing demands on our time and attention, but what about all those online 'friends' we work so hard to impress? Evolutionary anthropologist Dr Robin Dunbar suggests that, at most, human beings can only meaningfully connect with 150 people.

More than this, and our brains go into overload. Interestingly, 150 people was the average size of the hunter-gatherer communities in the distant past, and the size of the villages recorded in the Domesday Book in Britain over 900 years ago.[39] True connectivity involves building trust – getting to know a person, being there for them, sharing 'moments'. Friendship takes time and attention, and can be stretching. There are real bonuses to this level of caring. Where would we be without true, real-life friends?

Social media is great at reconnecting us with people from our past – those we grew up with, went to school or worked with – but reconnection doesn't necessarily lead to closeness. It's almost effortless to send a brief text, or to 'like' someone or something they're doing. All it takes is a click. Yet while we may be genuinely thrilled in the moment, it isn't the same as making the time to have a meal or a drink with someone we care about after a long day at work. Such moments take effort and, on some occasions, sacrifice. The bonus is that fully fledged friendships feed our humanity. With numerous digital ways out of face-to-face connection, too often we fall for what's easiest, preferring to text instead of phone, or 'like' instead of making time for a walk or a coffee.

> 'Instagram is my downfall. But let's be honest it's not keeping us up to date with the world. Real and reputable news as well as getting out in our communities does that. IG is just our crutch.'
> *Harry*

Is Likeability the Way to Go?

'We are biologically programmed to care', states child and adolescent psychologist Mitch Prinstein at the University of

North Carolina. He suggests that there are two very different types of popularity. There's likeability, where we're a feel-good person to be around, and then there are those who use status to get attention. Likeable people have a way of making others feel happy and valued. They're the individuals who are more likely to be hired and to be happier, and less likely to get sick.

However, brain changes in our teen years predispose us to focus on status, even though high-status (popular) teens are often disliked by their peers. Previous generations tended to grow out of the need for status on leaving school. Now though, says Prinstein, we're more focused on status than ever, 'mouse-clicking for status 24/7' over a number of platforms. Yet studies following the lives of high-status kids show that there's rarely a happy ending. Too often these individuals go on to experience relationship difficulties, anxiety and depression, and are less likely to keep their jobs.

We thrive when we can access an authentic connection with others, when we can enjoy a sense of community. The tragedy, Prinstein reflects, is that today's teens know no world other than the competitive, status-fuelled one we've created for them.[40] The decision to connect and not compare is a much more satisfying way forward. So, instead of being jealous of others when things are going well for them, concentrate on what you 'admire and appreciate' about them. 'Cultivate joy for their success,' exhorts San Francisco psychiatrist Ravi Chandra. 'It [this level of generosity] can be a catalyst for personal growth.'[41]

#ScrollFreeSeptember

Aware of our growing addiction to devices, the Royal Society for Public Health in the UK dreamt up #ScrollFreeSeptember, where people choose their level of social media shutdown for the month. You can be a Busy Bee, not accessing social media during work hours; a Social Butterfly, who attends events without engaging in social media; or a Night Owl, switching off your devices after 6 pm. Aside from going Cold Turkey, you can also opt to be a Sleeping Dog, with no connection overnight.

Not everyone is up for a digital detox, but it's interesting to hear from those who've gone the distance. When journalist Christina Hope signed up for #ScrollFreeSeptember, she decided to let go of Twitter, Facebook and Instagram for the month and, to her surprise, woke up feeling 'much more relaxed'. She reported reading more, writing 'more – and better', and generally feeling 'more present'. Her fear of missing out did also soar, and she did find herself checking her emails more than previously. Yet over the month, Christina became aware of those she only ever connected with on social media, which left her pondering what to do about this. Overall, she found #ScrollFreeSeptember an 'amazing month of very present, lived experiences'.[42]

Also signing up to #ScrollFreeSeptember, Pam soon realised how much more she could achieve by retreating from social media. When her #ScrollFreeSeptember was up, she admitted to being excited to get back onto Instagram:

> It was in that moment [of reconnecting with Instagram] I realised our brains aren't supposed to be processing so much information, constantly and at once. No wonder people report feeling more anxious after being on social media. In the span of 30 seconds you might see a new recipe you want to try, a motivational quote that reminds you of your grandmother, a funny meme about vegans, someone sharing their experience with anxiety, and so on and so forth. It never stops.[43]

That, it seems, goes straight to the heart of our bittersweet engagement with social media. While it's endlessly intriguing, it doesn't miss a beat. Never allowing for moments of reflection, it eats up more and more time, leaving us anxious, distracted and sometimes distressed. Yet we as human beings need the chance to pause and take a couple of deep breaths. We need time to ponder, to refresh and recharge if we want to thrive. We also need to see how our often addictive need for online connection prevents us from cultivating the authentic, caring relationships we ache for, thus leaving us lonelier still.

Reclaiming Precious Time Lost on Devices

Those emerging from a digital detox tell of the joy of having more freedom in their day – more time for themselves, and for the people and passions that matter. They report experiencing less anxiety, too. With the average person now checking their phone 150 times a day, it's time to pull back, and here's how to do it:

- Make time with friends and family device free. There's no better way to connect than feeling genuinely seen and heard.

- Switch your phone to silent whenever possible, and savour the sudden sense of 'spaciousness'.

- Turn off pop-ups and sound prompts, as they keep you chained to your device.

- Stow laptops and devices during your daily commute and enjoy the ride – the people, the passing locations, the chance to clear your head.

- Delete or prune the number of social media apps you use so you can welcome more space between your thoughts and enjoy more breathing space in the day.

- 'Follow' only those you truly care for on social media so that connection becomes an occasional pleasure instead of a source of constant stress.

- Whenever you fall into the comparison trap, make a habit of hauling yourself back. Everyone has a unique way of being in the world, so work on your uniqueness instead.

- Unsubscribe to all but essential emails. Life's too short to wade through junk mail.

- Place strict time limits on favourite online games, and stick to those limits.

- Decide on a regular time each evening to put away your devices so that you can 'come down' from your day and enjoy a good night's sleep.

- Treat yourself with one device-free evening a week for a yoga or dance class, for sport or home hobbies. Note how much you've achieved and how good you feel.

- Don't take your phone or laptop to bed. Luxuriate in the sweet comfort and relaxation there.

- Plan off-the-grid weekends away, and experience the bliss of letting go of everyone and everything that presses in on you.

5

Looking for Love

Why the Love Stakes Are Higher Now

Instant Attraction

Everyone Lies a Little

How to Avoid Dating Disasters

WHY THE LOVE STAKES ARE HIGHER NOW

Rarely are social media interactions more complex than in the world of online dating, with its numerous rabbit holes. And with so many of us moving cities, juggling demanding jobs and wrestling with long working hours and commutes, finding love can be burdensome, which is part of the reason that online dating has such appeal. Dating apps and websites do offer busy singles immediacy and convenience, keeping online daters motivated with a regular diet of dating tips and trends and, of course, success stories. The massive number of people using dating apps helps us glimpse the depth of loneliness that too many feel.

Match.com launched the first online dating service 25 years ago. Mobile dating followed, but was slow to take off until the arrival of smartphones. Today, half of British singles have only ever organised dates online, while millennials spend up to ten hours a week on dating apps.[1] Once seen as the domain of the desperate, online dating is now part of life for most singles, with a third of all marriages in the US, according to a 2013 study, resulting from online dates. It is not surprising that, in 2018, dating app Plenty of Fish reported having 90 million users. For the businesses that get the formula right, the rewards are considerable. In the latest figures, Tinder is set to double its turnover in just a year to around US$800 million,[2] while eHarmony's revenue is sitting at around US$350 million.[3]

> 'The first few days of being on an app for the first time in a while boosts my self-worth. You are receiving so much more attention than ever before, but it wears off pretty quickly. After a few weeks, my usage decreases alongside my self-worth ... no-one really seems to care about what you have to say, or even who you are.'
> *Rosa*

There are now more than 8000 websites worldwide,[4] from EliteSingles and OkCupid, to Tinder, Bumble, Grindr, Scruff, Chappy and Scissr and more, for LGBT audiences. With additional apps such as Christian Mingle, PURRsonals.com and FarmersOnly.com, you're able to hone in on what feels like your 'tribe'. Monique, who lives on her own, uses dating apps to meet other gay women she wouldn't normally come across. 'Not everyone likes the queer scene,' she explains. 'It's a very small community, and it tends to be the same people out there in rotation ... everyone knows everyone and everyone's business. It's very incestuous, tense and dysfunctional. The chance of meeting someone [online] that isn't part of this world is encouraging, and a big part of why I persist.'

Rise in Mature Daters

Figures also show that the over sixties are one of the fastest growing groups of online daters, reaching out for someone to be with.[5] There's also an increasing number of mid-life individuals using dating apps, enjoying the novelty and frisson of an online match, and all the flirting that follows. Mindful of the number of mature singles looking for a date or something more permanent, Debrett's, the last word in British etiquette, has released a guide for mature online daters, covering everything from how to handle the first kiss and who pays the bill, to overnight stays, follow-up texts and going 'exclusive'.[6]

Psychotherapist Melissa Ferrari understands the upsides of online dating both firsthand and from a professional viewpoint. 'Eight years ago I met my husband online,' she tells, adding that while 'the process has been great, it's taken some work with blended families'. There are issues, Ferrari admits. 'I feel there's been a bit of a turn in the dating culture lately.

With so much choice, we don't have to invest the same time and energy in relationships, which is a shame as relationships need to be worked on. It's as if we don't know how to work with what we don't like. It's creating a loneliness out there. The fun and excitement of dating is diminishing, feeding the belief that relationships don't work.'

> **'Shagging people you don't love can make you feel lonely.
> Dating apps are bleak.'**
> Roxanne[7]

For some, online dating ends up being a 'brutal' and 'toxic' business, while for others it's 'fun' and 'exciting'. For most, in attempting to push past their loneliness, their techno-dating experiences lie somewhere in between. 'Online dating is a way to meet men that would otherwise not happen. You don't feel as alone,' tells Izzy, but she's also acutely aware of the downsides. 'You don't know how many other women they are dating at the same time or how many women they are physical with. You have to find a way to trust and let it go.'

Most Are Looking for Love

So are dating apps really about getting together for sex? Not according to the research. In an international survey of over a million daters, three-quarters of participants stated that they were looking for love first and foremost,[8] although finding love proves elusive for many. Almost a third of all scam losses reported to Australia's Competition and Consumer Commission were dating and romance related.[9] Yet in spite of the bumpy bits, convenience tends to win out. 'It's fun, quick and easy,' Rosa tells. 'Talking to a lot of different people, albeit on a very surface level, is interesting and often makes me realise how easy it is to experience things out of your comfort zone.'

It's a myth that online dating is an easy way to push past loneliness. A great deal of effort and persistence is required. The ability to 'market' yourself is a key element to success, especially for those who are serious about finding someone to share their life with. A willingness to 'play the game' indicates how much people want to move beyond the often biting loneliness of singledom. If you want to be in with a fighting chance, you need a great profile and photos. Studies also suggest that women are drawn to men who look proud rather than kind, while men go for a kind appearance over proud.[10] This process can, and does, create additional stress. 'I worry that my photos don't look like "me",' admits Izzy. 'But you actually have to put great photos up to get men to look at your profile … I worry that the photos are "too good" and that I will disappoint when I meet them. This has happened in reverse.'

Did You Have to Ghost Me?

There are few guarantees in the online dating stakes, as you're swimming in a largely anonymous world, where everyone's looking out for themselves. One minute you're enjoying a pleasant date and the next you've been 'ghosted' – dumped without explanation, which is hardly a great experience if you're already feeling isolated. Yet while ghosting seems 'needlessly cruel', James, in his mid-thirties, insists it's the best way to extricate himself from a relationship he's not invested in.[11] This is a view shared by many online daters, who believe that disappearing without telling a person why is fine, and that there's no harm done. Not so, says psychotherapist Jennice Vilhauer. Indifferent behaviour hurts and leaves those dumped with nowhere to go. It's selfish too, because when you ghost someone, you're putting your feelings first.[12]

To have a love prospect evaporate isn't anything new, but the numbers of men and women treating each other poorly is. In a recent Plenty of Fish study, eight out of ten singles aged 18 to 33 admitted to experiencing ghosting.[13] Dumped daters talk constantly about how wounding and bewildering ghosting can be, while readily admitting to ghosting others. 'It's not the end of the world if you just drop off the face of the earth,' states Alexei, who took off after making out with someone on a first date.[14] The fault, some suggest, is due to the endless options online dating provides, and a sense of unreality that can make it feel more like the chance for some fun and entertainment – a kind of game-ification of love.

With individuals so readily available, the process can seem more like online shopping than reaching out to another person, leaving would-be daters feeling more like a commodity than a person with real needs and feelings. Monique agrees: 'You can be mid-conversation, arranging a meet-up, and when you go back they have blocked you. Deleted the app. Vanished. If you don't respond quickly some get angry, then block you.' Curious as to why online dating can be such a battlefield, journalist Rachel Hosie followed up on the men who had ghosted her. 'Adam', the most honest of her 'ghosters', told of feeling overwhelmed with the number of people he interacted with daily. He saw having to get back to someone he'd only had a few friendly messages with online as 'a chore', so decided to just disappear off the radar. Rachel's other ghosters were less forthcoming. After a series of exchanges, they ended up ghosting her all over again.[15]

'On all the dates I have been on so far, I've been treated as if I'm choice #2. Option B. The backup plan,' complains

Scarlett. 'And after it happening again and again, it's killed my self-confidence. Why am I not enough? … Am I just a side chick or "the one"? Does he actually like me, or is he just lonely and looking for a rebound?'

'The potential for someone richer, hotter, funnier, more intellectual, more interesting, more "your type" is forever just a Tinder swipe away,' admits New York lifestyle writer Aly Walansky. 'It can affect how you treat the people right in front of you,' he adds, aware that this behaviour can, and does, spill over into everyday life.[16] How can anyone exposed to such scenarios feel anything other than seriously undervalued and ever lonelier? Izzy tells of her dating experience:

> I had two dates with him. The chemistry was there and I thought we were going somewhere. We had a lot of mental chemistry as well. The third date was going to be 'serious' I thought, and I got excited. My girlfriend was also dating on the same website. It was the day before I was going on my third date that she contacted me and said he had emailed her a flirtatious email, 'Isn't it about time we got to know one another?' – she then called me and I was upset. She knew it was him, as I had sent her a photo of him a few weeks prior. I definitely felt betrayed.

Part of our journey beyond loneliness is getting clear about ourselves and our expectations, but it's too often compromised in this 'smoke and mirrors' world. 'The worst thing,' Izzy admits after learning of her date's questionable behaviour, is that 'I doubted I should [feel betrayed].' So daters end up getting caught between the desire for a committed courtship and those who wantonly cast a wide net, intrigued to discover what comes their way. It is this very real disconnect that causes a great deal of pain and uncertainty.

Online dating isn't focused so much on long-term relationships or real dates, as 'flings', one online dater reflects. Does it matter if people are 'on' with multiple partners, or dumping each other the way they do? It's convenient to suggest not, but breakthroughs in neuroscience indicate that rejection hurts, and hurts deeply, activating the same pain channels in the brain as those turned on by physical pain. So the pain felt when ditched by a date or a potential date is real, and can be intense.[17] Added to this, when you're ghosted, you have no real idea what went wrong, so you're left with no way forward. Being dumped undermines your self-confidence, striking at your ability to make good decisions, not to mention ruining any chance you had of moving beyond your desire for love that set you on this path in the first place. Some ghost out of carelessness. Often women ghost for fear of a vitriolic or hateful response. Either way, there seems less willingness or ability to have a real-life exchange about thoughts and feelings that may prove helpful and positive all round.

A Lot of Fish

The popularity of dating apps is partly due to the constant suggestion that there are limitless mates 'out there' – an attractive message for anyone feeling lonesome. This belief that there are countless perfect dates, says David Buss, an expert in the evolution of human sexuality, impacts the way men behave, since men tend to go for short-term encounters whenever there are plenty of available women.[18]

Online dating is definitely working out for Joshua, a self-professed 'world expert in online dating'. '[It] has provided me with access to a lifestyle that was once only obtainable by men of superior looks and stature. Stick me in a bar to meet women and I'm likely to freeze up and falter. But in the online world, I'm a god amongst men,' he tells. With each date, Joshua finds himself 'more superficial, more judgmental, and completely unrealistic with my expectations', and realises no-one comes close to his 'impossible standards'. He admits that he wasn't always like this. But previously, he reflects, he didn't have 'unlimited options'.[19] How isolating, though, for the dates that Joshua discards.

That Sudden Tingle of Excitement

Many would-be daters become addicted to the buzz of a new match. 'After using dating sites like Tinder you need a rehab,' admits Art. 'Swiping left and right is simple, and addictive. It gives you a thrill to the point that you forget there are real people behind those pretty, and some less pretty, faces.' In such situations, how easy it is to let go of what's kind or fair, to diminish our humanity. Often we don't realise that we've been drawn into the loneliness loop with our ache, however harmless, for validation. 'Online dating notifications are an added rush as you are being physically validated by someone else,' tells Rosa. 'With the emphasis our society places on physical attractiveness, it's not surprising you feel validated when someone "swipes right" on you, based on a few photos of your face. Also, I loved the rush when you speak to someone who's different. Someone where the conversation doesn't follow the same script as the fifty other men [I've spoken with].'

Accused by some of 'McDonaldising' romance, dating sites do provide wider access to a much larger pool of possible dates, and the chance to communicate and 'match' up with these dates. Is it any wonder that online dating can seem so appealing? Yet it can also sabotage outcomes, because no matter how well written an online profile is, experts warn that the profile is two-dimensional at best. 'Choice paralysis is a very common trap,' agrees Blake in an AskMen chat room. 'No-one will take risks and invest because there might be a better option one swipe away. Our great grandparents had almost no choice, now we have too much.' Swimming in an ocean of choice can be exhausting and alienating.

So where does this unwillingness to commit leave daters? While dating sites are quick to claim they've altered dating for the better, studies show that being exposed to multiple candidates makes people more judgemental and less realistic. Put simply, so many choices can be a double-edged sword. 'We're not programmed to be exposed to so much sexual opportunity,' says psychology lecturer and relationships expert Dr Wendy Walsh. 'We're also programmed to get really excited about a new [sexual] opportunity because it used to be rare.'[20] How this pans out for the next generation of kids will be interesting, as they have grown up with this new normal.

Honing Your Skills

Some would-be daters are grateful for the often-lengthy process of finding 'the one', as it helps them fine-tune their dating skills on the way. Joshua freely admits he was fairly hopeless around women before online dating. 'Online dating gave me a medium to practise and harness my skills with women,' he tells.[21] Rosa agrees. 'I'm more assertive in what I want in a partner. I don't search for reasons why things won't work. If I'm not being treated correctly, I will stand up for myself. I definitely didn't do this before my online dating experiences,' she tells, adding, 'I'm more inclined to want to learn from someone, talk to them, rather than approach someone who's just attractive.'

With so many people to choose from, online dating does tend to raise the bar. Expectations are too high, insists human behaviouralist Alfie Kohn, warning of the dangers of the quick sense of entitlement the world of online dating creates, given almost immediate access to an intimate yet impersonal space, where someone's personal hygiene and sexual proclivities are spelled out, but not their name.[22]

'With same-sex-women dating, expectations are the killer,' Monique says. 'If you chat for too long, some women start to think it's a relationship before you even meet IRL [in real life] … they arrive on the date emotionally ahead of reality and are disappointed when you aren't ready to move in after the first date.' If loneliness is biting, we can easily lose perspective. Having so many potential partners on offer, it's also easy to make 'lazy, ill-advised decisions', one study suggests. A hastily decided 'match' doesn't come close to the 'experiential richness of a face-to-face encounter' – a person's body language, tone of voice, sense of humour, in-depth conversation.[23]

While online dating offers more potential partners, experts insist that current dating algorithms are 'ill placed' to deliver long-term relationships, as everyone is looking for someone attractive and personable with good earning power. Yet there are so many other qualities also needed for two people to gel that get little attention in the online dating process – from a person's overall coping ability to their backstory and sense of humour. These qualities aren't immediately apparent when assessing a potential date, as these details need to be gauged face to face. Moving beyond loneliness is a tender process, and one often not served well in cyberspace.

INSTANT ATTRACTION

When we're feeling isolated, it's easy to become a little too eager. Romantic expectations aside, often it's hard to gel on the first date. Knowing this, is it possible to 'click' with someone online in just a few seconds? Patience, it seems, pays dividends. One Stanford University study, looking at four-minute rounds of speed dating, found that the longer participants took to choose a date, the greater the resulting bond. The women who gelled with men used appreciative and sympathetic language, while the men who talked more about women during their four-minute encounter ranked higher in the success stakes, as did speed daters of both sexes who took the time to share their stories.[24] What this study reveals is the importance of nuance in the love stakes.

There are many more would-be daters to choose from online. Yet finding who you're compatible with, and how long it will take to find 'the one', remains the burning question. Love is rarely instant. 'I've had women meet me and say they have seen me on the apps for a long time,' tells Monique, an attractive, well-educated gay woman in her early forties. '[When we meet face to face] they are pleasantly surprised, as they assume the fact that I have been on dating apps so long means there is something wrong with me.'

It's a Crowded World

When dating online, there's also the amount of competition to contend with. If you're at a party you can see who's getting all the attention, but online you have no idea where in the queue you stand. 'The challenge is getting noticed through the noise of all those other men who are clamouring for attention,' says Roy. Lucas agrees: 'On most dating sites men outnumber women by at least 2:1, often more.' He believes the imbalance is so great that most dating sites deliberately lie about the number of women on the site 'to entice men to sign up'. 'It's somewhat of a numbers game,' states Max. 'I had to fail 500 times to succeed 10 times.'

Searching for dates online takes time, and can dent your self-esteem. 'I started feeling like so many other discouraged guys online,' admits Brad. 'I mean, imagine you had a guest over for dinner every week. You brought out the good dishes and cooked them an immaculate meal every Friday night. Just to have them eat and say it was just all right. How long do you think you'd keep trying?' Dave agrees. 'Plain and simple, a woman's inbox is filled and entangled with hundreds of messages from men ... dating in real life can be hard, online dating is exponentially difficult.' The opposite, it seems, is true for lesbian women. 'With the pond of women so small, many women that pop up as prospects on the apps I have met, or know of. It's awkward,' Monique tells. 'Some people just ignore the people they know. I block them as I know them, and know we are not a fit. I figure blocking others saves any awkwardness if they like you and you don't like them back.' Still, there's an unspoken sense of anxiety in these interactions.

Handling the Let-downs

Many online daters admit to feeling gutted at the frequent disappointments. 'It's rare for a woman of our generation to meet a man who treats her like a priority instead of an option,' reflects dating coach and columnist Erica Gordon.[25] Still, there are plenty of women who admit to enjoying 'boy shopping' and ready access to a string of dates willing to buy them dinner, or 'Tinder stamps' as some call them. These kinds of transactional approaches reduce interactions to little more than a cold-hearted numbers game, where people are judged purely in terms of benefits they can deliver 'on the night'. That said, many women (and men) do actually want to commit, although often older women are done with full-on relationships and simply want a good friendship, which can be equally fulfilling in some settings.

In this world of endless choices, where all it takes is a swipe to choose or discard someone, it's easy to see others as disposable. Some daters tell of how efficient current apps are at finding them abundant matches to the extent that they no longer feel obliged to take someone out for a meal before sex. Others admit to thinking that while their date is engaging and they're having fun, they can't help but be aware that there's someone better out there, only a swipe away. The tell-all Whisper app is littered with online dating horror stories, including tales of singles who are straight back on Tinder the instant they've had sex.

However the let-down happens, it's inevitable that self-esteem takes a hit. 'I feel like dating online can expose someone to more dramatic emotional highs and lows than dating organically and in person,' admits Josh. 'You can have a streak of success and feel invincible – and then have a string of rejects that is terribly deflating. Because online dating exposes you to so many more people,' he adds, 'the scale of one's successes and failures can increase correspondingly.'

Many do enjoy the novelty of hooking up with new people, but it can also pall. 'I used to imagine everybody having a unique interesting life. Instead almost every account I come across is generic,' complains Spiro. 'Either they don't know how to sell themselves besides their looks or they don't have anything to sell.' Tony agrees. 'You become much more sceptical over time, at least I did. I think over the years I've met at least 40 girls and roughly half of these dates were a complete failure ... both visually and when having a conversation. Right now I only meet up with girls that I find super amazing to talk with/hot because I subconsciously expect them to be significantly less attractive/witty in person.'

In a powerful article, Melbourne writer Giselle Au-Nhien Nguyen describes the rush she gets with mobile dating – the 'skin on skin, whirlwind, heat, flash', that leaves her hungry for more, catapulting her into a 'rinse, repeat' cycle. Yet on reflection, Giselle can also see there's a darker side to this process that feeds a growing sense of insecurity.[26] Caught between the ache for love and the excitement of new encounters, sooner or later a weariness sets in. 'It's all 'a f**king waste of time,' Andy reflects. 'To put so much into something you get so little out of is not even worth it. And don't even get me started on that goddamned ghosting.'

New Territory

One of the difficulties for newcomers to online dating is that it has its own rules, which can leave new daters confused or bruised. Izzy talks of the rush she feels when a match takes himself offline. 'It is a way of signalling you are taking the relationship seriously and are "going exclusive",' she tells. 'Generally you don't say this, you just take off your profile.' In a recent *Vanity Fair* piece, one New Yorker noted that if she's texted before midnight, she has more chance of being genuinely 'liked', while a text after midnight tends to signal it's simply yet another guy trawling for sex.[27] Another woman talks of her surprise at learning the 'hobbies' field isn't meant for everyday passions, so much as sexual preferences. 'It's surface,' Rosa admits. 'You have the same conversations over and over again, and it can get very boring and repetitive. I rarely felt comfortable to actually meet people in real life, so was really just using the people connected to the other end of the phone conversation as ways to pass time and feed my ego.'

The 2015 OkCupid survey of gay, straight and bisexual men and women users emphasised that the dating culture is still evolving. Over the last decade, 19 per cent fewer daters considered sleeping with their match on the first date. Interestingly, the biggest drop was with gay men. Those dating purely for sex also fell across the board. That said, people are now more relaxed about multiple sexual partners, while the 'three dates before sex' rule still holds strong. However, once matches are sure about their date, they're less likely to hesitate to take the next step.[28]

When Things Go Wrong

Many online daters talk of struggling to navigate the humiliations of bad language, explicit photos and poor behaviour. Aside from ghosting, they run the risk of 'benching' – having a date suddenly distance them, while suggesting they may still be in with a chance. Then there's 'breadcrumbing' – receiving vaguely flirty messages from potential daters without any real effort to connect. Others complain of 'orbiting', where a date continues to follow them, liking their posts but never answering their texts.

Then there's the creepy trend towards catfishing, creating a fake identity to lure in likely date prospects. 'It's a contest to see who cares less,' tells one online dater, adding that generally guys win in these stakes.[29] The more we delve into the world of online dating, the more we see how dark and isolating it can be for many, but just how many we'll never really know. It's concerning and depressing to see that these unkind, if not highly dubious, behaviours are so widespread, and it helps explain why would-be daters talk more about the 'downs' than the 'ups'. Who can blame them?

Disappointment isn't just down to the failures of individual daters, experts suggest. Dating algorithms are in need of considerable refinement, according to Mick, who's grown tired of 'fake profiles and bots'.[20] Peta agrees. 'After attempting to weed out scammers and persons only interested in bed intimacy ... I had no less than 5 males from overseas contacting my profile over the 3 days I was signed up. I had no interest in meeting anyone from overseas or interstate for that matter.'[31] Apart from all the 'fake users' and 'very small volume of current users', Kaz complains of being plagued with 'women wanting me to sign up for Snapchat video and other sites'.[32]

Checks and Balances

Traditional dating offered more safeguards. When you met a friend of a friend or co-worker, even if you didn't click, you were at least motivated to treat the other person well, so there wouldn't be any repercussions in your friendship group. There's a sense of nostalgia amongst some of today's daters for what seem like simpler, more innocent times. 'You are better off face to face trying to chat someone up. It has worked for hundreds of years. It is hard and it is putting yourself out there, but I think you will have a better shot than online,' notes Guy in one chat room discussion. 'Online you have no benefit of a dimly lit bar, a few cocktails, and the anticipation that comes with approaching or being approached by a stranger,' he adds. 'Online is stark, in your face, bright light and creeptastic.'

The almost instant intimacy online dating offers is frequently misleading, creating what social commentators call 'thin trust' – an assumption that because a stranger seems to share similar interests and possibly your extended social circle, they are trustworthy. Another aspect of thin trust is 'loving the one you're near', the sudden intimacy felt when you discover a possible match lives in your neighbourhood, which, while convenient, has nothing to do with whether you're likely to gel.[33]

There's a personal safety aspect to online dating, too. Tinder-related police callouts in the UK were up by 50 per cent in three years following up on the actions of more than a thousand questionable individuals. One in three complainants allege sexual assault or rape. These figures are thought to be light on, as not everyone reports assaults and not all reported assaults made the figures.[34] In Australia and elsewhere, online dating crimes include harassment, blackmail and fraud. In Denver alone, there were 53 reported crimes in 2018. Police suggested the actual figures were probably much higher, with some victims choosing not to come forward. One male found his laptop and tablet stolen after 'intimate relations'.[35] Others have lost serious amounts of money.

Following a wider story on online dating for *The New York Times,* Jack Nicas came across 56-year-old Renee Holland, who arrived at Philadelphia airport to pick up her friend Michael in the Marine Corps, only to discover there was no such flight. Several months earlier, Renee had lost her mother, become depressed and ended up on Facebook, where she met Michael Chris, who defused bombs in Iraq.

Renee was cautious, but as Michael shared his life in a war zone, she relaxed and started to help out with iTunes gift cards, medicine for Michael's sick daughter, then US$5000 for an airfare, which he promised to repay. Shocked when Michael didn't turn up, Renee overdosed. Renee's husband, Mark, a veteran from deployments in Honduras and South Korea, was furious about her relationship with Michael, and soon their marriage had deteriorated.

Meanwhile, Michael explained that he'd been delayed in Iraq due to his work. Photos of war injuries followed, along with papers indicating he was due for a major insurance payout. Renee sent more money for airfares, but Michael never showed up. By now Renee had given Michael upwards of US$30,000. Needing to start over, she, Mark and her elderly father relocated to Florida, where Mark was arrested for domestic violence towards Renee, who dropped the charges. Then, two days before Christmas, Mark shot Renee and her father dead, before shooting himself. Renee was one of tens of thousands of women who are scammed every year.[36]

EVERYONE LIES A LITTLE

Online dating is a tough game, a highly competitive race to the finish line, especially for those feeling vulnerable. Unrealistic expectations seem to go hand in hand with internet dating. 'A lot of women have higher standards online than they do in real life,' notes Pierre. The same holds true for many men. Figures suggest that those defined as 'elitely attractive' do best in the online dating game. The more glamorous a photo, the less believable it is, yet it's the good-looking daters who receive most hits. Studies suggest that, overall, women are more deceptive when posting photos,[37] with a third of the 'hottest photos' online over a year old.[38] Men tend to stretch things, too, adding a couple of inches to their height. Both men and women also tend to earn 20 per cent less income than stated.[39]

With the stakes so high, it's tempting for those entering the dating game to go easy on the truth. One study suggests that almost six out of ten people are deceived online, while only 19 per cent admit to being 'intentionally dishonest'.[40] 'Most people in the world are, by definition, average,' reflects Jost. 'In a world where people pretend averages don't exist, and where everybody is effectively obliged to look and act awesome and stylish and smooth 100% of the time, is it … surprising [people end up disappointed]?' It is 'harder to stand out', Neil admits.

'You have to straddle that line between "memorable" and "trying way too hard that it comes off as creepy".'

What About the Cheats?

An estimated 40 per cent of frequent online daters are married,[41] which isn't surprising, with a number of sites, most notably Ashley Madison, targeting 'married daters'. In one British survey, a participant compared online relationships to fast food, 'ready when we are, naughty, cheap, very often eaten alone without the exhaustion of social niceties'. However, for victims of internet infidelity, the outcomes are far from sweet. 'My ex-husband is inherently a very shy man, but online he is able to act much more confidently and attract the attention of other women,' Gloria told after discovering his infidelity.[42]

So what constitutes cheating online? Is it simply cybersex – the exchange of the odd sexy or daring selfie? Does it include online flirting and dating? Given the private nature of the internet, it's easy for a person's inhibitions to drop away and for them to embark on a second secret life. 'The problem,' notes blogger Kris Gage, 'is that we've made "love" into a game of escapism, and measure potential partners by how they fit into that fantasy.'[43] Couples, experts suggest, need to get clear about what is acceptable, both online and offline.

Does Online Dating Work?

One of the many pluses of online dating is that it saves time. But according to behavioural economics professor Dan Ariely, that's not actually the case. On average, online dating takes six hours of searches and connecting to make one date happen.[44] Yet for many, with the absence of viable alternatives, online dating is the only solution to their dating needs. Many are grateful for this opportunity. 'There has never been a time before now that two people from such different and diverse backgrounds could be brought together by something as simple, yet significant as the internet,' reflects Chas.

'I've always felt like an average-looking woman,' admits Kim Brooks in an article on Tinder, 'but swiping through my matches and messages, I felt like a special species. I felt coveted and appreciated and valued and desired. Why isn't every married woman in the world on Tinder, I began to wonder. It all felt the way romance was supposed to feel – playful and exciting and unserious.' Kim loved that the men she encountered online desired her, beyond being seen 'exclusively as a wife or mother', but 'as a sexual being, a full and complicated and multifaceted person, [loving] the experience of being wooed, wanted, admired, acknowledged'.[45] Not all matches end up as love interests, but they can still be valuable. 'I've made a few friends from people I have gone on dates with. This means when I am out, I have more people I can say hi to,' Monique tells. 'And from a networking perspective, it increases reach, as they may have a cute friend.'

Falling in love used to mean that someone would have to pluck up the courage to initiate a conversation with a person, then get to know them, sharing their life story and feelings. Online apps remove this layer of vulnerability. Now you know instantly if there's someone close by who may turn out to be a potential partner, or someone simply up for sex. Tinder 'inoculates us from the reality of what we are doing when we swipe left', reflects philosopher and ethicist Matthew Baird. 'We are so desensitised by a society that consumes images – news, pornography, film, television, advertising – that human beings, embodied persons with lives, feelings and stories of their own are also ripe for consumption.'[46]

Where to Now?

There's an increasing restlessness around relationships – a need to keep moving, to be on a constant lookout for the perfect partner. Ours is a culture that's rarely satisfied, so we continue to consume, never quite managing to reach a 'sweet spot'. Online dating is 'changing people's ideas about ... commitment,' notes former Match.com CEO Greg Blatt, and whether or not this is for life.[47] Living in a world of growing impermanence, where does this leave us, especially if we're feeling lonely?

After a decent spell with an older woman, Scott tells of meeting Tessa online, who was 'young and beautiful'. They settled down, only to split after two years. Scott's immediate response was to go straight back to Match.com, confident there was someone else out there. Looking back, he admits that had he not met Tessa online, he was 'about 95 per cent certain' he'd have married her, but his online experiences changed his expectations.[48] Could this be a missed opportunity for long-term happiness? Where does this pattern leave us in a decade or more – as individuals, and as communities? What does this do to our children? There's a definite dehumanising factor at play here. Denise readily admits to viewing online matches as different from people she first encounters in real life. Even after meeting an online match, she notes, they still tend to seem more like a profile than a person.

'I find dating sites priceless. I've had several month-long relationships, with women I met at dating sites,' states Adrian, who by his own admission is no 'Don Juan' or 'Tom Cruise'. 'It never took me more than a couple of weeks, sometimes only a day, to meet a woman I liked, and make a relationship out of it,' adding, 'And I'm pretty bad with women. I never know what they want.' Online dating does 'increase your chances to meet someone you'll like,' states Des. 'But you need to prepare yourself to expend lots of effort, which you may not deem to be worthwhile.' Frankie agrees. 'There is nothing exceptional about me. I'm not particularly good looking. I don't take particularly great pictures … Yet, despite all these things, I have had fairly good success with online dating. My last six relationships were from online dating … So how, as an average straight male, did I achieve that success? Effort. I put effort into it. I put effort into myself. I made sure that I was always the best me I could be … Take the time and put in the effort and you will find success.'

What, we need to ask ourselves, if we're hoping to curb our loneliness, is a measure of true success? Is it a numbers game, or something more profound, more sustainable?

What Will Get You Past the Line?

'You won't go from lonely bachelor to swingin' casanova just by signing up for OkCupid,' Beau cautions. Los Angeles dating coach Laurel House agrees. 'At the end of the day, you shouldn't allow the app or website to control your style of communication to begin with. Take control yourself, and ask real substantive questions that will allow you to get to know someone on a substantial level before you meet in person.'[49] Ultimately there are no shortcuts. Online dating still requires considerable effort. 'Men typically put very little effort into their physical appearance and Tinder profiles, and then wonder why it's hard for them to get laid. It's just bizarre,' reflects Ryan in an AskMen chat room. 'Ask any bisexual person how often they see an attractive man on Tinder vs. an attractive woman on Tinder. It's like night and day.'

In one survey of over a million Plenty of Fish potential daters, those who used the word 'love' in their profiles were most likely to find love. Additional words such as 'life', 'friend', 'time' and 'music' also seemed to resonate, whereas women using the words 'shop', 'travel' and 'dinner' proved less successful, as did men using 'hang' and 'humour'.[50]

Online dating seems to make people hopeful yet cautious and more self-focused, thus ultimately less focused on the relationship. Does this, in part, indicate why 'success' is hard won and often fleeting? It's too early to tell where this new world is taking us. Online dating is, behavioural scientist Clarissa Silva notes, the perfect forum for 'vanity validation, to having one's ego stroked, but it's hardly the basis of a strong relationship'.[51] Concerns around online dating are shifting away from worries about our security, suggests digital anthropologist Chris Hurley, to the 'potentially catastrophic effect online dating can have on our traditional values such as love, intimacy and ultimately what it is to be human',[52] all vital elements if we want to move beyond our loneliness.

There's no doubt that dating apps offer wider choices, which can be reassuring, 'When my marriage ended 11 years ago, I went online. I hadn't dated in over 20 years,' tells science writer David Levine. 'So I signed up for Match.com, which has more than 21.5 million subscribers. I received 350 emails in a month.'[53] Still, there are no guarantees. 'It's not working for me,' Monique admits. 'I've been totally single for three years. In this time I have had a few first dates but zero intimacy. I've had no "skinship" in this time, and this brings with it a great sadness.' Intimacy, whatever that looks like, is what most crave. But where is it to be found?

'I encourage people to stay online,' says psychotherapist Melissa Ferrari, 'yet not to assume that their dating needs are sorted, so they don't miss out [on a real-life connection] – the twinkle in a barista's eye that could lead to something.' However, with less enthusiasm for 'being soothed or helped by another', Ferrari fears there'll be greater relationship issues in the future. 'We're losing the ability to stay with the other's flaws,' she reflects. 'People aren't perfect. They're going to make mistakes, it's human. But the ideal of the perfect romance is so high now, people leave relationships prematurely, because they expect their partner always to get things right.'

What's clear is that we're not designed to operate in a sea of endless choices, which leaves us stuck in our heads and increasingly detached from our physical bodies, not to mention 'dating app fatigue'. Why? Because our brains aren't wired to cope with hundreds of options. The most they can deal with is nine choices, explains Helen Fisher, chief scientific adviser for Match.com, so when you reach nine matches, she advises you cease additional swiping, and consider the possibilities before you.[54]

COVID-19 and subsequent fears about the health of would-be partners has sparked some intriguing changes to online dating. Internet daters are now spending a lot more time getting to know each other – chatting for extended periods on FaceTime, Zoom and other platforms before they meet in the flesh – and with their first real-life encounters socially distanced, they're investing far more into getting to know each other. As a result, we're seeing less churn and more slow burn in our approach to relationships. By getting to know each other better, perhaps we'll be motivated to treat each other with more thought.

The other side of this coin, experts insist, lies in our own self-belief and ongoing self-care. Perhaps Melbourne writer Giselle Au-Nhien Nguyen sums it up best when she says, 'If I can only Super Like one person a day … from now on I sure as hell am going to make it myself.'[55]

How to Avoid Dating Disasters

It's tempting to put the rest of your life on hold while searching for the perfect mate. But the narrower your life, the narrower your chance of finding that special someone. So follow your passions, and perhaps introduce a few more. You may meet someone who's equally passionate about something you love, be it rock-climbing, foreign movies, tattoos or Thai food. And check out Meetup. It's a great non-dating app that helps bring people with the same interests together.

If you do decide to go down the online dating path, here are some tips to consider.

1. Safety First

- When meeting someone new, meet somewhere neutral, where there are plenty of people around.
- Let friends know where you are on new or almost new dates.
- Organise a 'safe word' to text friends, should a date turn sour.
- Set up a 'testing the temperature' call – have a friend ring to check in on you while with a new date.

2. When You Meet Up

- Take a deep breath and try to relax.
- It's not a job interview, so don't give your résumé and don't try too hard to impress.
- Be interested in your date and listen closely to what they are saying – ask questions but don't pry.
- While not all dates work out, don't immediately ditch someone, as you may still end up being good friends.
- Offer to pay the bill – generosity is always attractive.
- Know that love comes in different packages, some of which may just surprise you.

3. When to Pull the Plug

- If there are worrying personality traits or behaviours, it's time to walk away.
- Should you no longer both contribute equally to the relationship, and support each other, the relationship needs to end.
- If your partner's family and friends make you feel inferior or uncomfortable, the relationship is not likely to be a happy one.

- A relationship is unlikely to work if your values constantly clash, and you find yourself on an emotional roller-coaster.
- Don't assume you can change someone to fit your ideal.

4. How to End It

- Endings can be messy. Try to make the break in a way that's kind but assertive.
- Face to face is always best. (If you have a history or fear of abuse, take the precaution of having a family member or close friend assist you in leaving.)
- Where possible, talk of the good moments you've had that you'll cherish.
- Don't get into a catalogue of what your partner has done wrong.
- Dare to admit that the break makes you sad and, if circumstances permit after you've both grieved, that you hope you'll continue to be friends.

5. If You've Been Ghosted

- Don't cling to a dream that's not going to eventuate.
- See this experience for what it is – a lucky break.
- Be prepared to feel shocked, saddened, angry, hurt.
- Allow for some healing time before more dating – time with friends who nurture you.
- Don't be tempted to follow suit and treat others in this way.
- Do yourself the kindess of getting professional help if you're finding it hard to move on.

6

When Love and Reality TV Collide

Train-wreck TV

The Impact on Viewers

Is it Time for a Reality TV Detox?

TRAIN-WRECK TV

Nowhere is the process of finding love more harrowing than on reality TV shows such as *Married At First Sight*, which for many is mesmerisingly awful and compulsive viewing at the same time. As far as reality TV shows go, *Married At First Sight* is up there with the most popular, knowing exactly how to capitalise on the 'love market'. Now produced in over a dozen countries from Portugal and Poland to Belgium and Israel, the Danish-inspired show rates its socks off. Sold as 'a ground-breaking social experiment', *Married At First Sight* has an audience nudging 2 million in Australia alone. As a social experiment, however, it's not exactly a runaway success. After eight seasons in the US to the end of 2019, only six couples are still together. Over this same time period in Australia, all but one couple have split, despite the 'scientific' matching of 35 straight and gay couples over five seasons.

Was *Married At First Sight* ever really a scientific experiment? The answer is probably not too hard to work out. The bigger, often more polarising question is whether the show is simply harmless entertainment. *Married At First Sight* is nothing more than 'the manipulation of the most intimate desires and fears' for TV ratings, insists Lou.[1] But Desney disagrees: 'These people are adults and they willingly sign up. They are not victims.'[2] Wherever you stand on this spectrum, no-one denies that *Married At First Sight* is a huge commercial success, with millions of viewers worldwide.

> '"Reality" TV. The modern-day freak show.'
> *Lyn*[3]

What's it Like to Be in a Reality TV Show?

When you dive behind the scenes, you get a better sense of how reality TV shows are set up. In a 2008 interview, Claire Molyneux, a 40-year-old council officer, shared what it was like to be part of the UK reality show *Take My Mother-In-Law*. Reflecting on her experience in a *Daily Mail* interview, Claire told how the show's researchers behaved like 'best friends', delivering everything they'd promised, until she signed the contract.

Looking back, Claire believes she was basically 'groomed'. As she got into the filming, she was shocked at her complete loss of control – from the unrelenting hours spent in front of the camera, to having her least flattering clothes laid out for her to wear the moment she was home from work, while at the same time being miked up. What also shocked Claire were the deliberate attempts to get her angry and make her cry. At one point the producer yelled at her in frustration, asking what it would take to break her.[4]

Beyond the glittering lights and dazzling possibility of nationwide attention, there are real risks in volunteering for these kinds of reality TV shows. Few hopefuls stop to think what it's like to navigate frequent outbursts of anger and other out-of-control behaviour from fellow participants, while the camera captures everything that's taking place; or to face the judgement of hundreds of thousands of strangers. Most participants have no idea of the struggle needed to stay strong amid countless misrepresentations of who they are. 'These ingredients,' suggests clinical psychotherapist Noosha Anzab, are 'the perfect environment for depression, anxiety, pain and isolation to grow.'[5]

Gillian Cooke and daughter Zoe from northern England also experienced firsthand how these programs are put together.

Having struggled with obesity, Gillian and Zoe signed up for reality TV show *The Family Weigh-In*. Thrilled to have access to expert help, and despite being filmed 16 hours a day, Gillian and Zoe were determined to go the distance. Participating in endless gruelling regimes, they desperately wanted to lose weight. Later, they were crushed to see themselves depicted as lazy and just 'in the game' to score the prize holiday for the winning weight-loss family. After all Gillian and Zoe had worked towards, they were left feeling devastated and stripped bare.[6]

Dealing with the Scrutiny

There are real consequences for those who participate in these kinds of reality TV shows. If life felt lonely before being a participant, it's often more so afterwards. Desperate to escape all the negative attention she had received during and following the 2018 Australian season of *Married At First Sight*, Tracey Jewel headed off to Berlin, finding herself in a 'headspin'. 'You've won, trolls. I give up,' she posted on Instagram. 'You've ruined my life. You've involved my friends, family, clients and sponsors. I have lost everything because of your relentless hate.'[7]

After fielding a year of hate messages, Tracey was in a difficult space and ended up overdosing a long way from home. Luckily, Tracey sought help. Her psychologist went so far as to suggest Tracey may be suffering from post-traumatic stress with all she'd been through.[8] Jan Melia also felt the full force of events after taking part in the UK reality TV show *Wife Swap*. Jan was so traumatised by her reality TV experience that she and her family sold up and moved countries. Like many participants, Jan tried to speak up about the way things were evolving during filming, only to have the crew assure her it was all simply 'harmless fun'.[9]

Whenever concerns about such programs as *Married At First Sight* arise, the stock response is that participants know exactly what they are getting into. But do they? How, for instance, do program-makers know exactly which buttons to press, when they're dealing with virtual strangers? One male participant in the UK version of *Married At First Sight* admits he's still unclear about how the 'scientific matching' on the show works. Before filming he went through a detailed procedure, where almost every part of him was measured – from his height and 'shoulder to waist ratio', to 'the size of [his] index fingers'. None of this seemed to have any bearing on helping him find 'the one', but he went along with the process, as the program-makers seemed to know what they were doing. Added to this, he was asked to fill out a '500 question questionnaire', which covered endless details, from his religious and political views, to past and current sexual encounters.[10]

> 'I find watching (un)reality TV belittling, degrading, embarrassing to the people involved and unworthy of my time.'
> *Marissa*[11]

Participants, Beware!

With so many searching questions, why doesn't this stop potential contestants from signing up? When mining-truck driver Susan Rawlings looks back on her time on *Married At First Sight*, she admits to feeling encouraged by the level of detail she was asked to provide before the show began. As she worked through all the psychological tests and paperwork, she read all this effort as a real attempt to get to know her, and thus give her a good shot at meeting the right person.

Added to this, Susan had the show's psychologists to fall back on, if she needed them. However, once filming began, Susan was shocked at how little thought was given to the likely fallout from the careless way participants were treated. And as for the resident psychologists, according to Susan, the only time she saw these experts was when they observed a dinner party from behind a curtain, and at the commitment ceremony.[12]

If you hand over your destiny, you need to expect a few surprises. How does this 'scientific matching' play out? The 2019 Australian season saw Heidi Latcham, who was raised in foster care, paired with Mike Gunner, who wasn't exactly a sensitive new-age male. Another participant that season was hairdresser Ning Surasiang, who'd been left in Thailand while small, and subsequently had her first baby at 16. Ning, who is no longer with the father of her children, was paired with Mark Scrivens. There are no prizes for guessing that their honeymoon was in Thailand.[13]

How do such scenarios help those with fragile pasts? As one viewer points out, 'Some contestants appear to demonstrate behaviour and ways of thinking that are indicators of mental health concerns', including a 'pattern of blaming others when confronted with problems, impulsivity, anger outbursts, extreme mood changes, lack of empathy, telling lies, lack of remorse and going against the "moral code" to meet one's own needs'.[14]

The challenge for the producers of reality TV shows is to keep viewers watching. Upping the shock factor is a sure-fire way to go. During the 2019 Australian *Married At First Sight* season, mental health and other experts raised a red flag, concerned that the show was pushing the boundaries too far and that contestants could be left with 'severe trauma and long-term emotional issues'.[15] Were they overstating the case? Not according to Australian participant Lauren Bran, who told of the unbearable conditions that she and fellow participants faced in an earlier season, with hour after hour of shooting, leaving them begging for toilet breaks. At Lauren's hens' night she was shocked to see jugs of water swiftly replaced with vodka and Red Bull. Added to this, some of the filming sessions she was involved in lasted up to 12 hours, finishing at three or four in the morning.[16]

A Culture of Abuse

Another aspect of reality TV shows is the seriously catty way some participants take each other apart. The question we all need to ask is: is what we're seeing just a handful of people letting off steam, or high-level emotional abuse? Everyone has their own opinion, but what we do know is that this show comes at a time when domestic violence and violence towards women in general are cause for massive concern. Witnessing the largely verbal abuse between participants over and over can desensitise viewers, leading them to believe that this is acceptable behaviour.

Abuse has a way of escalating – of becoming the norm in families and friendships, and at work. Currently, on average, one Australian woman is murdered every nine days, and one Australian man is killed every 29 days by a partner.[17] One in six women and one in nine men have experienced physical or emotional abuse before they were 15, while one in five women have been a victim of sexual violence from the age of 15.[18] These figures are echoed in too many countries across the globe.

It's also concerning that, increasingly, women are the ones dishing out the abuse. In the last decade or so there's been a shift in how female empowerment is depicted, with women sometimes behaving in violent and abusive ways, mirroring the behaviour of out-of-control men. In this race to the bottom, we constantly see dark, dysfunctional images and storylines – in movies and on-demand TV, and in shows such as *Married At First Sight*. Here women treat each other badly with impunity, bullying and lying, and deliberately setting out to take each other down. This is done in the name of empowerment, but all that's really happening is that bad behaviour is being used to justify despicable actions for ratings and revenue, allowing abuse to be regarded as the norm.

Cynics may suggest this is overstating the case. Yet abuse is like shrapnel – its shards have a way of harming everyone within range. Viewing abusive behaviour on TV glamorises it. What a world away this nastiness is from true empowerment where, for example, country music artist Kellie Pickler shaved off her hair to support her best friend who was diagnosed with breast cancer.

Stories of empowerment take us in a different direction, giving us hope. On New Year's Eve 2019, Aboriginal Elder Aunty Gloria was one of many to lose her home to bushfires. Devastated, she was desperate to stay on her land. When a complete stranger living 1200 kilometres away heard of Aunty Gloria's situation, they offered their caravan. With the help of the local community, they filled the caravan with much-needed items before it was driven down the coast in a relay to Aunty Gloria. A few months later in Florida, during the pandemic, a 96-year-old man asked the nurse giving him a blood test where he could buy toilet paper. She had no idea. That night, there was a knock at the man's door. The nurse had visited ten stores with a friend at the end of her shift, before she found a large pack of toilet paper for this elderly man.

THE IMPACT ON VIEWERS

In our already disconnected world, do we really need to watch men and women behaving badly, and tearing each other apart? It's not just participants who end up bruised. Viewing people hurting each other strikes at our humanity, leaving some feeling fragile, with less faith in the world. We saw this after the 2013 bombings in Boston, when a study into the aftermath found that those suffering acute stress from the bombings weren't so much those who had experienced this terror firsthand as those who had watched the terrible event over and over on TV and in social media. It was these latter viewers who were more likely to end up with post-traumatic stress symptoms – anxiety, flashbacks and hyper-vigilance.[19]

'The negative effects of exposure to other people's suffering have long been recognised,' affirms Dr Pam Ramsden, a senior lecturer in psychology at the University of Bradford, who was part of a study looking at the effects of individuals watching disturbing news coverage on social media. The study found that just over 20 per cent of participants were 'significantly affected' by their viewing, reporting clear signs of post-traumatic stress disorder.[20]

'Personally I was disgusted by the conduct of these so called "experts" [on *Married At First Sight*]. I found their behaviour to be that of callous disregard for the wellbeing of the participants. Blind Freddy can see they purposely mismatched participants for maximum drama.'
Mae[21]

Getting a ringside view of people tearing each other to pieces can also awaken past hurts – situations we thought we were over, only to find that we're not. Some of life's traumas get locked away, buried deep, as we're just not able to deal with them at the time. Then, when we face similar events, this past pain is triggered. We end up reliving our hurt in a sudden tsunami of unpleasant feelings and flashbacks. 'I stopped watching [*Married At First Sight*],' Jenny admits. 'I had to for my mental health. I felt very hopeless, like there was nothing out there for me.'

Jenny is one of a number of viewers, including entertainment writer Anita Lyons, who were affected by the show. Anita described her intense viewing of one *Married At First Sight* season for work, as like being on 'the mother of all benders'. As Anita immersed herself in the detail, it triggered this 32-year-old single's own romantic hurts and anxieties – from a series of stressful first dates, to trawling dating apps in search of love. Having viewed a whole season of people treating one another badly – lying and cheating and yelling at each other – and watching people happily gaslight and ghost others, Anita was left wondering if this is all a person can hope for and if love works.[22]

'Please tell me you're not buying the "social experiment" line
that the network trots out?'
Angela[23]

When Trauma Hangs Around

In a powerful article on her own relationship difficulties, Dr Imaan Joshi tells how trauma has a way of rewiring us, leaving us thinking our thoughts and beliefs aren't important, and prompting us to press ahead, ignoring 'our own feelings'. The end result is that we're often anxious, overthinking 'everything and everyone', and allowing 'poor behaviour' towards us 'long after it is appropriate'. Past baggage, she writes, has a way of impacting current relationships, and 'we end up distancing ourselves from someone that may actually be good for our healing'. We 'blame the other person' and keep our distance, then 'move on to the next "safe" person until they too lose their shine'. Looking back, Joshi can see how she blamed those she dated for past hurts. The way through, she now sees, is to focus on what she learns from each date, and to continue to work on her own growth.[24]

> 'Reality Trash TV is curated to place the basest human
> behaviour on show for voyeurs who have little else to do.'
> *Hans*[25]

Matching Contestants

Nothing is left to chance in these high-stakes shows. Producers know exactly how to get participants to behave badly. Just how does *Married At First Sight* manage to open old wounds? After taking a look at the questionnaire, writer Hannah-Rose Yee shared some of the questions, which ranged from a person being asked to share their greatest regret, and 'one major thing' about themselves they'd never told anyone, to details of previous relationships, and whether they were lonely and had ever been unfaithful.[26] This is highly sensitive information and, like all sensitive material, can be dangerous in the wrong hands.

Right from the start, participants' expectations are raised, then manipulated, for the purpose of the show. They have their hearts set on one scenario and assume it's all in place, only to find it's not and then feel let down. Before the 2016 UK season of *Married At First Sight*, Clark Sherwood was shown a presentation of his possible wedding choices, from different food offerings and the overall theme, to the kind of music he'd like, none of which he got on his big day. There was also money put aside should Clark divorce, which he did, although he had to wait a whole year after his 'marriage' before he could start divorce proceedings.[27]

These experiences are in sharp contrast to the *Married At First Sight* website, which welcomes those eager to be part of the new season's line-up, insisting the show only wants those who are 'genuine about finding love'. For this once-in-a-lifetime opportunity, all that's needed is '4 months of your life'. This is not a competition and there is no cash prize, the website stresses, but you could just win 'the most valuable prize of all ... true love'. And all you need, the website assures new hopefuls, is to 'put your fate in the hands of our relationship experts'.[28]

This all sounds so easy and, when you're in a vulnerable place, it's easy to revert to a child's view of the world, hoping that someone else will pick you up and sort out your life for you. If you're feeling down about finding your life partner, how appealing to have *Married At First Sight,* with its resident psychologists, help make this happen. When judged through this lens, it's not hard to see why signing up for the show is so appealing. Yet much as we'd like others to sort out crucial aspects of our lives when we're not in a great headspace, this is exactly the moment we need to take charge of our destiny and get professional help if needed, to make our own decisions and forge our own way ahead. To do anything less is disempowering. To enter a reality TV show with these goals is terrifyingly so.

> 'So the programme is setting a very, very low bar for human behaviour/relationships. Not a lot of good in that.'
> *Katie*[29]

To be fair, not everyone is negatively affected by the show. While psychologist Rachel Voysey doesn't condone its aggression, bullying and violence, she can see some value in viewing *Married At First Sight*. As women have a way of gossiping and insulting each other, Voysey suggests viewers may benefit from observing these dynamics at a safe distance. This may shed light on a viewer's own hurtful experiences and help them process past conflicts. That said, Voysey also stresses that watching people lying, cheating and tearing each other apart can lead some to believe this is acceptable behaviour.[30] Alan agrees: 'I am 64 years old happily married and I can honestly say it [*Married At First Sight* has made me] think about what sort of partner am I, what sort of friend am I and is there something I can do to have better relationships. I have certainly taken some positive action since the beginning of this season of *MAFS*.'[31]

Way too Cruel

Train-wreck TV shows such as *Married At First Sight* don't just push people's physical boundaries. At their essence these shows are psychologically cruel. Unsuspecting participants step into a dark world, where all the wonderful colour and diversity found in everyday life is reduced to people being branded winners or losers. This uncomfortable world is constantly shifting. One minute you're on top of the game, the next you're cut down, often by those closest to you. How can anyone feel safe in such set-ups, let alone valued? This kind of hothouse environment is designed to push participants' buttons, then capture the fallout. And with the almost forensic level of 'research' into individual contestants, there's plenty of material for producers to play with.

So how do participants feel about the program? In one interview, businesswoman Davina Rankin, who appeared in the 2018 Australian season of *Married At First Sight*, says she 'barely got out of this whole ordeal alive'.[32] This may seem an overstatement, yet as the 2019 Australian season drew to a close, there were reports of a 'shocking and unprecedented' number of threats against contestants. Branded as the season 'baddie', 28-year-old legal assistant Ines Basic was the subject of a street attack. Thousands signed up on social media for a revved-up city gathering close to her home. These and other incidents obviously had the network spooked. A number of participants were reported to have been whisked off to a rural retreat at the end of the show.[33]

There's good reason why Ines might unravel under pressure. She arrived in Australia aged four. Before this she had moved around Eastern Europe with her family, and had lived for a time in refugee camps. With her father largely absent from her life, it's not surprising that Ines admitted: 'my biggest thing is I need to be protected and I need to feel safe'.[34] Participants like Ines are reality TV gold, but where was the tangible sense of safety for Ines during the show? One heartbreaking moment towards the end of the season summed up so much that's unhelpful to women about the show when fellow participant Lizzie Sobinoff broke down, saying, 'We get so much thrown at us [as women]', then went on to talk of how relentless men's expectations of women are. Her implied question: do women need to be at each other's throats as well? This is a critical point, because while the show might not leave visible bruising, verbal threats and abuse strip away a person's sense of self, impacting them physically and mentally.

Not All Hurt Is Physical

Recent research shows that it's difficult to distinguish the psychological effect of physical torture from that of intense psychological pressure.[35] More than this, when someone has a shock in everyday life, normally there's time to rebalance. However, when placed in an ongoing high-stress situation, such as on *Married At First Sight*, there's little chance for anyone to readjust. So as the stress ramps up, it's not surprising that people lash out.[36]

'It's pathetic to see what people will do, desperate for 15 minutes of fame,' claims Yolande.[37] But is the situation participants find themselves in so straightforward? Some of the techniques used on the show, such as sleep deprivation, are the very same tools used in torture, and in keeping people under control in cult situations. Sleep deprivation is also very effective at wearing down a person's resistance, making it hard for them to think straight, make positive decisions, or be articulate. Such techniques also alter a person's moods.[38] One paper looking at the impact of torture on the brain notes that such 'non-injurious' techniques can also impair the brain's ability to renew its cells, impacting the part of our brain responsible for long-term memory and how we navigate our environment.[39]

So why participate in this complicated charade? Yes, there's the chance of fame, and the ache to find love, but ultimately we can only speculate about why participants do what they do. Interestingly, we now know considerably more about those joining cults. Often cult members suffer self-esteem issues. They're people in search of solace and answers outside themselves. Psychoanalyst Dr Stanley H. Cath, who has worked with people emerging from cults, also tells of how cults keep people constantly fatigued and controlled as a way of getting them to cooperate.[40] When people first enter the cult they are often 'love bombed' – made to feel special. They're the centre of attention, feeling nurtured and accepted. Then they are slowly taken apart as the focus shifts to their shortcomings. Sound familiar? Members are pitted against each other, leading to a climate of distrust and public humiliation, creating a loss of joy, increased irritability and heightened paranoia.[41] In cults, people are made to believe they're the 'chosen ones', all the while slaving and sacrificing themselves for 'the cause'. With so much at stake, often cult members resort to lying and cheating to stay ahead of the game, and are soon in survival mode. The great fear is always that they'll fall short and be ostracised from the group, that they'll be back where they started – out in the cold.[42]

Where Does This Leave Us?

Falling in love is scary. It's one of the most vulnerable steps we as human beings can take – to reveal our innermost self to another person, and hope we'll be loved back. At the heart of this vulnerability lie the two great human fears – of rejection and abandonment. Deep down we know we're not perfect, so we often try to hide our vulnerability by trying to prove how special we are. Shows such as *Married At First Sight* play to our deepest aches and fears and, in spite of their promises, leave many feeling even more isolated.

The final question is where we as viewers sit watching the show, and contributing to *Married At First Sight* ratings. We all like to feel our humanity is intact, all the while watching people being manipulated, falling in and out of love in graphic ways, and saying and doing hurtful things to each other. Shouldn't seeing participants' extreme disappointment and hurts sadden us? To 'enjoy' their pain is a questionable pursuit. How does this help build our connection with each other?

When I was researching my book *What's Happening to Our Girls?*, one school counsellor told me of seeing an escalation in bullying when reality TV arrived on our screens. Following this thread, I came to see how teens had begun mimicking the behaviour seen on reality TV, escalating their judgements about who's 'in' and who's 'out'. And soon this pattern becomes a new way of relating – of treating each other, including best friends, with blatant disregard. Or, as one teen commented at the time, 'It's not like hurting people physically. It's very mental. It's very much an emotional kind of like breaking you down mentally. It does break people down very systematically until there's not much left.'[43]

Reality TV does have a wintry feel, often lacking any warmth, hope or genuine love. Ultimately, most of these shows leave us with the uncomfortable sense of being on the outer: a fear that life is less certain than we'd hoped; that no-one is truly on our side; that with so many expectations, we can't possibly measure up. In this climate of growing isolation, we each have to find our own ways to dull our fears and uncertainties. Perversely, seeing someone else subjected to unkind behaviour can deliver a sense of relief that we're not the ones standing under the spotlight.

Like it or not, reality TV does impact people's lives, and none more so than the lives of its contestants. Claims have been made that as many as 38 reality TV stars worldwide may have taken their own lives[44] after appearing in such shows as *Let's Dance, Survivor, The Bachelor, The X Factor* and *The Voice*.[45] Former Miss Great Britain, Sophie Gradon, who was part of the UK's 2016 *Love Island* season, committed suicide two years later. According to Sophie's mother, Sophie was upfront with the *Love Island* crew about her struggles with mental health issues, and made several attempts to leave the show.[46] In June 2018, Sophie's body was discovered by her boyfriend Aaron Armstrong, who was so grief-stricken that he took his own life just weeks later.

Almost a year on, professional soccer player Mike Thalassitis, described as an 'absolute gent' and 'thoughtful, caring, and so fiercely loyal to his friends and family',[47] hanged himself after appearing on the 2017 UK *Love Island* season. Meanwhile, the *Love Island* offering moves on, picking up additional franchises and turnover around the globe. The show does now offer contestants social media training, therapy and financial management.[48] Time will tell whether this is sufficient support for contestants. Certainly Matt Hancock, the UK's Health Secretary, has his doubts, admitting to being 'very worried about the support for mental health' given to reality TV contestants.[49]

At the end of the day these participants may well be flirting with fame, but it's important to dig deeper and question why. When we step back a little, we see how often these on-screen contestants look like they're barely surviving, rather than living the dream. But that is also how an increasing number of us are feeling – like we never truly measure up or belong. These are some of the many faces of isolation we're continuing to grapple with in our post-pandemic world. Surely there are more uplifting ways for TV stations to make money, and for us to be entertained.

Is it Time for a Reality TV Detox?

Given there's little that's 'real' about reality TV, why give so much time to it? These questions and points are designed to help you examine the reasons you watch reality TV, and point the way forward.

- What draws you to reality TV?
- Do these shows leave you feeling optimistic about people?
- Is reality TV behaviour the way you'd like others to treat you?
- Watching others struggle to feel good isn't healthy. Why get hooked in to all the negative vibes? What's causing your need for drama?
- Train-wreck TV is addictive. Be aware that we tend to turn to an addiction to hide our personal pain – our isolation, extreme exhaustion, and so on.
- Why are you so fascinated by the shortcomings of others? Could it be an attempt to avoid your own?
- How do you handle conflict? Is your approach working, or do you need to refine how you interact with others?
- Try to catch yourself judging people through a reality TV lens, seeing others as winners and losers. Life's more complex than that – we're all good in certain areas, and less than perfect in others.
- Make an effort to understand where others are coming from, and what it's like to walk in their shoes.
- When it comes to managing conflict and differences, try to model the behaviour you'd like to experience.

'The world is full of kind people … If you can't find one, be one.'
Unknown

7

Home Alone

Living Alone

Ordering In

Binge-watching

Powerful Ways Back to Connection

LIVING ALONE

Aloneness comes in many forms and is a curious thing. Currently, singles occupy one in four Australian homes.[1] This pretty much aligns with US figures, where just over a quarter of homes are one-person households – eight times that of 1950, when there were only 4 million people living on their own.[2] Sweden tops these figures, with almost half of its population living in single-person dwellings.[3]

This is a trend that looks set to continue. In New South Wales alone, the market for studio or one-bedroom apartments is expected to rise. In 2011, there were around 630,000 people living alone. It's suggested that we're set to see a 60 per cent increase in lone households in 25 years' time.[4] This demand is driven by young people and a mature-age market, who are finding themselves single after a separation or due to the loss of a partner.

However, warns Eric Klinenberg, author of *Going Solo*, living on your own doesn't necessarily equate to loneliness. Given the hyper-connected environment we live in, time on our own can provide what he calls 'restorative solitude'. The singles' culture can also be a very positive trend, especially in urban areas. 'The spike of living alone has played a large and overlooked role in revitalizing cities,' Klinenberg suggests, 'because singletons are so likely to go out in the world, to be in cafes and restaurants, to volunteer in civic organizations, to attend lectures and concerts, to spend time in parks and other public spaces. They have played a big role in reanimating central cities.' Not so, however, for singles living in regional and in rural areas.[5]

Part of the reason for the growth in lone households is people partnering later. One Deloitte paper suggests that singles tend to spend more on housing, preferring to rent rather than buy. As our population ages, if this singles trend continues, it will impact the health industry, with an increased number of people needing access to 'outside' care because they don't have the informal care that a partner brings during times of sickness or disablement.[6]

ORDERING IN

As well as living alone, we're now eating entirely alone, or 'together but not together' as we're glued to a screen. All this is possible thanks to food delivery services such as Uber Eats, Deliveroo, Foodora, Menulog and more. Ordering in seems the perfect solution for the time poor, or those who are weary after a big day at work. In 2017, Australians outlaid $2.6 billion on food and drink home deliveries, a staggering figure given Uber Eats had been available for less than two years.[7] A third of all adults in Australian capital cities now order food prepared away from home, with millennials three times more likely than others to have a meal delivered. This new trend can cost households, on average, $4000 a year.[8]

No Need to Go Out

As seasoned online shoppers, who also enjoy the not-so-guilty pleasure of binge-watching TV, the arrival of Uber Eats and similar apps has meant that we have less and less reason to leave home. There's a wealth of new apps helping us conduct whole aspects of our lives from home. This new eating revolution has rapidly become a way of life – so much so that Samsung Smart TVs now come with a TV takeaway app and, if you have a smartwatch, you can also order food through Order Up! and others.[9]

'We could be at the first stage of industrializing meal production and delivery.'
Is the Kitchen Dead? *UBS report*[10]

Food has always offered us the chance to get together with those we care about – to share our days, our thoughts and plans, our concerns, our wins and moments of despair. Certainly there are nights when we need to batten down the hatches and enjoy our own space. However, as Sam Dick from the Campaign to End Loneliness notes, 'Choosing to eat alone is very different to having to eat alone.'[11]

There are concerns about this new trend of ordering in. Some worry we'll lose the ability to cook, the way we have let go of other skills such as gardening and sewing, instead relying on others to grow our food, to mend a tear or replace a button. Also disappearing is yet another opportunity to connect with nature, because we are no longer intimately engaged with the food we eat.

Food offers us many wonderful benefits. It has the capacity to take us out of ourselves, to warm our space. And, according to psychologist Fiona Martin, it offers real physical and mental health benefits – the joy of togetherness, not to mention the chance for kids to work on their verbal and social skills. By contrast, eating in front of the TV offers few benefits as it's a basically 'passive and anti-social' activity.[12]

Given the number of things we have to get through in a week, it is getting harder to eat together. Even if we are living with others, the rise in flexible work schedules has meant that often people in the same household end up eating alone. In one study into social eating, over six out of ten UK respondents reported never having had a meal with neighbours, while just over a third had never eaten in a community group. Most poignant is that one in eight respondents confessed that it was over six months since they'd had a lunch with friends or family.[13]

Health Impacts of Eating Alone

Another major study of several thousand South Koreans revealed that men eating two meals alone a day were more vulnerable to elevated blood pressure and cholesterol, and to being pre-diabetic. This study also found that men eating solo are 45 per cent more likely to be obese, and have a 65 per cent increased risk of metabolic syndrome, even when allowances were made for their age and exercise regime, their smoking and alcohol habits, and their work status.[14]

We also know that those with disordered eating and other mental health issues are more likely to eat alone. One Oxford University study indicated that the more we eat with others, the happier and more fulfilled we feel. Eating, this UK study suggests, helps us bond with those around us, connect with our community and benefit from the resulting sense of wellbeing.[15]

Creating a new network can be hard for those moving cities or countries for work. This is a growing problem, as many of us are now relocating a number of times for work. We then have to establish a series of networks over time, which can be exacting. Added to this, the advent of microwaves and other kitchen technology, along with the availability of pre-packaged meals, means food can now be prepared quickly, making mealtimes even more fluid.

With a quarter of Australian households now single-person dwellings,[16] statistics also suggest that those living alone tend to spend 90 per cent of their free time on their own.[17] Connecting with others is important. It helps us deal with life's inevitable ups and downs. It boosts our physical and mental wellbeing.

We now know there are clear links between solo eating and depression, sleep issues and low energy.[18] Countries such as Italy celebrate the joy of getting together over a meal, regardless of how simple that may be. Sharing a meal with those we care about warms our space, dissolving any sense of isolation.

BINGE-WATCHING

The rise in people eating alone comes at a time when more people are staying home to stream TV series and movies. This trend is proving to be very lucrative, with Amazon and Netflix alone returning around 2000 per cent and 7800 per cent profits respectively in just a decade.[19] According to a recent *Hollywood Reporter* poll, six out of ten adults now binge-watch TV. Of this group, more than one in four individuals binge several times a week. The younger the viewer, the more likely they are to binge-watch. Concerningly, almost a quarter of respondents admit to cancelling plans to meet up with friends, purely to keep watching. This figure nudges even higher for those aged 18 to 29. Almost half of this group are choosing to stay at home rather than honour commitments to friends. Over 40 per cent of this age group also admit to viewing on-demand TV while at work.[20]

In their 2017 Media Report, Netflix uses the words 'bingeing' and 'devouring' – language that's commonly associated with addiction – to describe customer habits.[21] Super-bingers are known to devour a show within 24 hours. Syd has refined this questionable art, admitting, 'I speed my shows up to x2 using a browser extension, so I can fit a whole season into about a day (less for some shows).' In a 2016 statement, Netflix revealed that horror, sci-fi and thriller series are most likely to be binge-watched, while viewers are more likely to savour irreverent comedies, political and historical dramas.[22] There is, suggests Derek Johnson, an associate professor of media and culture studies, a sense of using Netflix to the point that the consumer feels they can't live without it.[23]

> 'I get to the end of the episode and I want more. And if I have the time I will play the next one. Some days I just have 10+ episodes worth of time, so I watch them all.'
> *Matt*

Health Impacts of Bingeing

A joint US/Belgian study of 18- to 25-year-olds compared regular TV viewing with binge-watching to see if the different viewing styles impacted participants' sleep and vitality. Those with regular TV viewing habits didn't seem to have any sleep issues, while the binge-watchers clearly did.[24] Aside from fatigue and sleep deprivation, there are definite links between binge-watching and depression. Experts aren't yet sure whether those who are depressed are drawn to intense viewing, or if bingeing creates depression, although Greg's take on this offers insight into the state of mind of some binge-watchers: 'Having no life, or depression helps [encourage binge-watching],' he says. 'Cause you're gonna be sitting there doing nothing anyway. Or sleeping.'

Binge-watching is a growing habit, and for many it is rapidly becoming the new normal. In a brilliant piece in *The Cut*, comedy writer and essayist Elissa Bassist describes binge-watching the 52 episodes of *Dance Academy* in seven days. Newly arrived in New York, Bassist tells of sitting in her one-bedroom Brooklyn apartment in need of a distraction. Her response? 'To watch something frivolous and chill out, to think tiny nothing thoughts and mentally exit my body, to tune in and tune out.' Bassist isn't alone in turning to long-form TV when feeling down. She describes how in one day she moved from 'beatitude to heartbreak in twenty episodes'. Looking back, Bassist can see that her 24/7 bingeing gave her the chance to park her real life and immerse herself for a few hours in another world – a fantasy – helping divert her from the issues she was wrestling with, in therapy.[25]

Why Binge?

So what prompts people to keep viewing and viewing? Research suggests that serial viewers get hooked in to the storyline and need to see how it plays out. Many also find passive viewing relaxing.[26] When you're viewing you're not worrying about work, the mortgage or the energy bills. Over eight out of ten people also admitted to staying up beyond their normal bedtime to continue viewing. Half of this number said they made less healthy food or exercise choices when glued to the screen. The health impacts from 'mindless eating' while viewing, along with what happens to the body when it is inactive for so long, is getting the attention of health professionals. Sitting for long spells is now regarded as being as harmful, if not more so, than smoking.

A recent study into why people binge-watch TV found that there needs to be a strong emotional connection between viewers, a character/s and the storyline. Some viewers also tune in to experience specific feelings, such as love, excitement or fear. Others even replay a series they've already seen just to revisit those same emotions while they wait for new episodes to screen. Re-watching is a familiar route for those who just can't bear to let a season go. Viewing is often a different experience the second or third time around, according to media scholar

Jason Mittell. It can be 'a form of companionship or therapy', he explains, 'replaying a familiar, positive experience as a controlled and predictable bit of pleasure', with the added fun of anticipating dramatic moments.[27]

There's also the joy of sharing a series we've fallen for with others, and enjoying discussing the series with the same intensity and interest we'd give to a conversation about real-life friends. 'I love getting all my friends to watch or at least try the shows I love,' admits Martin. 'So satisfying when you lend them the first few episodes and a few days later you get that phone call, "I've just finished that first disc you gave me, I watched them all in one go. I lost sleep because of you!"'[28]

When You Can't Stop Viewing

The addictive nature of some series is clear. Anticipating the release of the next episode can be nerve-racking. 'I get so antsy waiting for new episodes of things,' Damien admits. 'I can easily sit down and get sucked into a show for hours on end.' Some viewers admit to rushing through their commitments and chores so they can get back to their program. Others feel compelled to keep going with a series even though they're not enjoying it, while keeping a close eye out for information on new episodes.[29]

Serial binge-watchers keep viewing every possible moment – at the gym, during meals and, as we've already seen, in some cases at work. The end result? Viewing erodes the chance to connect with others, to follow other passions, to catch up with family or relax with friends. Danny gives a sense of just how full-on this viewing can be. 'If I'm not super into the show,' he says, 'I will watch it on my second monitor while working ... if I want a break, I'll watch an episode. Usually my bingeing goes on at night though when I'm bored out of my mind.

I'll also watch TV on the treadmill. Lately I've been super into TV for some reason and I've watched five to six episodes in a row, though this is not a daily occurrence by any means. I've gone through depressions where I watch TV all day but that is different.'

The Dopamine Effect

Why are these series so enticing? Clinical psychologist Dr Renee Carr says that the chemicals released during viewing prompt us to keep going. 'When binge watching your favorite show, your brain is continually producing dopamine, [creating] a drug-like high.' Enjoying this sudden injection of dopamine, our body is keen for more. 'The neuronal pathways that cause heroin and sex addictions are the same as [those that create] an addiction to binge watching.' The body, Carr explains, can become addicted to 'any activity or substance that consistently produces dopamine'.[30]

Added to this, our bodies don't distinguish between something we're personally experiencing, and something we're viewing. So when we watch a drama, we're watching with all the intensity and connection to characters that we would feel if the scene were playing out in real life. We start to bond with characters, to care about them, get mad at them and worry for them, making the viewing experience even more real.

It Can't Be the End!

After all this investment in a story and its characters, there can be a sharp sense of loss, if not mourning, when a series is complete. How many of us have gone straight to the net after finishing a series to see when the next round will be released, only to feel stricken to discover this journey has come to an end? When a show does finish, studies show that some viewers genuinely feel blue.[31]

Jessica Kruger, a clinical assistant professor of community health and behaviour, describes the end of a series as a 'showhole'. People feel 'really sad, lost, a sense of emptiness because their favorite characters, who now feel like friends, are gone until either the next season,' she says, 'or, if they don't create [another] season, it's over'.[32] Daniel agrees. 'I just have to know what happens,' he admits, adding, 'it's still always sad to get to the end of a series though.'

> **'Then there are the societal impacts of millions of people isolating themselves for hours at a time to watch their favorite TV shows.'**
> *David J. Hill*[33]

The darker the content of a show, the more it can alienate us from others. One 2015 study looked at the five most binge-watched TV shows at the time – *House of Cards, Unbreakable Kimmy Schmidt, Marco Polo, Bloodline* and *Daredevil*. One of the hallmarks of such shows is often frequent graphic content. And many characters who stray beyond the law are presented as being morally justified for their behaviour, however extreme. What impact do these shows have? A clear link amongst those surveyed was found between the frequency of viewing and a belief that the world was a 'mean and scary place'.[34]

There is another less obvious but still important point about isolation with regard to streaming. When we view endless documentaries and dramas on global and social justice issues, where does all this viewing lead? While we may be more *aware* of the challenges, if we never do something tangible or practical, however humble, to help with the issues, then what difference are we making sitting on our sofas? It's important that we don't fool ourselves here.

Where does this leave us? 'We are wired to connect,' insists psychologist Dr Judy Rosenberg, 'and when we disconnect from humans and over-connect to TV at the cost of human connection, eventually we will "starve to death" emotionally.'[35] This is a big claim, but as we consider the many forces adding to our isolation, this statement gives us pause. Elissa Bassist makes an equally valid point when she says, 'With Internet-streaming media, we're overwhelmed by choice and robbed of choice at the same time.'[36]

Powerful Ways Back to Connection

As we emerge from our COVID-19 lockdowns, we have the chance to reconfigure how we are in the world – to seek out nuanced ways to move beyond our isolation and rediscover the joy of connection. One of the traps that has held us back in the past, I suspect, is the need to make a grand gesture. But the truly powerful moments are often the most simple. A few years back I was in London for work, and was invited home by a colleague. We could have eaten out as we both had expense accounts. But as we sat at her kitchen table eating her homemade lasagne with salad, it was one of the most enjoyable meals I've ever had, because it was over that delicious, loving meal that a lifelong friendship developed.

EATING TOGETHER
- **Eat with Others**
  Dining with other people has real benefits. Perhaps it's time to push past our passive lifestyles and find effortless ways to nudge us out of entrenched habits that create a subtle (or not-so-subtle) sense of loneliness – to have an impromptu coffee, casual pasta, potluck supper or weekend picnic with those we care about. (In my apartment block, we enjoy impromptu meals with different groups of neighbours. The guest list is flexible and inclusive. Everyone brings a dish to share, and we've had some amazing nights.)

- **Share Family Meals**
  Eating together as a family helps build social skills. It's a great way to catch up on the day, allowing the day's wins and worries to be aired, and solutions to be found for tricky moments. Best of all, it gives you the chance to relax and savour being with those you love.

- **Eat Together at Work**
  Some major organisations are now using shared meals to help grow morale. Google's AR/VR team make time to eat together, renting out house spaces and kitchens for shared meals and bake-offs. And in its Brooklyn headquarters, Etsy has set up 'Eatsy', its twice-weekly staff lunch where staff get together to enjoy and support local, artisan-produced food.

- **Make it a Habit**
  Weekly rituals around food really help, affirms the Food and Mood Centre, which researches nutritional psychiatry. This world-first centre focuses on the use of diet and nutrition to prevent and combat mental health issues. Why not set up a regular breakfast catch-up or picnic with friends, or encourage shared lunches at work? The secret is to choose effortless ways to get together – you can share the load by having everyone bring some food or drinks to share.

TIME TO GET OUT AND ABOUT

- **Monitor Your Mood**
  Be aware of when you feel vulnerable and isolated. Instead of flopping on the sofa, get moving – go for a walk or ring a friend for a coffee catch-up. Everyone gets bored. Recognise that boredom can boost creativity and help us chill out. Why not indulge in a hobby? Keep a box, drawer or shelf handy for any materials and tools you need so it's easy to get going. Once you've started, note how much better you feel.

- **Cherish Your Local Cafe**
  Even a casual coffee catch-up can help keep isolation at bay. Remember how much those trips for takeaway coffees helped during the pandemic? While you're grabbing a coffee or some lunch, there's also the chance to connect briefly with those serving you – ask their name and take an interest in *their* day. A lot can be shared in a couple of sentences. This is how we grow community, and enjoy the resulting feel-good chemicals firing through our bodies.

- **Get Your Explorer Groove On**
  Visit a part of your city or local area that you don't know, or haven't visited recently – browse the unusual stores there, explore hidden alleyways, wander through a graveyard, meander through the local market, visit a gallery, and take a break in an interesting cafe.

- **Become a Friday Forager**
  To get out of our 'bubble' and see more of each other, my friends
  and I seek out different ethnic family-run restaurants in our city that
  we wouldn't normally visit. One Friday a month, we have a meal at
  a different eatery. Seated at simple formica tables, we've had some
  brilliant meals, and we now make a point of taking out-of-town
  friends to these tiny hole-in-the-wall restaurants. We've connected
  with people whose paths we wouldn't otherwise cross, and we've
  also found some amazing providores.

- **Give Meetup a Go**
  Now the biggest 'in person' social network, with around 20 million
  members, Meetup posts half a million events globally every month.
  With its geo-location feature, it can connect you with interest groups
  near you, from yoga and book clubs, to rock-climbing and everything
  in between.

- **Shared Movies Can Make a Day or Weekend**
  Whether you're at a cinema or having friends home, shared viewing
  changes the whole dynamic, especially when you can make some
  time afterwards to sit and reflect together on what you've just seen —
  thoughts you can agree on, laugh about and debate — and enjoy each
  other's company.

8

A Curated Life

Who Gets to Choose?
When Perfect Is too Perfect
Reclaim Your Unique Self

WHO GETS TO CHOOSE?

With so much pressure to present ourselves in a certain way, we've become hypersensitive to how others see us. But how do we settle on the winning formula? There is now a string of curators and influencers out there, determined to grab our attention and tell us exactly how we should be living our lives. These self-proclaimed 'experts' are bursting with advice on everything from the length of our lashes to the hottest holiday locations. And it seems that people all over the globe are tuning in. Why is this opportunity to be told what to do so appealing?

'In a time in which information, population and ambition continue to accelerate unmanageably, there is an attendant desire to control, contain, organize,' suggests Canadian art writer David Balzer.[1] Given the massive speed of technological changes, and amid wider changes, we're certainly treading new ground. Through social media, we've seen political movements, the work of obscure artists, and new fashion trends ignited in just a few short years. We've been entertained and appalled by the best and worst of human behaviour on our devices, accessed financial and weather forecasts in real time, and been tutored online and offline across a whole range of skills.

All these spectacular advances, and more, have taken us further than we could have ever dreamed. They've also left many of us with a keen sense of our insignificance – how can our story have value, amongst millions of others? And how do we want to show up in the world? As our sense of self shrinks, we agonise over what kind of look to aspire to – do we want to be on trend, or leaning more towards the avant-garde? Or are we drawn to one-of-a-kind upcycled pieces? Thousands of voices whisper to us daily, offering us the chance to be more playful, more elegant, more nostalgic, to try a more androgynous or surreal look.

How Am I Meant to Show Up?

With so much detail, it can be hard to decide on what's needed to be accepted and admired. 'On average,' notes psychology professor Daniel Levitin, 'we take in five times as much information every day as we did in 1986 – the equivalent of 175 newspapers.'[2] In addition, we're desperately busy. We don't have the time or energy to navigate so much choice, and yet we don't want to miss out. The beauty of curation is that it offers us much-needed shortcuts that will take us where we most yearn to be – to a place of belonging. Why would we miss this chance for even a little certainty in the middle of the constantly shifting sands of our times?

Grateful for a step up, we start to rely on others to point the way. We find ourselves embracing their tips on everything from the best in radiance-inducing skin products and the books we should read, to affordable and not-so-affordable little luxuries that we're told we deserve. Following the suggestions of those in the know, we dash off to 'must see' films, exhibitions and shows, until any impulse to follow our own curiosity seems a tad unsophisticated and possibly perilous, too. Who are we to know what's best?

Curation does offer many gifts, but it can so easily imprison us. And what we choose to exclude from our lives also has a story to tell. Yet as we're all so time poor, what are we to do? With everything from clothing to tech accessories moving so fast, and new items often losing their lustre within weeks of hitting stores, how do we keep up? Daily we're encouraged, incentivised or badgered into elevating our style and breaking new ground, so we learn to be more particular, until we too become would-be curators and can expound in depth on the merits of limited-edition super-soft wool socks, or an eco-luxe garment in colours that pop that we've just purchased.

Without realising it, we're being driven into a circle of striving without ever arriving. Rarely, if ever, do we reach that sweet spot where we can relax a little and simply enjoy where we are. Where does that leave us? We're facing a 'relentless anxiety around the self as a product: what it means, who owns it, what it costs, what it's worth', suggests India Ennenga, a New York-based actor and filmmaker.[3]

Too Much to Choose From

Choice can be a complicated thing. In *The Organized Mind*, Daniel Levitin tells of one of his students who grew up in communist Romania. Out of a class of several hundred students, this student shone with her inquiring mind, thoughtful questions and willingness to experiment. When Levitin ran into her in the stationery aisle of a college bookshop, she confessed to how 'terrible' it was living in America at times. This was her fourth trip to the bookshop that day. In Romania there were three types of pens at most, sometimes none at all. Confronted with a whole bank of pens, she had no idea which pen she needed for her biology class, or for poetry. 'Do I want felt tip, ink, gel, cartridge, erasable? Ballpoint, razor point, rollerball?' she asked in despair.[4]

Curation can help us deal with overload. However, there's often a subtle, or not-so-subtle, desire to compete also at play here – a determination to ensure we're always ahead of the pack. One recent blog on the art of curation offered 'the secret sauce of getting noticed', promising to show readers how to be 'an influencer', to establish 'your authority', to gain a competitive advantage. Tellingly, it told of how to 'curate the curators'.[5]

Curation's Not What it Used to Be

Until recently, curation was regarded as a painstaking skill honed over decades – a long and winding journey, with bittersweet moments of searching and longing, of disappointment and serendipity, and the delights of unlikely discoveries along the way. Trawling through interesting links, sites and blogs, information and images, and passing on what you deem of value to others, doesn't equate with the vast knowledge that the curators of museums and art galleries possess. As one ex-curator notes, 'Just because you like playing doctor doesn't mean you are one!'[6]

That doesn't mean our attempts at curation aren't sometimes worthwhile. But is it possible that we've elevated the idea of curation to a place it may not deserve? Curation has become code for a fine eye and the last word in taste. It points the way ahead, offering us the chance to stand out, to elevate ourselves. There's a plethora of curators out there, offering to help with everything from removing toxic people from our lives, to dealing with divorce or job loss. These 'it list' individuals promise to help keep us on track and, more importantly, to help relieve us of our unspoken fear that we might just be about to disappear from sight.

> 'Anyone who spends time actually "carefully curating" their home … has too much time on their hands! I just want to call it what it is: It's just how you decide to fill your home with stuff.'
> *Siobhan*[7]

How Did We Get Here?

It's interesting to consider the recent history of curators. In his book *Curationism*, David Balzer traces the rise of curation as we now know it, back to the sixties and seventies, when artists struck out against the 'commodification and institutionalisation' of their works. Deliberately moving away from art as an object, they began to embrace edgier, less tangible, sometimes transitory art concepts, which, they felt, spoke to the heart of creativity.[8] This move left the art world shaken. How could you judge the difference between good and hopeless art, when it was suddenly all so intangible?

This growing uncertainty left the perfect opening for the curator or, as Balzer describes it, the 'imparter of value … whether or not it [real value] actually exists'.[9] With the curator came the cashed-up eighties, when there was money to burn. Those with means began purchasing huge art collections, resulting in many pieces being locked away. Suddenly curation was no longer just about the care and deep knowledge of objects, so much as being the one who settles on the 'going rate' for an artwork.

With so many choices and every part of our lives under the microscope, how do we settle on our own value? How can we find a way through the maze of choice to ensure we come out on top? Living in a hype-infested culture, we're acutely aware that our every move and purchase – from our home décor and the way we plate our food, the music and magazines we consume, to where we buy our coffee – makes a statement about us. Then there's our online presence to manage – Facebook, Instagram, Twitter, Pinterest, TikTok and more. These platforms need constant attention if we have any chance of growing our brand.

All this would be so much easier if we weren't drowning in choices. Aided and abetted by powerful insights gleaned from psychology, neuroscience and anthropology, advertising slogans and visuals have become so sophisticated that marketers are busy messing with our heads. Is it any surprise that we're left wondering if we can possibly trust our own judgement?

Do we like what we like because we like it, or because we've been persuaded to like it? A few decades back, ground-breaking sociologist Erving Goffman described this process as 'impression management', where we start to see ourselves how others see us – to live our lives from the outside in. To some extent we all do this, and have been doing so for millennia, but now we're objectifying ourselves to the point that the authentic 'us' is nowhere to be seen. We're becoming isolated from our unique take on the world.

Do We Have What it Takes?

This takes us back to the question of detail, and our growing need to be vigilant to ensure we're living up to expectation. Could this mean we're getting hopelessly lost in the minutiae – in worrying about what we should be doing the instant we arrive at our holiday destination, or what we're meant to be wearing at the back end of this season, to always guarantee we hit the desired note? For tweens and teens still working on their identity, this level of detail can be unbearable. As my previous research has indicated, even preschoolers are exhibiting increasing anxiety around their looks and possessions, worrying about whether they have the right branded backpack and lunch box to take to kindy, the 'right' body and hair.[10]

> 'I think overuse [of 'curate'] cheapens the word, sort of like what happened with "artisanal". Instead of thinking about something as handmade and special, you think of a loaf of overpriced bread at the store.'
> Bethany[11]

Living in a fiercely competitive performance culture, few of us are brave enough to settle on our own intrinsic worth. So we look for that special someone who can give us a boost. The word 'curate' is now code for 'iconic'. But how much room in our lives is there for iconic statements, with almost every aspect of our lives and bodies already under scrutiny?

Frankly, the detail required of us can be dizzying. All this effort doesn't do a great deal to help bring us closer to each other, either. Living in a highly competitive culture isn't for the faint-hearted, when even those closest to us feel the need to compete. And now that we can create digital mood boards, make our own short films, stage mini exhibitions, write blogs and more, we're constantly looking for 'content', trawling through our lives and those of friends, foes and acquaintances in an attempt to stay on top. We become the concept, the image, the article, the video clip. Or, as blogger Katy Huie Harrison puts it, 'We take things that are already good, already precious, and search for ways to make them better – for the consumption of others. And we're taking time out of our lives for this.'[12] How poignant and isolating this is.

WHEN PERFECT IS TOO PERFECT

Psychologists suggest that this growing need to put ourselves 'out there' – to appear perfect, to constantly assess how we're coming across – feeds a deep-seated ache to belong. Added to this is our almost voracious appetite for perfection, which leaves us anxious lest we let ourselves down and end up looking stupid, or worse. For many of us, striving for 'perfect' becomes a kind of insurance policy – a hope that our version of perfect will keep us safe. We tell ourselves that if we're meticulous about ticking all the boxes, nothing can possibly go wrong. But that's not realistic, as we saw in our recent pandemic. And what's the ultimate cost of this approach? In the past there was a handful of people to compare ourselves to. The landscape has changed, notes Hilde Holsten, communications adviser at the University of Oslo, telling of how people 'have the possibility to compare themselves to many other users worldwide. Reference groups are now expanding to include a wider social circle as well as the world itself.'[13]

Is it any surprise that we feel a little nervous about anything and everything we do? Let's face it, there's a lot of talent out there, which means we need to be vigilant in everything we do. Chicago-based writer Julia Brenner reflects:

> Take an event like a baby shower. How many hostesses now feel pressure to craft some perfect brunch display with pins and 'likes' in mind. No longer is food simply set out for guests, but rather it's curated within an inch of its life with the pin-worthiest pompoms, a ridiculously ornate finger food situation, and precisely-placed-paper-straw-filled-punch cups arranged just *so* for that one perfect Instagram picture that happens after 30 other Instagram pictures were deleted.[15]

We can probably all recognise aspects of our own behaviour here. While we mightn't be guilty of stressing out over a baby shower, social media has impacted how most of us meet the world.

'Stop normalising glamour and glitz. Nobody lives on a perpetual mountaintop.'
Mindi Palm, mindipalm.com[16]

Health Choices

With so much to manage, it's tempting to look for curators and influencers to deliver quick fixes and miracle cures. Nowhere is this more evident than in the health arena. It's interesting to see how even those who are genuine health professionals choose to spruik their services – with one group offering would-be patients a 'Health for Everyone Superclinic ... committed to providing the care you deserve'.[17] Another talks of their 'handpicked holistic health squad: a tightly curated group that gives the best advice this side of your own personal guru'.[18] Yet another tells of their 'community of psychologists, wellbeing and performance professionals', working with you 'to make room for your mind to grow'.[19] No doubt these are caring professionals, but the hype can leave one a little breathless.

Sadly, not everyone's health credentials do check out, sometimes with disastrous consequences. Australia's Belle Gibson, the girl from the wrong side of the tracks, saw an opportunity to take on the world. Aware of the need to have 'a good hook', Belle misrepresented herself to thousands, then to Apple, and then to her publisher. As a major social media influencer she built a lucrative business, detailing in her blog The Whole Pantry her epic journey to wellness after being diagnosed with multiple cancers and given only weeks to live. Forgoing her prescribed chemotherapy, Belle told of her own journey of healing, soon earning the status of a top wellness guru. As a result, some of Gibson's followers abandoned their chemotherapy, including Kate, who doubts she would be here today had it not been for the intervention of her mother-in-law, a nurse, who set her back on track.[20]

One of the difficulties of social media is that it can deliver an instant sense of connection – the feeling that you know someone because you like what they say, or how they look. Because someone appears authoritative, 'looks' professional and has an attractive online presence with plenty of followers, those in search of answers are drawn to such figures to a level that rarely occurred before the internet. Is this trend, in part, a result of our yearning for meaningful connection? And why, in finding it, we grab onto it as hard as we can?

Living in what can feel like an impersonal world creates in us an ever-deepening hunger to experience all the intimate, joyous and validating experiences we can. Yet our never-ending catalogue of 'must have' objects, and bucket lists of mountains to climb, can make life feel relentless. When we live at this pace there's no time for reflection, or to draw out the fullness of the moment. There's no time to weigh up all these experiences and newly acquired possessions against the deep longings of our essential selves.

> **'I'm not really interested in perfect. I'm interested in the hills and the valleys, the triumphs and the failures, the f**k ups and the fantasies.'**
> *Jennifer Rabin, Jennifer + Rabin*[14]

Often these traits creep up on us. 'One of my friends analyzed me recently and told me that she realized that I curate my entire life,' tells Amanda J. Slavin, founder of CatalystCreativ, in a *Huffington Post* piece. Reflecting on this comment, Slavin admits her friend's observations were probably true, yet is quick to point out that curation is a 'very delicate' process. 'My passion,' she explains, 'is to create relationships that provide people with their "aha" moments. I will notice something in someone that can be brought out in a bigger way through knowing someone else, and I literally thrive on the adrenaline of creating this chemistry.' However, her expert curation isn't without its pitfalls, Slavin warns, telling how she became so focused on 'everyone else's dreams' that she neglected her own.[21]

Those who know their Latin will recall that to curate comes from the word *curare*, meaning to care, worry about or heal.

In the Christian tradition, the curator is charged with the 'care of souls'. It's the kind of caring that offers deep nurture – a willingness to give something as much time as is needed, to reach a place that sustains. In our rush to curate almost every aspect our lives, to become 'our own advertisers', we're close to extinguishing the quiet longings of our true selves, which is a desperately lonely place to be.

In spite of all the hurry and the hype, and the lack of personal reflection, it's reassuring to learn that there's been a renewed interest in visiting museums. In a recent paper, curator and academic Dr Anna Edmundson tells of an American survey of visitors to the country's living history sites, which looked at why people were visiting these locations. Respondents told of how they felt life had become so complicated and unreal, they wanted to connect with something authentic by seeing real objects from history.[22] I suspect we are all aching for what is real and authentic, and perhaps it's closer than we imagine.

Reclaim Your Unique Self

Each and every one of us has unique ways of meeting the world. By giving voice to our essential self, we help make life more fulfilling and we inspire others, freeing them up to be a whole lot more authentic, too. They, in turn, give us a lift and so this upward cycle continues.

- **Mindful Moments**
  We hear a lot about mindfulness, and that's because time for reflection, meditation or for simply taking a break actively replenishes our energy and sense of self, balancing out the activities that do deplete and drain us.

- **Follow Your Nose**
  There's something seductive about the almost forgotten art of the *flâneur* – those with a bent for quiet exploration, who revel in seeking out the hidden and the forgotten people and places in our cities and towns that quietly exist beyond the humdrum. How might your life be if you were to awaken your inner *flâneuse* and reignite your curiosity – to seek out the extraordinary concealed in seemingly ordinary locations and individuals wherever you find yourself?

- **Embrace the 'Real'**
  Think about what 'real' looks like for you right now. What are your real passions? What of the real friendships you enjoy? What gives you a real sense of purpose? What if you were to spend more time with uplifting people and immersed in stimulating conversations, where you toss around ideas that are similar to your own, as well as those that are wildly divergent? What might you learn? Look at the 'real-life' locations that deliver joy and inspiration, which are close to where you live or work. Perhaps it's time to spend more time there.

- **'Enough-ness'**
  What if you already have everything you need to thrive? Only you can decide what 'enough-ness' looks like for you. Often lack comes from our culture of comparison. Yet what if you were to change your fixation with comparison and competition and instead focus on curiosity, seeking out the unusual and valuing the different qualities we each bring to a family, community or workplace? Enough-ness doesn't mean you're not ambitious, more that you're choosing to 'travel light', to craft your own goals. It's exhausting to be continually chasing this season's 'must have' items, attempting to see every noteworthy film or series, to read every well-reviewed book. Choose, savour, and allow time for enjoyment and reflection.

9
Narcissism Rules

And Now, Back to Me

Living in a Narcissistic World

How to Handle Narcissism

AND NOW, BACK TO ME

With our focus turning inwards, perhaps it's no surprise that there's a lot of talk of narcissism right now, from narcissistic young people and bosses, to neighbours, partners and politicians – people whose presence is powerfully and destructively isolating. Given the often devastating fallout experienced by those trying to navigate such individuals, it's also no surprise that there has been an explosion of books, articles and blogs on the subject. Describing narcissism as anything from a malignancy to an epidemic, these tools offer to help us handle, disarm and escape narcissists. Added to this, a surprising number of bloggers, themselves survivors of narcissistic partners or supervisors, are now life coaches or fully fledged psychologists seeking to assist others find their way through the haze of abuse, which often leaves us intensely lonely, and even frightened.

The burning question remains: is narcissism simply a hot topic, or a worrying trend? H.G. Tudor, a self-confessed narcissistic psychopath, who writes the blog Knowing the Narcissist, believes society is not only more narcissistic, it's busy 'cultivating more narcissists'. Admitting to finding 'gratification from manipulating individuals to [his] own ends', Tudor is now putting his 'dark art' to good use. And, for a modest fee, he will shine a light on narcissism and help you deal with the narcissists in your life.[1]

> 'Our "me" culture is perfectly served, exploited, and promoted by Instagram as a platform for display of narcissism.'
> *kristibruno*[2]

How to Spot a Narcissist

What is narcissism? Key traits include an overarching belief in one's abilities and importance, and a need to be noticed and made to feel special, to be admired. With these traits comes a strong sense of entitlement, a willingness to take advantage of others, and an inability to empathise with others. Narcissists work hard to appear strong and in control, to mask an extremely fragile sense of self, which can be partly due to a complete lack of validation or excessive validation as a child. For Netflix viewers, narcissism at its most acute – pathological narcissism – is starkly evident in the depiction of the life of American serial killer Andrew Cunanan, who murdered five men, including Gianni Versace.[3]

Narcissism isn't only a topic of recent debates. In the late seventies, historian Christopher Lasch warned of the pitfalls of a culture where individuals put their own happiness first, in his bestselling book *The Culture of Narcissism*. 'We demand too much of life,' Lasch reflected, and 'too little of ourselves.'[4] So are we increasingly putting ourselves first, or is all this talk of narcissism simply hype? One study, which analysed the use of 'I' and 'me' in popular songs from 1980 to 2007, found a 'statistically significant trend toward narcissism and hostility'. Finding fewer references to 'us' and 'we' in these lyrics, psychologist Dr Nathan DeWall also notes that 'late adolescents and college students love themselves more today than ever before'.[5] One thing is certain: there's little room for you or me when we're around 'back to me' individuals, who can so easily leave us thinking no-one cares about our lives or issues.

Is Narcissism on the Rise?

What does narcissism look like right now? The results of an informal poll overwhelmingly suggested that we are indeed living in a narcissistic age. 'Narcissism is definitely more prevalent given our very materialistic consumer-oriented society, and is encouraged greatly by social media, advertising and the high regard for celebrities, often seen as role models. It comes in part from being self-absorbed and living in a bubble,' reflects Ellie, who sees the rise in plastic surgery as yet another aspect of current narcissism.

Other respondents weren't so sure. 'I think the word is often wrongly assigned to people who are self-centred/self-preoccupied/self-serving, whose friendship networks are vicarious and who have a distorted sense of self-worth,' tells Jane, who has spent her life working in the media. Mim, who has a background in the corporate and care sectors, agrees: 'There appears to be a rise in narcissism, but it may be that people are just more open about looking after themselves. Perhaps the actual level has not changed, it is just more socially acceptable to put yourself first.'

'Keep in mind,' warns psychology professor Ramani Durvasula in her book *Should I Stay or Should I Go?*, 'that we all engage in some of the "bad narcissism" patterns from time to time, but when it hits critical mass and characterizes your behavior in a predictable manner, that is when it jumps the rails into "pathological narcissism"'.[6]

So where does this leave us? In a BBC Radio 4 interview, Dr Tennyson Lee, who specialises in narcissistic personality disorder, says narcissism is 'more common than we realise'.[7] Professor W. Keith Campbell, who heads up the University of Georgia's psychology department, also believes narcissism is on the rise. 'You can look at individual scores of narcissism, you can look at data on lifetime prevalence of Narcissistic Personality Disorder, you can look at related cultural trends' and, he states, they all indicate this same rise.[8] Narcissism is a measurable sliding scale, which takes us from those with few or an abundance of narcissistic personality traits, to those with a pathological personality disorder. In 1979, the Narcissistic Personality Inventory was put together to help professionals evaluate where individuals sit on this spectrum. Now this measure is even used in some hiring procedures.

> 'I don't care. Show me pictures of coffins, show me bodies floating in water, play violins and show me skinny people looking sad. I still don't care.'
> *Former* Sun *columnist Katie Hopkins, responding to the 2015 Mediterranean refugee crisis*[9]

How Does Narcissism Play Out?

'What is heightened in such individuals,' Anoushka Marcin of Balance Psychologies explains, 'is their inability to connect in an interpersonal relationship and the inability to feel empathy. This makes it very hard or impossible for narcissists to understand how another person is feeling.' She offers this warning:

> Look out for when someone is paying you more compliments and attention, or promising you the world. If it sounds amazing there probably is a catch. Similarly, if someone has an uncanny way of making you feel 'less than' most of the time, or in front of others, then this can be a tell-tale sign also. It's about trusting your gut feeling; no-one should make you feel like you have to question yourself, but narcissists enjoy playing on emotions and vulnerability to get a result. This is why educating yourself about what is involved will help you recognise when someone is playing with your emotions to get a reaction.

It's important we understand that the dynamic here is to render us invisible – of little or no consequence, beyond bolstering their out-of-control ego. Is it any wonder those who spend their lives around narcissists end up feeling horribly alone?

Given their ability to win over and dominate others, how do narcissists fare in real life? It's tempting to assume these individuals are more powerful or effective than they really are. While charming, often highly motivated and intelligent, narcissists are frequently problematic in the workplace as they're not team players. They may present well, but can find it hard to follow through on commitments. And while full of grandiose ideas and inflated views of their abilities, narcissists are highly sensitive to criticism. Frequently rule-breakers, they think nothing of missing deadlines and overspending budgets, and rarely take the rap when things go wrong. Apart from having a devastating impact on a work culture and morale, those higher on the Narcissistic Personality Index are more likely to commit white-collar crime.[10] Mim, one of the respondents to an informal poll on narcissism, made an interesting observation about narcissists in the workplace: 'Perhaps that is why it is so common to change jobs after only a short period of time. The job has not delivered the "specialness" that is required to bolster an ego that is very self-centred.'

While being interviewed about their experience of work, a number of people brought up what they saw as a rise in toxic workplaces. When questioned further, some felt this was partly due to a rise in narcissistic work cultures. 'I've noticed less willingness to give credit to the good work others are doing,' Jaimie told. 'A latent jealousy and extreme competitiveness has crept in, that undermines individual connections and group performance.' Another acquaintance told of a banking dinner where his boss produced a gold crown that he'd had made. The crown was handed to each guest in turn, who was then expected to extol the virtues of their superior. When everyone had heaped praise on this man, he placed the crown on his head and this surreal dinner continued.

Narcissists have a way of sucking the oxygen out of a room, leaving others feeling 'less than', if not useless and completely out on a limb. 'They will take you from being an empathetic person with lots of love to give to everyone, to feeling hopeless and lost,' one victim reports, adding, 'they will take you from having friends and hanging out, to not speaking to anyone else and staying behind closed doors most of the time ... making you feel worthless and alone ... just like they do.'

'Narcissistic Personality Disorder does its greatest harm in close, intimate relationships,' states Ramani Durvasula in *Should I Stay or Should I Go?*. 'Many people have narcissistic bosses, colleagues, siblings, friends, and neighbours. They are not easy situations, but they do not have the same impact that a romantic partner would have. The primitive and emotional nature of a close personal relationship means that the lack of empathy, the rage, the distance, the control, the inconsistency have tremendous power in shaping the life and the inner world of a person in a narcissistic relationship.'[11] Given the huge rise in domestic abuse, we might wonder how many people are living in extreme isolation in their own homes, imprisoned in a very dark place.

> 'Instagram's ability to easily, quickly and cheaply cater to narcissism has exponentially grown narcissistic behaviour in our culture.'
> *kristibruno*[12]

When the Mask Slips

Working with the fallout from narcissistic personality disorder, Anoushka Marcin notes that 'what is disabling in these situations is that the person that you got to know, is not actually the person you got to know. And it's about trying to fathom that cognitively, which is very challenging (this is called cognitive dissonance). In many people this causes trust issues, and in severe instances survivors have post-traumatic stress disorder.'

Harvard's Craig Malkin, author of *Rethinking Narcissism*, warns that narcissism comes in many, sometimes unexpected, forms: 'Not all narcissists care about looks or fame or money. If you focus too much on the stereotype, you'll miss red flags that have nothing to do with vanity or greed.' Some narcissists may, for example, be more community-minded and spend all their time and energy assisting others. 'Everyone has met grandiosely altruistic martyrs, self-sacrificing to the point where you can't stand to be in the room with them.' And there are also those narcissists who are extremely introverted, or 'vulnerable'. Hugely sensitive, these individuals are averse to even mild criticism and need to be constantly propped up.[13]

It's essential that we start to recognise the warning signs so we don't get drawn into this isolating vortex. Equally, we need to keep ourselves in check so as not to harm others.

There's a fine line between healthy self-esteem and narcissism. It's important to recognise that the more attention there is on us, the less room there is for anyone else. Added to this, our growing emphasis as a society on individuality encourages us to place ourselves centre stage. Healthy connection is about balancing giving and taking. Narcissists are focused on taking. It's essential we temper our own needs with accommodating others, and learning to spot the cues as to what is and isn't appropriate.

When Narcissism Takes Root in Childhood

Educational psychologist Peter Gray believes the growth of narcissists is, in part, down to the increased early pressure on kids to succeed. If a child is brought up to win above all else, then the child is going to be focused on number one. Gray also suggests that children need unsupervised play with other children. Kids, he explains, love playing with other children and, if they want to keep playing, they soon learn they need to keep other children on side. And while kids rarely praise each other, they are adept at calling out each other's bad behaviour, using insults and jokes to pull each other into line. With a generation of helicopter parenting and children playing alone, Gray believes that many children are missing out on opportunities to connect, and to hone these vital social skills.[14]

'Most narcissists are simply doing what feels good to them in the moment, without regard for your feelings.'
Clinical psychotherapist Karen Arluck

While narcissism is on the rise, Dr Kostas Papageorgiou of Queen's University Belfast suggests that it isn't necessarily a 'malevolent trait'. His research into adolescents revealed that those with more narcissistic tendencies scored better at school. He states that, 'People who score high on subclinical narcissism may be at an advantage because their heightened sense of self-worth may mean they are more motivated, assertive, and successful in certain contexts.'[15] Psychology professor Brent Roberts of the University of Illinois views narcissism as being more of a product of age. Far from seeing a rise in narcissism, his research suggests the opposite, with the added observation that we become less narcissistic as we age.[16]

Is Narcissism on the Rise?

Most definitely, states psychology professor Jean Twenge, whose research focuses on generational differences. For almost four decades now, her studies reveal, college students have been exhibiting heightened self-confidence, and are more likely than previous generations to affirm, 'I will never be satisfied until I get all that I deserve' and 'If I ruled the world it would be a better place',[17] questions taken from the Narcissistic Personality Inventory.[18] This trend isn't just down to social media, suggests Twenge, although it does play a part, allowing people to assume the minutiae of their lives are mesmerising to others.

Clear links have been drawn between heavy users of social media – those with more online friends – and those who rank higher on the narcissism scale.[19] Added to this, family sizes have been shrinking. With many families now with only one child, that child is often the centre of attention, and constantly made to feel special. Some also point to the growth in the human potential movement from the seventies, with its resulting explosion of self-esteem books, for a rise in narcissistic traits. What is noteworthy is that studies indicate a spike in narcissism since 2000, which coincides with faster, more widespread connectivity, along with the introduction of more sophisticated devices such as tablets and smartphones, to the resulting growth of social media platforms.

There are positive signs on the horizon. According to Professor Twenge, narcissism might be plateauing or even falling, due in part to the global financial crisis, which dented people's ability to appear powerful and successful. There's still the impact of indulgent parenting and the power of the internet to counter, but at least this is a start, and backed up in part by the 2012 Josephson Institute of Ethics survey of high school students, which noted that for the first time in a decade, students were found to be stealing, lying and cheating less. Just over half of this sample still admitted to cheating in an exam, or lying to a teacher about something significant, while one in five had shoplifted in the previous year.[20] Over half these teenagers also felt that successful people did what they had to do, including cheating, to get across the line. There's clearly room for improvement here, but hopefully this is the beginning of a downward trend in the narcissism stakes, as the last thing we need is a society bent on pushing each other out of the way. That's not how we thrive, how we live happy, empowered and empowering lives.

LIVING IN A NARCISSISTIC WORLD

As we continue to witness the daily rants and bragging of the narcissists in our midst, it's tempting to just switch off, not realising how destructive such individuals can be. 'It seems that we are beset with global leaders who take narcissism to new heights,' reflects Sydney-based marketing consultant Jane Adams. 'Their erratic behaviours, egoism, conceit, lack of empathy and insatiable need for admiration are capable of distorting world order. And, at worst, legitimising these behaviours.'

Chuck Robinson, former bookseller and president of the American Booksellers Association, is also concerned:

> I certainly believe we've seen a continuing rise in narcissism in the US. There have been constant references to the 'me generation' for some time, though there's some belief that the younger generation may be retreating from that. The election of President Trump, who is the epitome of narcissism, is in keeping with a nation of individuals who can only see issues in relation to themselves. I worry that we, as a nation, are losing – or perhaps have already lost – any claim we may have to moral leadership.

This is a crucial point. When we can only see life through the filter of our own needs, and neediness, there's little room to connect meaningfully and happily with others.

So where does our current narcissistic bent leave us? 'I have concerns about this self-focus for the future care of others,' reflects Sydney-based Annie Willems, who has spent over a decade working as a court support for victims of serious crime. 'If you only put your own needs in the picture, then voluntary work will cease, as will care for friends and relatives during periods of ill health, and when [people are] needing friendship and kindness ... I wonder what this will do to the suicide rate.'

No Room for Apathy

What do we do about the narcissists we face? There's power in numbers so perhaps, like kids in the playground, it's time we call out the narcissists. There's too much at stake for us to sit back, allowing them to fracture workplaces, communities and even whole countries. Apathy is the perfect breeding ground for narcissists, as there's no-one to stand in their way. There are few winners in narcissistic, winner-takes-all cultures, as narcissism is isolating for all concerned. The resulting fragmented societies can so easily slide from dysfunctional to dangerous – dangerous to any form of dissent, to the vulnerable, to the environment – and this isn't where we want our communities or nations to be. '[The rise in narcissism] deeply concerns me,' says Jill, mother of two adopted boys and a biological daughter, 'because it encourages a disregard for humanity, a disregard for common decency, a disregard for diversity and thus, we have the insidious rise of the Far Right.'

In one telling study, participants were placed in different teams. Each was assigned to run a notional forestry company, harvesting timber from a renewable forest. Interestingly, the groups wanting to push the boat out most, and harvest ever more timber than was sustainable, displayed more narcissistic tendencies. Ultimately, the 'narcissistic group' managed to harvest less timber overall, as their forest was soon depleted.[21]

London psychoanalyst Pat MacDonald, who sees an increasing number of clients 'on the narcissistic spectrum', warns of the dangers of group greed and grandiosity. 'Perhaps most sinister of all,' she reflects, 'is our attitude to the planet that supports us, as we play a part in the destruction of much of the environment and many of the species that share the earth with us.' When asked how we turn things around, MacDonald states, 'Having compassion for one's self and recognising how ordinary we really are make for a good start.'[22]

Ordinary is a concept that's fallen out of favour, yet it is one out of which extraordinary insights and talents can emerge. Why? Because we're not weighing down our fledgling ideas, talents and solutions with huge expectations. Jill sees the route forward as 'the same as has been advocated for centuries, from John Stuart Mill who said in 1867, "Bad men need nothing more to compass their ends, than that good men should look on and do nothing", through to the #MeToo and other movements, rightly calling out unacceptable opinions or behaviours.' Narcissism has fractured much of what is good in our homes, workplaces, communities and beyond. As we adjust to the new 'normal' in our post-COVID-19 world, we can't afford to allow people to remain isolated, which in turn means we can't afford to let narcissists run the show.

How to Handle Narcissism

Here are some tips for dealing with less harmful forms of narcissism. Should you ever feel endangered physically, mentally or emotionally, extract yourself from that relationship as quickly as possible.

Don't hesitate to reach out to professionals for help.

Narcissism in Children
- When your kids are small, nurture a safe, sharing culture.
- Be firm about rules and expected behaviour. Nip entitlement in the bud.
- Ensure visiting children are heard and accommodated.

Narcissism in Relationships
- Don't indulge, or make excuses for, narcissistic behaviour.
- Set clear boundaries and rules.
- Never make yourself small to accommodate a burgeoning ego.
- Don't mistake bullying and self-centred behaviour for strength.

Narcissism at Work
- Be aware that narcissists spend a lot of time talking about themselves.
- Narcissists are sensitive to how others see them – if they're being unhelpful, it may help to ask them how others are likely to react.
- As narcissists are likely to steal your ideas, be sure to document your thoughts and ensure others know about them before sharing with your narcissistic co-worker or boss.
- Narcissists are good at discrediting others, tend to bully others and fail to follow through. Be aware of this, and be assertive, not aggressive.

Overall
- Be clear about how toxic your relationship is, and whether you can sustain it.
- Depending on where a person is on the Narcissistic Personality Inventory, they may well need professional help.

10

The Empathy Deficit

Doesn't Anyone Care Anymore?

I Feel Your Pain

Invite More Empathy into Your Life

DOESN'T ANYONE CARE ANYMORE?

With the rise in narcissism comes a resulting drop in empathy, in the ability to feel how it is for others, to walk in their shoes. But it's not just narcissists who are found lacking when it comes to empathy. The speed and complexity of contemporary life seems to have lessened our ability to care about others. 'Our interactions with each other are often thinned out, anonymous and tribal,' reflects Stanford neuroscientist Jamil Zaki. It's a state he describes as 'barren soil for empathy'.[1]

As humans we're wired to connect, and there are real wins for us when we do reach out. As the feel-good hormones oxytocin and progesterone flood our system, our cortisol levels start to drop, helping reduce stress. Simply holding hands or hugging can also raise our oxytocin levels, as can putting ourselves out for someone else, thus creating a further lift in progesterone levels.[2]

> 'You never really understand a person until you consider things from his point of view ... until you climb inside his skin and walk around in it.'
> Atticus Finch, To Kill A Mockingbird[3]

Being able to empathise isn't the same as being a doormat. When we're overanxious for others, it is also detrimental. Amongst other impacts, our cells age more rapidly – an occupational hazard for parents and carers, who can so easily become burnt out. The way through is to feel for others without getting drawn into their pain. There are real benefits for those who strike the right balance. A life lived with a willingness to help others creates greater happiness and the likelihood of a longer life.

Why Has Empathy Taken a Dive?

What can we do about our current fall in empathy? Some blame the trend on our growing inability to see the injustices and vulnerabilities around us, and to be willing to do something about them.[4] In his 2016 *Atlantic Monthly* article, teacher Paul Barnwell suggests that the decline in empathy is due, in part, to our emphasis on academic achievement in the classroom – on promoting a success-oriented school curriculum above all else. Yet, while disheartened by the ongoing bullying and unhelpful stereotyping he witnesses at school, and the rubbish strewn around outside the school cafeteria, Barnwell has also noticed how his students 'crave more meaningful discussions and instruction relating to character, morality, and ethics'.[5] Taking these insights on board, could our focus on exam success be undermining our children's preparation for life, and the resulting choices they make?

Some years ago I was presenting my research on the invasive levels of marketing to kids, to an audience of nine- and ten-year-olds. To my surprise, they grasped the ethical issues with ease. Their questions were some of the most probing I've had, even when presenting to adults. Afterwards, one of the teachers told how they had begun to weave philosophical inquiry into the curriculum. This, she explained, was partly why such young students could grasp this level of detail, and draw out the salient points. What struck me about this remarkable group of kids was their ability not only to think, but to empathise with the victims of excessive marketing, struggling with body image and other self-esteem issues. Surely this ability to think more inclusively, to take a body of material and draw out the ethical and other considerations beyond our own personal agenda is a crucial life skill in this, our complex global world? But rarely is this happening.

'If you want to cultivate empathy, my suggestion is to stop thinking that everyone thinks and acts like you do or would.'
Jeff Rotmeyer, ImpactHK[6]

Is the Media Partly to Blame?

One University of Michigan study charted a dramatic drop in empathy amongst university students between the 1970s and the 2000s, and most dramatically since 2000. This is due, in part, to the explosion of online platforms and people being connected 24/7.[7] In recent years, numerous teachers have expressed their concerns at the sudden growing need for pastoral care in schools. Are we all too busy to stop and be with our young? Amid the avalanche of posts and texts, and a hunger to feel special, lies a deep ache amongst our children and teenagers to be listened to deeply, to be understood. But to empathise, we first need to know what empathy looks like and feels like.

Another of the many challenges with our ability to empathise is the growing sense of overwhelm people are feeling in viewing the news, a large portion of which is about all the disasters on the planet. How different would our worldview be if we were to hear more of miracle breakthroughs in science and hard-fought dreams coming true? So why turn on the news? Is it to inform ourselves of world affairs – to think about issues and work to find solutions? Or perhaps we've become addicted to viewing the next awful instalment of the nightly news for the adrenaline, and to back up our assumption that the world is a dark and dangerous place.

The flood of graphic information and images we see daily is so confronting that many have stopped turning on the news. Others watch the news purely for entertainment. Where does this leave us in the empathy stakes? When asked for the lessons from the Holocaust, Jewish mystic Rabbi Heschel warned that 'the opposite of good is not evil, but indifference',[8] also reflecting, 'indifference to evil is worse than evil itself'.[9] Not everyone is indifferent to the huge challenges the planet faces, but many are distancing themselves from essential issues as they're suffering compassion fatigue.

Too Busy to See What's Happening

It's difficult to empathise with others when we're feeling overwhelmed. We're also so distracted that we're often scarcely aware of each other. Yet something powerful happens when people feel heard – real empathy grows. One Pew Research study revealed that almost 90 per cent of people admitted to using their phone during a recent social gathering to send or read a message, call someone, raise an alert, or take a photo or video, even though most admitted that mobile phone use harms conversation. Of those surveyed, women were more conscious than men of how disruptive mobile phones can be. A third of this sample also admitted to using their devices in a gathering when bored.[10]

> '**The happy moments aren't the big Hollywood ones – they're little glimpses of hope … when you're least expecting it to, someone's humanity will astonish you.**'
> *Tobias Jones,* A Place of Refuge[11]

Of all the aspects of empathy we need to focus on, studies suggest that empathetic concern for others is top of the list. We need to be much more aware of others around us, and learn to see life from their perspective more.[12] Yet another study into mobile phones showed that simply having a phone in sight while two people were talking impacted their conversation and the closeness they felt. The mere presence of the mobile phone prompted people to stick to more superficial subjects. That way it didn't matter if they were interrupted.[13]

> **'A wealth of information creates a poverty of attention.'**
> *Herbert A. Simon, economist and psychologist*[14]

Let Go of the Need to Be Perfect

There are additional trends that may impact our ability to empathise, including a growing need to come across as perfect. One study of university students across the UK, America and Canada over almost three decades revealed a 33 per cent rise in young people feeling the need to be perfect in order to gain the approval of others.[15] Reflecting on the results, the study authors fear 'a hidden epidemic' of perfection is emerging.[16] This spike in perfectionist traits – what millennials, especially, demand of themselves and others, and in what they think society expects of them – keeps people focused on their need to come across as perfect 24/7. And, in pitching for perfect, there's little room to think about how others are travelling.

We're worried about our appearance to never before experienced levels, not just focusing on our wrinkles and pimples, but prompting us to have breast implants and botox, to extend our penises and reshape our vaginas, and buy a whole wardrobe full of new clothes each season. Added to this, the world seems less safe, with terrorism and daily reports of muggings and murders making us more reluctant to embrace more adventurous travel, or even to go out at night. With all these details needing our consideration, the world has become a mind-numbingly complex place. In a recent

Global Risks Report, John Scott, head of sustainability risk at Zurich Insurance Group, spoke of our growing levels of anxiety. 'We are going to need new ways of managing technology and globalization that respond to the insecurity that many people experience,' he stated.[17] One fact is clear: anxiety and empathy don't make for good bedfellows. It's essential that we get on top of our overwhelm, lest it crush us, inspiring us to lead unnecessarily isolated lives.

I FEEL YOUR PAIN

If we want to help empathy along, we need to look at what's not working. Dr Tim Elmore, founder and president of Growing Leaders, a not-for-profit organisation set up to nurture tomorrow's leaders, believes we're failing this emerging generation by allowing them to grow up in a world where mistakes and bad judgements are ignored. These kids are also spending their days in a virtual world, where they can switch off from situations whenever they like. Kids, Elmore believes, need to be exposed to real-life experiences that challenge them, to help them grow up and expand their ability to see the world from other people's viewpoint.[18]

Something meaningful happens when we genuinely connect. One Harvard study, which tracked the lives of adults over the last 80 years, found that the quality of relationships people had with others had a huge impact on their health. Close ties, the study concluded, protect people from life's ups and downs, help delay our mental and physical decline, and are better predictors of long and happy lives than social class, IQ or one's genes. As psychiatrist and director of the study Professor Robert Waldinger observed, 'The people who were the most satisfied in their relationships at age 50 were the healthiest at age 80.'[19]

There's Strength and Healing in Numbers

When we expand our personal space to include others, our sense of isolation fades. Recent brain-mapping shows how such activities as communal singing can work well for people who don't have a great sense of connection with those around them, delivering real enjoyment as they synchronise their voices with others, creating a greater sense of trust and cooperation.[20] Inspired by Montreal's Homeless Men's Choir, Australia's Dr Jonathon Welch AM set up the Choir of Hard Knocks, bringing together the homeless and disadvantaged, rebuilding confidence and creating a space that fostered friendships and self-esteem. One of the original choir members, who grappled with homelessness and addiction issues, has since completed a masters degree in organisational psychology. Winning numerous awards and performing in some of Australia's most prestigious performance venues, the Choir of Hard Knocks has now inspired the establishment of 'street choirs' across the globe.

Following 56 individuals who joined the first two Queensland intakes for the School of Hard Knocks (part of the Upbeat Arts program working with marginalised communities), music psychologist Associate Professor Genevieve Dingle described how after initially struggling with the anxiety of making it to rehearsals and meeting others, participants reported 'increased energy', 'optimism' and 'closeness with others'.[21]

Reaching Out

Essential to empathy is our ability to understand how life is for someone else – to feel what they feel and respond kindly to them. Do we have to be in physical contact to create meaningful connections? A recent study into the effectiveness of two online forums – one for those suffering breast cancer, the other for those diagnosed with motor neuron disease – produced some interesting results. Most of those joining these forums were still coming to terms with their diagnosis and the uncertainties around their future health. Forum members described the information and emotional support they received online as 'invaluable'. Interviewees talked of the 'welcoming', 'warmth' and 'understanding' they enjoyed, and how connecting with others helped them talk about their experiences and feelings with online members in a way that they couldn't share with family and friends.

The personal messaging functions on these platforms also helped users link up. Friendships developed and even more information was shared. Here people were able to let fly, knowing others understood where they were coming from. These online friendships helped with the isolation that comes with ill health. In these forums, people also appreciated that they were able to take their time to get to know each other, which in turn increased their ability to empathise.[22]

Empathy Has an Impact

There are many benefits for those able to create an empathetic space. In his book *The War for Kindness*, Jamil Zaki tells of how employees with an understanding boss are less likely to call in sick; how teams that genuinely connect with each other also collaborate better; and how organisations that prioritise kindness benefit from greater loyalty and a strong sense of morale. Growing up with parents from Peru and Pakistan, whose marriage subsequently fell apart, Zaki found his way through this emotional and cultural minefield by learning to see events from both parents' perspective. An empathetic approach, he states, is an essential 'survival skill'.[23]

Invite More Empathy into Your Life

While we may often feel isolated, we needn't remain this way. By reaching out kindly to others, often with the simplest of gestures, we build bridges that help sustain ourselves and others through life's ups and downs, as seen most powerfully during the worst days of our recent pandemic.

Get to Know Yourself
- Too many of us are hard on ourselves, with impossibly high standards that can also affect the way we view others – learn how to be kinder to yourself.
- Take small pockets of time out of your day just to 'chill'.
- Join a mindfulness class.
- Download a meditation app to use daily.

When You're with Friends and Family
- Commit to spending time together without distraction.
- Be open and authentic.
- Connect eye to eye, and listen closely so people feel seen and understood.
- Organise one-on-one catch-ups where you can.

How to Better Understand Strangers
- Recognise that learning how to 'read' others takes time, patience and practice.
- There are so many approaches to life, and personality types – challenge any kneejerk reactions you have to those who are different.
- Experts suggest reading good fiction to expand your understanding of others.
- Volunteer – it helps connect us with others in potentially life-changing moments.
- Make friends outside your social group – you may be surprised where those friendships take you.
- Practise random acts of kindness, paying forward coffees and meals.

When Someone Is in a Difficult Space
- Don't avoid those you care about when they're experiencing hard times, just because you don't have all the answers – often what people most need is simply to be heard and, if we know them well, perhaps to be held.
- In a genuine listening space, something significant often happens, even though it can't always be put into words.

11
Brain Fatigue

Who's Messing with Our Brains?

What's Happened to Our Memories?

Time for a Brain Reset?

WHO'S MESSING WITH OUR BRAINS?

Personal computers, smartphones and other devices arrived in our lives promising to save us time and effort, but the outcome isn't always so straightforward. With an avalanche of material to wade through daily, our schedules are busier than ever. Rarely do we get the chance to switch off. Have you noticed how your brain begins to tire, or how you start to feel a little twitchy when you're facing too much detail? With the amount of information and choices available to us, we're finding it harder to read complex material.

Some people, including a number of academics, now admit to struggling to read long papers, while others find themselves more forgetful, or losing their thread in the middle of a conversation. 'I am a fairly good reader. I can read well, it's just that now, when I open a book, my mind just can't let me read,' Dot confesses. 'I have to skip through paragraphs, I forget sentences that I read literally one second ago, I feel sleepy and tired the moment I start reading, and I have no clue what to do.'

> 'Nowadays everything is in small, bite-sized doses, that the attention span has been diminished to 5–10 minute pieces.'
> *Stan*

There are other changes, too. Many of those using e-readers – Kindle, Kobo and the like – tell of how much harder it is to recall the title and author of the book they're reading, as they no longer have a physical book lying around. One of the advantages of the new technologies is their ability to take care of non-essential information for us. So does it matter if we can't remember the name of the book we're reading? Isn't that what Goodreads, Litsy, Shelfie and other apps are for? Or is there something more fundamental at stake?

Reflection is an essential life skill that helps us connect with each other. It's also good for our concentration and imagination. Yet we're finding it increasingly hard to just sit and think. In one University of Virginia study, students were asked to sit quietly in a room for six and 15 minutes without using a mobile phone. Almost a third of participants broke the rules – taking out their phone or getting up and wandering around. Assuming this was due to the age of the sample, the researchers widened the age range of participants to include people from a farmers' market and local church. These additional participants proved to be just as restless as the original group, even when given the opportunity to plan for this short time of reflection. Some even chose to self-administer a mild electric shock rather than sit still. More than eight out of ten participants aged 18 to 77 years also admitted to having no time to relax or think in the previous 24 hours.[1]

The Myth of Multitasking

One of the great advantages of new technologies is that they allow us to multitask – to be more efficient, to cram more into our days. While we're busy writing a report, we can check our emails or Twitter feed, pay a couple of bills, jump onto a travel website and browse a future holiday destination, or book a restaurant for dinner. But is all this multitasking really making us more efficient?

According to Stanford psychology professor Anthony Wagner (and others), we can't do two or more things at the same time. Why? Because our brains can only focus on one task at once. In short: brains don't multitask. They switch from one task to the next, and are expected to do so ever more rapidly. So, far from being more efficient, our constant 'switching' takes its toll on the brain, which then struggles to recalibrate and focus on each new task it's presented with. Multitasking also taxes our memory and undermines our ability to concentrate. The more we multitask, the more easily distracted we are, and the less recall we have.[2]

> 'The computer screen bulldozes our doubts with its bounties and conveniences.'
> Nicholas Carr, The Shallows: What the Internet Is Doing to Our Brains[3]

Information Overload

Studies show that the more we move from screen to screen, scrolling through whole bodies of text and skipping over information, the more likely we are to accept the ideas presented to us, rather than think about what we're reading, reflect on it and possibly end up with a different point of view. We are not only *what* we read, but *how* we read, insists neuroscientist Maryanne Wolf.[4] And, unfortunately, our growing digital distraction is fracturing our attention. The way forward, suggests digital wellbeing expert Dr Kristy Goodwin, is to learn to concentrate on one task at a time, and to ensure there's time for some 'quiet space and boredom' in the day, to boost our creativity and focus.[5]

The ease and speed of access to information on the net is seductive, but is it working for us? One piece of research found that participants accessing information online were able to do so more rapidly than those consulting encyclopedias. However, those searching online had less recall of the material they came across.[6] Now that we're in the habit of skimming, where is all this superficial reading taking us? Studies show that, increasingly, we're assuming the first piece of information we come across is the most important.[7]

Keep it Brief

Maryanne Wolf has no doubt that our digital culture is changing how we read and think. This was brought home to her when she found herself less able to embark on 'sustained, deep reading'. She decided to set aside time every day to re-read a Hermann Hesse novel she'd loved decades earlier, and was shocked to find she now 'hated' the book. The story was slow, with 'unnecessarily difficult words and sentences' that didn't seem to go anywhere. 'I now read on the surface and very quickly,' she tells. 'In fact, I read too fast to comprehend deeper levels, which forced me constantly to go back and re-read the same sentence over and over with increasing frustration.'[8] Journalist Xenia Kessler also finds her reading style has changed. 'Even if I'm interested in a subject, reading over 25 pages all in one [go] is exhausting,' she admits, adding, 'but when I have to read for example, 5 shorter texts, which can be summed up to this extent, it doesn't feel that hard anymore.'[9]

WHAT'S HAPPENED TO OUR MEMORIES?

While we may have some difficulty reading whole screeds of text, are our new technologies impacting memory? A Trending Machine poll revealed that those aged between 18 and 34 were more likely to leave their keys and lunch behind, and to be confused about what day it was, than those aged 55 plus. Why is this? 'Stress often leads to forgetfulness, depression and poor judgment,' suggests family and occupational therapist Patricia Gutentag. 'We find higher rates of ADHD diagnoses in young adults. This is a population that has grown up multitasking using technology, often compounded by lack of sleep, all of which results in high levels of forgetfulness.'[10]

It's not just the fact that we're forgetting things that's concerning. The way we use information is changing, too. Until recently, we made a habit of remembering facts so we could recall them later. With easy access to the internet, we don't have to commit details to memory, so we don't. Now we're more likely to remember *where* we accessed a piece of information, than the information itself.[12] While this frees up our brains for more important concerns, often in our spare time we end up engaged in more of the same – scrolling and skimming, and trying to keep up.

When we forget the name of the book we're reading, we no longer worry because our e-reader has that information. However, in spite of the convenience of these new technologies, are we losing something essential? My dad loved nature and was skilled at 'reading' the weather. He taught me how to observe a whole range of details around the weather – from the behaviour of birds, to the formation of clouds – which helped give me a sense of where the weather was heading. Now, though, we simply consult our smartphones, and the opportunity for a deeper connection with the natural world is lost.

'The Net seizes our attention only to scatter it,' states Nicholas Carr in his groundbreaking book, *The Shallows*.[13] And when our attention is scattered, we're more easily distracted and confused. Yes, we can access a world of information and entertainment on our phones. But as our online experience becomes ever more intimate, immediate and intense, we can't help but check in on our phones and other devices throughout the day. Why this compulsive behaviour? In part it's because we've come to enjoy the 'information rewards' that ready access to smartphones, tablets and laptops deliver. Where is this increasing dependence on our devices taking us?

Declining Recall and Concentration

In one US study, students installed a tracking app on their phones, revealing that on average they unlocked their phone more than 60 times a day, totalling almost four hours. 'That means,' notes psychology professor Larry Rosen, who led the study, 'that even when they [students] are supposed to be studying, they are unlocking their phone three to four times an hour for about three to four minutes at a time.'[14] This distraction does little for stress levels and concentration, let alone recall.

Accessing information is very different from taking it on board. To fully *absorb* a piece of information, it needs to be shunted from our working memory into our long-term memory, and we need to be attentive for this to happen. Our short-term memory has a limited capacity to hold information, while our long-term memory is where our accumulated knowledge sits. When our short-term memory is overloaded, details that might be useful, or critical even, end up getting discarded.

'We prefer to collect a lot of information quickly and superficially in order to have a general idea about a topic.'
Xenia Kessler[11]

Learning happens best when it aligns with the way our brains operate. Our neural pathways absorb new information, creating new structures or 'scaffolds' of linked information. As our knowledge in an area grows, it adds to this structure. And these structures help us make sense of the world. The more substantial our 'information structures', the more we're able to think through issues or ideas and solve problems. Put simply, the more familiar we are with a body of knowledge, the easier it is for our working memory to handle further information in this area.

> '**I used to read all the time no problem, now I'm constantly distracted (I blame overuse of my phone).**'
> *Colin*

To get the best out of our memory, we need to ensure we don't overload our working memory.[15] However, making the most of our memory is a bit of a balancing act. Like our muscles, our brains grow and strengthen when challenged, which explains why the brains of London taxi drivers, who have to memorise all the city's streets, lanes, avenues and more, have larger memory centres than taxi drivers who rely on navigation devices.[16]

Glued to Our Phones

One of the challenges of our 'always on' culture is that our use of technology is growing exponentially. In a 2018 report published by British telecom regulator Ofcom, people admitted to spending, on average, a day a week online – more than double the time reported in 2007. People also said that they looked at their smartphones, on average, every 12 minutes while awake, while six out of ten people felt they couldn't live without their phones.[17]

Cynthia, a regular smartphone user, reflects on how her attention span has been affected:

> In the past decade, our lives have become highly dependent on tech and internet. A lot of time has been spent on instant gratifying stuff such as Facebook, YouTube, movies etc. This has caused my attention span to go down to peanuts. I keep feeling the need for something new every moment, and get distracted and open something, anything from FB to reading and learning about stuff. It seems to have seriously affected a lot of my life.

How Does Taking Photos Affect the Memory?

Our habit of snapping endless photos is also impacting memory. In 2013, psychological scientist Linda Henkel took a number of people through a museum. The group was free to take photos of any object they wished. Afterwards, those who took a lot of photos had greater difficulty remembering the objects as a whole and in detail, as well as their location in the museum, compared with those who simply chose to take in the whole museum experience.[18]

Keen to challenge this finding, two researchers from the University of California got a group of undergraduates to look at artwork on a computer. First the group was asked to simply look at the art. In the second round they viewed the art, then took a photo. Finally, they studied the art and then took a photo with a Snapchat equivalent, which participants knew would soon disappear. The results showed that those simply looking at the art had the best recall of the images, followed by those studying the art before photographing it. The poorest recall was from participants using the Snapchat scenario.[19]

And Now Let's Move On

As our consumption of content grows, so does the speed at which we absorb it. Danish computer scientist Sune Lehmann Jørgensen recently analysed a variety of measures, from box office sales to how long popular tweets remain in the top 50, to track how quickly subjects catch our interest, then disappear. Jørgensen found that incidents such as a successful event or high-rating TV show are now becoming popular more rapidly than previously. The downside is that we're losing interest in these same highlights faster than was previously the case. Each of us, Jørgensen reflects, is 'constantly triaging' the tsunami of information that comes our way – from personal posts and the news, to ads, live streams and on-demand TV shows – leaving us grabbing at the most popular, so as not to be left behind.[20]

My Brain Hurts

Our diminishing ability to comprehend and absorb information is causing concern in a number of fields, including the intelligence community. Experts are worried about what will happen to the integrity of future intelligence gathering, with a generation in the workplace used to hurried reading and moving swiftly from site to site. While the net gives analysts more data than ever before, the reality is that human intelligence-gathering is a slow process. One report, 'Thinking in 140 Characters', expresses concern that the 'sustained concentration, deep thinking, and creativity' needed in good analysts may elude this new generation of intelligence recruits, as intelligence is a painstaking occupation, needing time and attention to check and refine one's analyses. In a world that now also values speed, this further adds to the challenge, creating what could very well turn out to be 'poorly vetted information'.[21]

Where does this leave us? It's clear that we're experiencing tech fatigue. Our brains are getting tired, making it harder to be productive or to think straight, with an endless stream of information delivered to us almost instantaneously. Brain fatigue leads to wider exhaustion – to sleep and eating issues, and to irritability. It's not just our brains that suffer from our mental exhaustion – our cognitive fatigue can impact us physically as well. Participants in one UK study rode a stationary bicycle until exhausted. Half did so after a 90-minute, mentally stretching test, the remainder after feeling rested. The study found that mental exhaustion impedes physical performance, with those who were mentally fatigued tiring more quickly.[22]

With so much pressure on us, could our increasing love affair with our devices, and the resulting overload, be ageing our brains? A 2019 trial found that those engaged in an online role-playing game for six weeks experienced 'significant reductions in grey matter in the brain region involved in impulse control and decision-making'.[23] Constant interruptions don't help, either. A 2005 University of London study, led by psychologist Dr Glenn Wilson, found that those experiencing continual interruptions – emails, texts and phone calls – saw a ten-point drop in their IQ – double the impact of participants taking an IQ test after smoking marijuana. A high level of interruptions, Wilson concluded, has the same effect on the brain as sleep deprivation.[24]

Pleasure/Pain

One of the real difficulties in this new environment, suggests psychology professor Larry Rosen, is that it's easy to get caught in a pleasure/pain cycle – between the pleasure of constant stimulation and 24/7 entertainment, and our anxieties around keeping up.[25] Our resulting 'always on' habits keep us alert and make us hyper-vigilant – constantly checking our environment the way we would if we were in survival mode. Our bodies are then flooded with the stress hormones cortisol and adrenaline, in response to what they perceive as an imminent threat. When our bodies are put under pressure in this way, our immune systems suffer and this can lead to inflammation in our brain cells, which, Cambridge psychiatry professor Edward Bullmore says, can spark anxiety and depression. And depression, along with anxiety, he explains, is 'a known factor in knocking out concentration'.[26]

The more we get drawn into new technologies, the less time and headspace we have for real life and real-life connections – for being able to make sense of our lives and those around us. 'I've been toying with the idea that I'm a dopamine addict for a little while now,' Troy confesses. 'Smokes, beers, video games, porn, weight lifting, constant switching between websites/shitty mobile games/sports pools/dating sites … it's always something, there's always a dopamine drip to look forward to. Dozens of them every day.' To be fully awake to life and those around you, you need a clear head – without it, you end up spending your life in a daze.

Time for a Brain Reset?

Given our growing addiction to our devices, it's essential that we factor time and space into the day to relax and recalibrate, to help us step out of the pleasure–pain cycle that constant connectivity offers.

Here are some ideas to get you started.

- Do not fear boredom as it allows us to chill out a little, balancing our busyness and giving our creativity a lift, too.

- Set aside time every day to work away from your devices, then make good use of this time by seeking out quiet spaces.

- Make a habit of diving back into real life and taking in the detail around you, such as the expression on a friend's face, and how the trees in your street appear over different seasons and during all kinds of weather.

- Get tactile – our cognitive skills are refined during sensory experiences. Touch helps connect us with those around us and with the wider world. Tactile play also improves our children's descriptive and expressive language.

- Spend contemplative time in nature – in a park or wooded area. Countless studies show a reduction in blood pressure and stress, and improved mood and focus, for those who make nature time a habit.

- Limit checking in on your devices, so that there's time just to pause, reflect and reset.

- Challenge yourself by reading more complex material, and reflecting on it.

- Make sure you're getting enough sleep.

- If you want to improve your memory and focus, take regular exercise.

12
Working Life Doesn't Appear to Be Working

Why Is Everyone so Stressed?

Vocation Frustration

Lost in Self-absorption and Spin

Workplace Solutions

WHY IS EVERYONE SO STRESSED?

One of the times we get the greatest brain work-out is during the working day. Work matters, not just because it pays the bills. If we work full-time, we'll spend around 40 per cent, if not more, of our lives at work. That's why we also need our jobs to deliver for us – to provide a supportive environment to help us achieve everything that's asked of us. If we're lucky, there will be the possibility of career advancement and the chance to learn new skills. Work is often the place where lifelong friendships are forged. And when work isn't working, it can cause huge stress, if not distress, a feeling that we're out on a limb.

There's a lot of energy spent in the workplace on building up human resources, redesigning office layouts, rethinking organisational structures, and introducing flexible work arrangements, along with new rounds of technology. Yet in spite of all this effort many are feeling alienated at work. A recent UK workplace survey revealed that seven out of ten employees expected to move jobs within the year. Just over half admitted to looking for a new position during work hours,[1] while a recent worldwide Gallup poll revealed that only 15 per cent of employees felt engaged in their work.[2] These figures are sobering, hinting at just how disengaged so many people are feeling right now.

According to the American Institute of Stress, work stress is 'far and away' the biggest stress adults currently face. Job stress, it claims, has grown steadily in recent decades, leaving individuals feeling they have little or no control over their working lives. People are also facing 'lots of demands' at work. Currently, employee workloads cause the greatest on-the-job stress. The levels of anxiety are such that one in four workers admit to being so stressed that they feel like 'screaming or shouting'.[3] Factor in the additional stress of a post-pandemic workplace, and it's not hard to sense how difficult work has become for many, and how isolated they must feel.

The Impact of Constant Change

In this climate of rolling retrenchments and the increasing complexity of work, it's little surprise that many are finding these volatile workplaces difficult to navigate. In some 2017 research by global recruitment company Robert Half, three-quarters of the Australian senior financial executives surveyed expected the stress levels in their organisations to rise, due to increasing workloads, rising expectations of what people can deliver at work and ever-shortening deadlines.[4] It's little surprise, then, that companies such as IBM believe some of the key skills now needed are communication, creativity, critical thinking and adaptability (a growth mindset).[5]

Our workplaces are under a lot of pressure right now. Aside from the fallout from COVID-19, we're still facing the rigours of global competition, the speed and 24/7 nature of communication, constant changes in technology and the ever-present pressure of shareholder expectations, all of which are proving more than a little stretching. Most organisations are also much leaner than they were two or three decades ago, with fewer people but often the same amount of work. These changes come at a cost, with loyalty and longevity in short supply. This means that far fewer employees are aware of an organisation's history – past wins and vulnerabilities, competition that came out of left field – and of the collective wisdom garnered along the way, and probably don't expect to stay long enough to gain this depth of knowledge.

One of the many consequences of a constant turnover of staff is that employees can no longer expect technical guidance from their supervisors. Yet, unlike their supervisors, they won't necessarily have access to consultants to fill in their knowledge gaps. Another consequence of so much workplace upheaval is that employees have less incentive to invest in their workplace – to go the extra mile or share new ideas – further weakening the long-term health of an organisation. With jobs more scarce now, people are more likely to stay put, as they have rents or mortgages to pay. How will they fare in a climate that was already under a great deal of pressure before the pandemic hit?

The Rise in Toxic Workplaces

For many, the work environment has become a less than benign place. In one Australian study, around half of respondents felt their workplace was mentally unhealthy.[6] This number indicates there is something fundamentally wrong. It's hard not to notice how often the word 'toxic' comes up in conversations about work. Recently, a friend applied for a senior position with a leading media company, and was taken aback at having a large part of the interview devoted to her ability to fire staff. She had been keen to join the organisation, and was well aware of what a senior position entailed, but didn't want to work in such a dysfunctional work culture, so she withdrew her application.

What are we to make of all the stress and resulting sense of estrangement currently felt by many at work? Work stress, some experts claim, is highly individual. What weighs one person down may be effortless for others. No doubt this is true, but it doesn't fully explain why there's so much anxiety and disillusionment right now. In one Global Benefits Attitudes Survey, over half the employees who were consulted talked of not having enough people to do the work. Impossible workloads, they said, were their main source of stress. Yet only 15 per cent of the managers in this same survey saw rising workloads as an issue, suggesting a real disconnect between managers and their teams.[7]

Currently almost 30 per cent of working Australians are experiencing high levels of on-the-job stress. The younger the employee, the greater the stress.[8] So what can we do about this? Leadership is a key issue, because the way an organisation is managed and the values it upholds have a significant impact on how people are able to work together. Celebrated professor of organisational change, Sir Gary Cooper, insists that people need the right physical and psychological environment to give their best at work,[9] but this doesn't seem to happening. A recent Staples survey of desk-based office workers across ten European countries found a growing 'vocation frustration' amongst employees. This survey revealed that a staggering 97 per cent of participating UK workers experience ongoing frustration at work.[10]

In our current climate of constant organisational changes and lay-offs, lack of job security, and on-the-job pressures, many are feeling disempowered and disconnected. No-one wants to work in a toxic environment. We instinctively know that it's not good for us, but we're starting to understand the short- and long-term health implications of working in an organisation that brings us no joy. In one UK study, healthcare workers who disliked their boss presented with significantly higher blood pressure than is considered safe. Scientist and psychotherapist George Fieldman warns that if you work long term for a boss you really don't get on with, you could be at a heightened risk of coronary heart disease or a stroke, due to sustained high blood pressure over an extended time.[11]

Work Without Boundaries

The toughening of corporate culture has also heralded the arrival of the cult of busyness. Those who are busy are seen as important – a breed apart. They're immensely competitive, too, eager to prove they work ten times harder than everyone else. This need to be busy has expanded, thanks to technology, to an expectation that we will be available 24/7. Yet OECD research indicates that productivity actually drops off when people are working longer hours.[12] Conversely, when Swedish nurses at a retirement home were put on a six-hour day on their usual salary, their productivity rose and sick leave fell by half. These nurses reported feeling happier and having more energy for work and for life outside of work.[13]

As work pressure and the fear of job loss ramps up, so does the expectation that calls and emails will be answered promptly out of work hours. Some don't think to question this trend. Others feel obliged to be accessible all hours, to hold onto their job. This 'always on' culture creates even more pressure within work teams to always be seen to 'deliver'. One professional told of how, as their work culture became more toxic, colleagues stopped helping each other out, refusing to share information with someone unable to make an out-of-hours conference call. When everyone retreats to their own silo, work can become an impossibly lonely place. Whatever our work dynamic, private time is being squeezed, as is the chance to have any real work–life balance. But what impact does being available outside of work hours have?

Always at Work

It's not working flexible hours *per se* that impacts us, one study suggests, so much as whether or not we get to *choose* when to switch off.[14] What we also know is that responding to work out of hours is constraining, and can't be counted as leisure time.[15] Whether or not an employee ends up taking the out-of-hours call they've been expecting doesn't matter. The *anticipation* of doing so leaves them in a state of heightened vigilance, which often leads to poor sleep and feeling less refreshed on waking.[16]

Far from raising productivity, responding to work calls and emails outside work time creates increased anxiety and can lead to burnout, not to mention its impact on family life. Management professor William Blecker, who was part of the 'Killing Me Softly' study, describes today's 'always on' work culture as 'insidious',[17] claiming that 'every time you check your email or glance at your phone to see if you have an email or other communication, your brain actually shifts back to work mode..[18] The stress of answering work emails out of hours, or expecting to do so, also impacts a person's wider health, as it's hard to switch off from work.[19]

Some organisations, and countries, are realising the impact of never leaving work behind. As far back as 2004, the French courts stated that it wasn't an offence to be unavailable for after-hours calls. Then, in 2017, France brought in the 'Right to Disconnect' legislation, insisting employers negotiate with staff on how connected they will be after work. While Germany is still working on the detail, in 2012 Volkswagen implemented a company-wide rule ensuring emails are not sent to employees after 6.15 pm and before 7 am. Two years later, Daimler determined that all emails sent to staff while they were on holidays would be deleted.[20]

Along with all this busyness and endless demands from employers, there often comes a mean-spirited culture, which doesn't serve anyone well. 'We'd gone through two massive takeovers back to back,' Paula tells. 'Everyone was stressed out with all the additional work, learning to work well together in blended teams, as well as getting to know endless new products. Once a week the company used to provide a savoury platter. It gave everyone a lift. Then we got a new CEO and the savouries and other small gestures went, and so did the goodwill.'

With everyone working longer and harder, there are the inevitable casualties. Beyond the statistics are real-life stories that can't be ignored. 'I have also had the misfortune to see someone have a full-blown nervous breakdown,' tells Harry, who describes watching a senior commodities trader in an unstable market become 'overwhelmed with information and sheer volume of calls, calculations to keep his position steady'.

'It was a classic sort of scene from a film with traders on their feet, waving their arms around,' he reflects. This trader was under a lot of pressure and 'all of a sudden he stopped: put the phones down, and standing on one leg exclaimed that he was a tree! The whole trading room burst into laughter, thinking he was just playing around. After 20 minutes, still standing on one leg, we realised that this was now serious and phoned for a rapid-response paramedic. The man was sedated and taken to hospital, in the meantime still persisting he was a tree and crying because "he was being cut down". It is probably one of the most frightening things I have seen,' Harry says. 'Needless to say, he never traded again; indeed we do not know what happened to him other than that at the time he was sectioned.'

This incident resonated with Harry, a fraud investigator, as he too went on to have a breakdown. 'Employers seem to think that this unnecessary pressure is something to be applauded and seen as being "effective and efficient" management,' he reflects. 'Nothing could be further from the truth,' he adds, calling the 'hire and fire' approach to management 'a disease ... inherited from America of the 1970s'.

Technology Alone Is Not the Answer

Increasingly, we're looking to technology to solve our job issues, which isn't surprising as technology has literally brought us the world, helping us communicate, process and share information to levels and at a speed that we could not have imagined a few decades ago. And we are grateful for this, but there are certainly downsides.

Technology is also redefining our concept of the ideal worker – someone who operates more like a machine, notes associate professor of philosophy Laura Rediehs. It's a person who's efficient, tireless, endlessly amenable and willing to give their all, without any suggestion of additional pay. This trend, she believes, is dehumanising, as it comes with a growing distaste for the 'inconvenience of feelings' and the intrusion of a person's life into work. Rediehs also notes how, with the constant changes in technology and major upgrades at work, huge amounts of time are spent updating and training staff. Instead of making our lives easier, increasingly it is dictating how we work.[21]

Gig Workers Need More Consideration

If work is tricky in mainstream organisations, it is even more so in the gig economy, where work is based on contracts and one-off jobs. Beyond the initial excitement of being their own boss, and of leaving behind the slog of nine-to-five work, enabling them to work when they like, workers in the gig economy soon discover they have few rights. One 2019 Canadian study reported an increase in loneliness amongst gig workers, who are twice as likely to feel isolated much of the time, and be more prone to depression and anxiety. The gig workers studied were also 50 per cent more likely to admit to feeling helpless, while four in ten felt they had little control over their lives. The study concluded that the freedom gig work offers may come at a 'considerable psychological cost', not to mention financial cost, as these workers don't have paid sick leave or holidays.[22]

> 'I've been a "gig" and contract worker for 3 years now, and while I'm doing relatively well financially, the instability, the ebbs and flows, and the pressure to "get while the getting is good" is really f**king bad psychologically.'
> *Sophie*

There's no doubt that many single mums, creatives and students, along with retired people enjoying the chance to pick up a little extra money on the side, benefit from the job flexibility the gig economy offers. Many, however, do not. Shawn Cadeau, Chief Revenue Officer of software app Jobber, admits that the gig economy has 'shifted nearly all risk away from employers and onto contract workers'. This means that companies are now able to 'profit off the substandard working conditions of their contractors, purely because they are not recognized as employees with applicable expenses'.[23] 'As sociologists,' the authors of the Canadian study conclude, 'we envision a decentralized workforce, bereft of regular human contact or continuous employment.'[24] What a desperately lonely space to inhabit.

VOCATION FRUSTRATION

What is happening to create all this workplace unease? We're currently seeing a 'disturbing lack of confidence' in leaders and managers, states British psychologist and business consultant, Sheila Keegan. Trust, she states, is at an 'all-time low'.[25] An Ernst & Young survey of upcoming professionals in eight countries bears this out, with less than half of respondents feeling they can trust their employer, due to poor pay, inadequate leadership and the lack of a team environment at work.[26]

Why this disconnect between employees and the organisations they work for? Fear, it seems, is a key factor, with the fallout from the global financial crisis still felt in organisations more than a decade after the event. Added to this are the challenges of sluggish economies, trade wars and escalating national debt; all the upsizing, downsizing and rightsizing at work; and the upskilling and multiskilling of staff. It's no surprise that many employees are feeling fearful and insecure, especially when we factor in our new post-pandemic 'normal'. And now we know that the anxiety people experience about the possibility of losing their job can actually equal the deep trauma felt by those who suddenly find themselves out of work,[27] we start to sense just how tenuous working life can be for those lucky enough to have a job.

'In a fear-based workplace the smartest and most capable employees don't get promoted. The people who get promoted are the ones who most wholeheartedly embrace the fear-based culture.'
Liz Ryan, Human Workplace movement[28]

Everyone's Scared

Fear is permeating our working lives, states Sheila Keegan, and it wears many faces. There's a fear of losing control of our working lives, fear of a loss of status and of being made redundant. There's also fear of the unknown, and doubly so since we're all still dealing with the fallout from COVID-19. And when we're fearful, Keegan notes, we tend to regress. We become reluctant to take responsibility. Basically, we 'close in and close down' and just want to 'blend in'.[29] Fear also promotes a controlling mentality in the workplace – leaders who are more interested in rules, protocols and red tape than in working relationships – creating managers with an over-reliance on numbers and targets, and bosses who can't see beyond head counts and organisational charts. In this roller-coaster climate, people are expendable, as they're seen as little more than numbers on a balance sheet. Yet one of the giants of corporate leadership, Max De Pree, the former CEO of Herman Miller (a world leader in high-end office furniture), warned against 'leaders who rely on structures instead of people', and what he saw as 'a loss of grace and style and civility' in work cultures.[30]

Alongside forging a stellar corporate career, De Pree, whose company was ranked fourth amongst the Fortune 500 companies for more than a decade, advocated for what he described as 'inclusive capitalism', where employees are part of decision-making and get a share of the profits. It's a concept some would call naive, others dangerous, fearing it strikes at the heart of capitalism. But in the mid-eighties, when Herman Miller's profits fell sharply due to a slump in the computer industry, De Pree put his inclusive principles to work. Employees were consulted on how best to move forward. They came up with a strategy to trim $12 million from annual costs. The sales team homed in on markets that hadn't been fully realised, expanding sales. And, remarkably, the Herman Miller team also found a way to slash delivery times for the company's new Ethospace office furniture from 22 weeks to just eight weeks. This company was soon back on track.[31] Could this same result be achieved in our fragmented workplaces, where so many feel bruised, near invisible and of little worth?

Belonging and inclusion are powerful drivers for success. They elevate the individual and help build a powerful work culture, giving people a sense of purpose.[33] Such qualities seem rare at work right now. Dignity is also 'in short supply', reflects Dr Tim Baker, a thought leader in organisational change: 'Morale levels are low.' Dignity isn't a word used much in relation to work at present. Instead we are obsessed with the bottom line and simply getting the job done. Is it possible that we've lost the skills to authentically connect in the workplace, to achieve shared goals, to find a way to genuinely support each other, and to take a truly collegiate approach to the challenges we face?

> **'Businesses and society still fundamentally depend on the resilience and creativity of human beings.'**
> *Paul Polman, former CEO of Unilever*[32]

Afraid to Speak Up

It's hard to feel confident in a workplace that feels hostile or shaky. One British survey revealed there is a startling lack of confidence in the nation's workforce, where over a third of people didn't have the courage to ask for a pay rise, and a quarter were too scared to ask for time off that they were owed. Just under a third of employees were worried about putting their ideas forward, while a quarter felt intimidated at the idea of working closely with someone more senior than them on a daily basis.[34]

Nigel Oseland, a UK environmental psychologist and workplace strategist and researcher, states there is hard evidence that insecurity affects performance. 'Studies have shown that lack of control has a negative effect on performance,' he says. 'And it persists 24 hours later. If we feel we have no control one day, it still affects our performance the next day.'[35]

With all this fear and what have become, for many, crushing workloads caused by a continual collapsing of jobs, we're seeing a new on-the-job phenomenon – presenteeism, where people drag themselves into work even though they're unfit to do any, or are so disengaged that they might as well not be at work. Presenteeism costs companies considerably more than absenteeism, and contributes to further workplace sickness, spreading germs as well as demotivating workmates. Productivity and customer satisfaction also take a hit. This trend of turning up for work either when sick or not in a frame of mind to be effective is higher in organisations that have suffered a shake-up, where there have been job losses or a reassignment of roles. Workers on low pay are also more likely to come in to work when unwell, for fear of losing their jobs. Again, what a lonely space to inhabit.

Too Many Bullies

Bullying is also alive and well in the workplace, and more prevalent in organisations as a whole than in individual instances, costing the workforce billions each year. People are more vulnerable to bullying where work descriptions are poorly defined, where people are under pressure and have little control, and where there are no clear policies on bullying behaviour. Bullying can be anything from ongoing teasing and being gossiped about, to unfair treatment, harassment and abuse. Organisations with a bullying culture can expect higher staff turnover, more absenteeism or people turning up for work unable to give their best. In one Australian study, a third of those bullied experienced some forms of bullying 'at least once a week',[36] while over a third of workers reported being verbally abused or shouted at. Alarmingly, just over one in four of these workers aged 20 to 27 had experienced some form of workplace violence.[37]

> '[My boss] simply told me to harden up and that I shouldn't take it to heart when people bully me! ... I have been becoming increasingly anxious and stressed and often cry as soon as I get home from work. I have to keep going back because I cannot afford rent and food otherwise.'
>
> *Adele*

The health impacts of bullying can't be underestimated. Victims, we now know, are at heightened risk of chronic diseases, headaches, dizziness, chest pains, heart issues and obesity, as well as a range of mental health issues, from depression to extreme stress. Those witnessing bullying at work are also impacted by this behaviour, and experience poorer physical and mental health.[38]

'The impact of workplace bullying on some people is extreme and incapacitating,' says psychologist Stephanie Thompson. 'Often people end up suffering from post-traumatic stress disorder. They're distressed and hyper-vigilant as they try to grapple with the "madness" of the person [bullying them].' Drawing on company research, Diane Utatao, head of Drake Personnel Australia, once stated that one serial bully at work could diminish the output of their victims by half, and surrounding employees by as much as a third.[39] These findings cannot be ignored.

'For decades the mantras of shareholder value and the view that the "business of business is business" has pervaded Western developed economies. Increasingly in a more global, technology-dominated world, with less certainty, especially for younger people, there is a consumer and employee-led desire for something more meaningful in their lives,' states John Scott, head of sustainability risk at Zurich Insurance Group, in the 2019 *Global Risks Report*.[40] While these insights are depressing, they also help point the way forward. One of the gifts of the pandemic is the chance to do things better and differently.

LOST IN SELF-ABSORPTION AND SPIN

It doesn't matter how experienced we are, we still thrive on having our efforts at work recognised. When this doesn't happen, we become disheartened and are likely to leave. The organisation loses yet another member of staff, and the company culture takes an additional hit. Pat, a content manager, tells of her experience:

> More than a year ago I got a job offer that made me very enthusiastic and gave me a feeling that I finally found the perfect workplace for myself. I was ready to spend days and nights at the office trying to make more than I was asked, reaching the goals I established for myself. But in quite a short period of time I burnt out completely … So I quit that job very soon after … The reason why I got burnt out is pretty simple. I've never felt appreciated for what I did.

Appreciation warms our space, drawing us out of any sense of isolation. The opposite is also true. At a time when employees are in need of reassurance and support, too many managers are failing to meaningfully connect with their teams. This is evident in a growing inability or unwillingness to 'tell it how it is', choosing instead to hide behind glib patter, to appear on top of things, or to whitewash situations that are less than comfortable. A lot more is demanded of managers as we struggle with the realities of our post-COVID-19 world. To be effective, it's essential to be able to see a situation from multiple perspectives, and respond accordingly.

Jargon Is Isolating

Sadly, too many hide behind 'management speak' in an attempt to bulldoze their way through tricky situations, leaving a shattered workforce in their wake. It's telling how much military jargon has crept into business language, most notably in the finance sector. While talk of staking out new prospects, rallying the troops and targeting new clients is relatively harmless, other phrases such as 'sweating [underperforming] assets' or taking a 'slash and burn' approach to problematic situations are less so. How can people give of their best in a 'take no prisoners' culture, in a workplace that sees people purely as 'winners or losers' or 'the quick or the dead'?

While jargon 'is tribal and reinforces belonging', notes Alan Stevens, who assists organisations in nurturing their culture, it is less than helpful in a work setting.[41] When faced with business babble, people are often left feeling confused, stupid or just plain resentful. 'Insecure managers create complexity [by using jargon] and that's too common in workplaces the world over,' states presentation coach and writer David Yewman. 'Jargon builds a wall between people at work. Often these people don't realize it; instead they think they sound smart. But what they're really doing is making the new team member or the boss feel dumb. The most poisonous part of jargon is that no-one in the audience is going to put up a hand and say, "What does that mean?" because we don't want to be perceived as stupid.'

Attempts to shape workplace values using jargon, often for the very best reasons, rarely hit the mark. 'It's [mention of core values] plastered all over my work,' Jamie tells. 'Nobody gives a f**k. We make a product that saves lives but we're so disconnected from the patients we really have no visual on our impact … We just want to go in, make sure it's safe and get the f**k out.' Vera agrees: 'I always hated that at IKEA I was a "co-worker" until I started working at Starbucks and became a "partner". I'm not a f**king partner in anything.'

Managers frequently use jargon to impress, but this can be risky.[42] In one US study led by psychology professor Daniel M. Oppenheimer, shorter words were replaced in a handful of essays by longer words. The result? The essays with longer words were judged as less capable and confident. The easier information is to understand, the more self-assured and intelligent it comes across.[43] There's another interesting detail here. The clearer a communication, the more likely it is to be believed. Basically, jargon makes people uneasy because they're unsure whether they're being lied to.[44]

Don't Sugar-coat Your Message!

All too often, jargon is used to gloss over unpleasant situations or decisions at work. Yet if someone is losing their job, no amount of fast-talking will lessen the inevitable hurt and confusion. 'Corporate performance – having to use fakery, having to perform in certain ways, pretend something doesn't matter when it does, is going on all the time,' explains psychologist Julia Noakes, noting how counterproductive this approach is.[45]

No-one wants an ITL (invitation to leave), but should it happen, co-workers aren't fooled by talk of rewiring for growth, rightsizing, decruiting, streamlining or rebalancing the company's human capital. 'Communicating is not about talking. Communicating is about connecting,'[46] insists communications expert Karen Friedman. 'How you share ideas on a daily basis determines how you make others feel.'[47] Julia Noakes agrees: 'The best leaders I've worked with have a confidence that narcissists don't have to listen to another person's point-of-view, to hear that point-of-view.'[48]

Language that shuts people out or skims over key facts distances those it seeks to win over. So why use jargon at work? This brings us back to the question of dignity. It's essential to 'speak the truth out of respect', states employee advocate and human resources innovator Michael Schneider.[49] Respect means having a *genuine* awareness of others – a willingness to communicate in a way that's accessible, that acknowledges the hurt and confusion felt in the stretching moments at work. It's about having the courage to tell things how they are, even when it's not what someone wants to hear. But that takes assured leadership and emotional intelligence – two qualities that are currently in short supply in many workplaces.

Finding Ways to Collide

Working in a 'time is money' culture has left many people afraid of interacting unless they're discussing work, as no-one wants to be branded a time-waster. However, research shows that chitchat helps employees connect and be more engaged at work. It's an excellent way to let off steam and keep stress levels at a reasonable level. Whether you're an introvert or an extrovert, studies show that connection boosts happiness.[50] We're not talking here about someone who collars you, launching into a half-hour conversation, but bursts of chatter, which help lift the day. In talking about one of Samsung's new buildings, Scott Birnbaum, a vice president at Samsung, states that if you want a creative company, you don't want people glued to their screens. Collaboration and innovation are sparked, he suggests, 'when people collide', when they meet unexpectedly.[51]

The co-founders of the people analytics company, Humanyze, are all for workplace collisions. 'Our data suggest that creating collisions – chance encounters and unplanned interactions between knowledge workers, both inside and outside the organization – improves performance,' they say. The quality of the interactions doesn't seem to matter. 'When collisions occur, regardless of their content,' they reflect, 'improvement typically follows.'[52]

One call centre gave its telephone reps a bigger break room and more time to spend there. Productivity shot up, as people were able to share their work knowhow during breaks. Data showed that when a salesperson increased their communication with co-workers from different departments by ten per cent, their sales grew by this same amount.[53] This need for interaction from a wide variety of sources has encouraged a growing number of companies to open cafes in their buildings, which are also available to passersby, while Airbnb allows outsiders in its San Francisco headquarters to book one of its conference rooms for free. Who would have imagined the add-on benefits from simply allowing people to connect?

The simple fact that it takes time to build a company's culture, and far less time to trash it, is evidenced in this anecdote that Susan shared:

> Our company went through a series of messy takeovers, and a couple of different managing directors. Then a new CEO was appointed with shiny business qualifications. Overnight our workloads trebled. We spent hours in meetings and writing countless briefs. It took all the joy out of work, and my team were cranky as I was rarely at my desk. I resigned within months. The CEO's final words to me were 'I hope I've learned

all I need to know from you.' What a joke! I'd just spent several months writing crib sheets for someone on a ridiculous salary, who still had a frightening amount to learn about the business.

A Better Way Forward

Although corporations often get a bad rap, it's important not to forget their capacity to generate immense good, while taking care of their core business. One towering figure in the corporate world is the Dutch high-flyer Paul Polman. In a 2014 interview with *Het Financieele Dagblad*, Polman told of ending up in business, as 'I can help more people here to improve their lives.' While CEO of Unilever, Polman directed the company to install toilets in Africa through its Domestos brand and encouraged Asian schoolchildren to wash their hands, using the company's Lifebuoy soap, to reduce disease spread.[54] Then in 2019, Polman moved on to create a sustainability consulting firm, Imagine, with co-founders Valerie Keller and Jeff Seabright, to help businesses 'eradicate poverty and inequality and stem runaway climate change'.[55]

Work has been a torrid, intensely lonely experience for many in recent years. Hopefully the balancing out of past practices focused purely on the bottom line, with more personal investment in staff and the opportunity for more innovation, will create calmer, more effective and sustainable workplaces. It's time, suggests Dr Tim Baker, a thought leader in organisational change, to 'invite [the] human spirit into the workplace'.[56] After everything that we've been through in the pandemic, taking greater care of the human dimension of our work is most likely something we all ache for.

Workplace Solutions

TRANSFORMING WORK CULTURE

A healthy work culture is one that acknowledges that communication and connection matter. There are many steps you can take to demonstrate that you value your team.

- Relate authentically. Be honest when difficult decisions have to be made. Underscore that with your actions by being a strong, supportive co-worker or leader.

- Value dignity, as dignity touches the heart of what makes us human and able to give of our best.

- Treat everyone with respect. Hierarchy is an antiquated approach to team-building. Acknowledge everyone's contribution, building trust.

- Challenge all forms of bullying, as it's destructive and a sign of a culture that's struggling.

- Minimise out-of-hours work. Everyone needs rest and relaxation. We're all more creative and productive when we've had time out. Does your workplace need a 'right to disconnect' policy, so everyone is clear about boundaries?

- Create an environment where people can speak out and engage in occasional banter, feeding your organisation's individual and collective joy, creativity, problem-solving and 'buy-in'.

- Shared food has a way of breaking down boundaries, and of creating a sense of informal celebration. Trial opportunities to eat together, and note the results.

- Provide good-quality tea, coffee and snacks. When companies skimp on these details, while senior staff enjoy overly generous perks and expense accounts, what message does this send?

- Include families in occasional gatherings, such as Christmas parties, as a way of acknowledging that people's lives are bigger and more complex than their work lives.

- Provide wider pastoral care, with such gestures as yoga classes and lunchtime talks, so people feel 'invested in' their workplace.

- Encourage out-of-hours sports and hobby groups, to help build bridges between different parts of the organisation and lighten the mood.

- Develop office rituals, such as casual dress Fridays and 'bring your pet to work' days, to enliven the company culture. Capture photos of these and other events on a company mood board.

LEADERSHIP ESSENTIALS

Good leaders champion best practice, leading by example to help create a new generation of future leaders. To achieve this we need to understand that:

- Change is a constant at present, so you need to learn to be comfortable with change, by being consistent and reliable.

- When you create a tangible sense of security around you amid all the change, you calm others, helping everyone to navigate unsettling times.

- Tomorrow belongs to the relationship-builders, as relationships are about building bridges, and making the effort to understand those you're working with.

- Leadership is changing from being a person issuing orders to a passionate coach for those you work with, helping bring out the very best in every person in your organisation.

- You must be accountable for your decisions, and be generous enough when you have a collective win, to step back and allow those working with you to shine.

- The workplace is often a highly charged emotional landscape, which you need to move through wisely and calmly, avoiding the temptation to blame, or to sidestep crucial issues.

- You don't help yourself or others when you get sidetracked by needy co-workers. These individuals are massively draining, and rarely interested in personal change.

- Committing regular time to personal development is important, as everyone is at their best when they're growing as an individual.

- When someone acts out, essentially they're feeling out of control. First create a space of calm to help take the charge out of any emotional responses. Then you can settle down to a more rational exchange.

13

Understanding Our Current Work Ethos

The MBA Workplace

When Greed Became Good

Generosity Mindset

Humanising the Workplace

THE MBA WORKPLACE

'Boss-induced' stress, it seems, is alive and well, and linked by some to the prevalence of business graduates, especially master of business administration graduates (MBAs) now in the workforce – from traditional corporate settings, to the arts and not-for-profit sectors. It's a trend that British psychologist Julia Noakes calls 'the tragedy of the MBA', which she believes has changed the whole climate of London banking. 'The MBA yoke,' she observes, 'kills people's spirit with procedures, rules and governance.'[1] Henry Mintzberg, professor of management studies at McGill University in Montreal, agrees about the negative impacts business graduates have had on the workforce. Managers, he insists, aren't created in the classroom, and nor are leaders.[2] Yet until recently, MBA graduates were regarded as the brightest of the bright and, in some cases, could expect a 75 per cent increase in their salary, if not more, on graduation.[3]

What does an MBA bring to the workforce? 'Risk averse individuals looking for a fast track to a certain lifestyle', claims journalist Phillip Delves Broughton, who captured his two years studying for a Harvard MBA in engaging detail in his bestselling book *Ahead of the Curve*.[4] At Harvard Business School, Broughton found himself part of 'an elite brand', amid a bright, highly ambitious group of people with 'a huge sense of entitlement'.

Where's the Spreadsheet?

When MBA graduates began entering businesses in the eighties and nineties, this new uber class brought with them an obsession with numbers and measurement, time and motion, creating what Mintzberg calls businesses 'contaminated' by analysis. An uneasy two-tier situation soon developed, where newly minted

MBAs who joined companies were preoccupied with their remuneration and enjoying life in the fast lane, while established staff, who were also capable and knowledgeable, and genuinely invested in their organisation, found their careers stalling.[5] This is not to suggest that MBA graduates have nothing to offer a workplace, but simply to underline the fact that no one person has all the answers and capabilities.

The Birth of the Corporation

To fully understand how radically the workplace has changed in recent years, it's helpful to backtrack a little to the beginnings of what we now know as the corporation. Former investment banker Will Hopper suggests the corporation grew out of a Puritan worldview, with its strong sense of moral purpose, innovation and cooperation, and exceptional organisational skills. In his book, *The Puritan Gift*, Hopper notes how these values were still strong in many of the top American companies for a large part of last century, including such organisations as AT&T, Johnson & Johnson and General Electric – all companies that operated with a strong social conscience, and a firm belief in quality over profit.[6]

This ethos was seen in other burgeoning corporations around the world, including Cadbury in Britain, where, on taking over the business from their father, Quaker brothers Richard and George Cadbury founded the Bourneville estate for their workers on more than 300 acres of land, building 313 roomy cottages, each with their own garden. Later the Cadburys went on to set up sporting fields, bowling greens and a large swimming pool free of charge for employees and their families.

During this time, companies also took a much greater interest in people's families. Company Christmas parties centred around employee's children, and work hampers were designed for the whole family to share. At this time career progression was based on merit. A person worked their way up through the business, learning the 'craft' of management under someone who had mastered these skills. This was also the era where companies aimed for what they felt was a 'decent profit'.

The Entrepreneur Rules

When economic growth slowed in the seventies, companies were encouraged to be more entrepreneurial, to take on debt to help them grow, to invite people from outside the company to join their boards and to focus on shareholder value. Corporate cultures shifted rapidly. As the concept of shareholder value took hold, few investors had any connection with the businesses they were investing in, or any interest in these companies beyond the profit they generated. Investors had no idea of the company's values or culture, or what these organisations were hoping to achieve beyond the balance sheet. This critical change in direction placed companies under huge pressure to meet the expectations of market analysts.

Then, in the eighties and nineties, a flock of MBA graduates arrived in the workforce, as glittering examples of a new concept – the 'professional manager', someone who was able to 'manage anything'. These were individuals with a strong grasp of the balance sheet, and thus well placed to deliver strong profits for shareholders. It's the period Will Hopper labels 'the years the locusts ate'.[7]

The presence of MBA graduates brought about additional changes to corporate life, and also to government organisations. Many public servants are grateful to MBAs for helping nudge government departments beyond the paralysis of lifelong tenure – an archaic system where managers, including those who were inept or out of date, enjoyed a job for life simply because they had 'done their time'. Few would question that organisations run better when efficient, and MBAs excel at efficiency. However, the 'slash and burn' tactics often employed to achieve these organisational changes were, and remain, often blunt at best. It's an approach, states UK psychologist Sheila Keegan, that assumes people need to be constantly controlled or chaos will ensue – a way of managing that tends to come with an 'us and them' mentality.[8]

> 'I have lost count of [the MBA] managers unskilled in the technical demands of their departments, who fell for the canard that management of a department was one thing (ie their job) and that technical realities were another thing (not their job) and that all they needed was to … manage.'
> Jeff[9]

I'll Fix the Problem for You

With the MBA focus on the balance sheet, and a determination to make organisations lean and mean, came a slew of hatchet men, corporate warriors prepared to do 'whatever it took' to fulfil the company's financial goals. Most notable amongst these ranks was Al Dunlap, also known as Chainsaw Dunlap, who was voted by *Time Magazine* as one of the top ten worst bosses.[10] During Dunlap's time as CEO of US company Scott Paper in the nineties, 11,200 employees lost their jobs, while he earned around $100 million in a mix of salary, stocks and additional compensation. When asked about his large remuneration, Dunlap likened himself to superstars Michael Jordan and Bruce Springsteen, stating that as a superstar in his field, he deserved serious compensation.[11]

In this new climate of hiring and firing, no-one felt safe. The loyalty and trust shared between employers and their staff was shattered. Employees watched on as workmates were escorted from the building without notice under the watchful eye of a security guard. When reflecting on the corporate men and women who emerged from the MBA culture, Julia Noakes noted what she calls a type of psychological 'splitting' in these individuals, which she describes as 'I'm going to be this person now, and then I'm going to be this other person later.' It is, she observes, 'one of the biggest and saddest illusions ... That somehow this pure amazing man [or woman] is going to emerge when he [or she] retires. He [she] doesn't. It's an illusion.'[12]

Concentrate on the Figures

With the arrival of the MBAs in the workforce, bean counters now reigned and, with the new focus on shareholder value, these managers were more interested in short-term fiscal fixes than more sustainable long-term solutions. These new corporate leaders saw themselves as 'bulletproof'. Standing outside the work culture, these elites 'didn't need anyone', and were determined to best everyone else, observes Noakes.[13] Always with an eye on their next career move, these individuals were, and remain, a highly mobile group of professionals who did what they had to do and then moved on, leaving others to deal with what was often a decimated work culture. How different this is from Max De Pree's ideals of leadership, of 'liberating people to do what is required of them in the most effective and humane way possible'.[14]

Keeping an eye on the figures and the organisational chart is one thing, but what kind of management culture did the MBAs issue in? In one Ohio State University study, MBA students were placed in small groups and asked to put together a pitch for a significant financial deal from a made-up company to a school board. What emerged from this study was how the more narcissistic group members tended to become group leaders. This is a cause for concern, reflects psychologist Amy Brunell, the lead author of the study. While narcissists tend to be charming and confident, they often have an inflated view of their abilities and, as leaders, are prone to 'volatile and risky decision-making', often proving ineffective and 'potentially destructive' to organisations in the long run.[15]

One issue that comes through when talking to people about working with MBAs is the self-righteousness of this new breed – their near-messianic zeal as they set about demolishing current work practices and structures in companies and government organisations. Impatient for results, these individuals focus purely on the balance sheets. This approach soon filters through organisations, creating very different workplaces. With stability a thing of the past, these newly volatile organisations become hostile and aggressive, as successive waves of staff are hired and fired.

Where Are We Heading?

Our narrow focus on profit and the mechanics of business to the exclusion of all else means our workplaces are seen more like an engine in need of repair than a culture made up of individuals. Happily taking apart pieces of a business, we replace a few nuts and bolts, then put everything back together again and wait for the engine to purr back to life. We forget that workplaces are made up of people with feelings and differing capabilities, and lives beyond work – people who need motivation and appreciation to help them reach their full potential.

> 'Sometimes we think we're a little too gifted to show up,
> you know. But none of us truly is.'
> *Max De Pree,* Leading Without Power[16]

We've dehumanised the workplace, notes international organisational change expert Tim Baker, turning people into 'an abstract piece of the machinery of production'.[17] This dehumanisation has consequences. The ideal worker is now seen as someone who is unendingly efficient and obedient and never late, and willing to work extra hours without extra pay. They're individuals who don't trouble others with their feelings, or have the 'inconvenience' of a life outside work.[18] When we fail to take into account the humanity of those around us at work, people feel ignored and isolated, and lacking in positive motivation.

The Numbers Game

'Managers,' reflects Baker, have 'become obsessed with processes, procedures, methods, and systems', systematising, homogenising, processing and mechanising human work.[19] What, then, asks New York-based business journalist Duff McDonald, is the true value of MBAs, who are only able to 'manage what they can measure', given that not all the answers can be found on a spreadsheet?

Surely a focus on numbers needs to be balanced with wider considerations and resources that also help make a business work – by recognising, for example, the importance of research and innovation, and of taking care of staff. Carla, a human resources manager for a large government organisation, agrees. 'We still put the process before the person,' she admits. 'Yet true human resource professionals shouldn't be doing that, we should be people-centred.'

One of the difficulties for MBA managers is that when they began entering the workforce, they knew little about the companies they joined, beyond their financials. This was a tricky moment, given that they were supposed to be able to manage anything. Not knowing the intricacies of a particular business did have its drawbacks. Outside help arrived in the form of the consultant – people who were able to fill in the gaps in an MBA graduate's 'domain intelligence' or company knowledge. With consultants came executive summaries, which, Henry Mintzberg suggests, can have far-reaching consequences. 'Give me a 20-page case study on Iraq,' he reflects, 'and I'll give you a war.'[20]

All the while MBAs flourished, seemingly unaware of what Sydney Finkelstein, a professor at Tuck School of Business in New Hampshire, calls the 'expertise trap'. When you're seen as the expert, Finkelstein suggests, it's easy to be overconfident, to let go of the need to consult others, or to take on other approaches. Yet just because you've had past success in one area doesn't mean future success is a given in another. Or, as Finkelstein puts it, 'there's no replacement for self-awareness', a quality that often seems lacking amongst MBAs. It is, Finkelstein states, like assuming that you know the answer to a question before you've even set out on the journey.[21]

The human cost of this hubris, I suspect, has been immense. This is a management style far too many have endured – being forced to look on as all the nuances of their carefully honed work practices, all the knowledge and expertise that's been garnered over years, is replaced in a handful of weeks by a flurry of charts and edicts about how things will be done 'from now on'. While betraying a stark lack of understanding of this particular workplace – be it a corporation, museum, or a not-for-profit organisation – too often these managers have ploughed on regardless, collecting hefty bonuses along the way, and then, with an eye on their career prospects, moved on.

MBA Rethink

Some of the fiercest criticism of business schools and its graduates has come from within the very same hallowed halls (now often the most lucrative faculty on campus, and thus extremely powerful). Harvard Business School's Professor Rakesh Khurana points out that while university-based business schools were founded out of a genuine desire to create professional, highly capable managers, along the lines of doctors and lawyers – people who understood their broader social responsibilities – the MBA culture has ended up creating 'self interest in the extreme', where managers demand huge stock options in exchange for their services. This trend, he believes, has left a 'gaping moral hole' in business education. He likens the new normal to the difference between 'a marine or mercenary'. Both are technically capable. The mercenary's focus, however, is on selling their skills to the highest bidder.[22]

> **'Corporate man is dangerous from a moral sense because he really does believe he can be a good man in the evening.'**
> *Psychologist Julia Noakes*[23]

There's also an ethical dimension absent in MBA decision-making, reflects Duff McDonald. With such a fixation on figures, how do you determine what's right and wrong, when MBA students are told repeatedly that there's no single right answer to a scenario, simply solutions that are more or less articulated? This surely is a concerning message, suggesting an action or decision is acceptable, given you've developed a compelling and coherent explanation for it[24] – an approach now witnessed in a number of arenas, including that of politics.

When Harvard professor Scott Snook conducted a recent survey of MBA students, he discovered that a third of them judged right and wrong in terms of whatever was considered the norm at the time. This helps explain, in part, the ethical shortcomings seen in investment banking, and private equity and hedge funds, all of which are favoured destinations for MBA graduates.[25] Nobel prize-winner Robert Shiller, founder of the field of behavioural finance, is another to voice his concerns about business schools producing students with 'an ethic of selfishness and limited accountability'.[26]

Where's the Line Between Right and Wrong?

The MBA has changed the face of senior management, admits sociologist Joel Podolny, currently dean of Apple University, the tech giant's corporate training centre. He views these individuals as being focused on the big picture – on strategy, vision and agendas – leaving their underlings to 'sweat the details'.[27] That's not to say that MBAs aren't smart and don't have a contribution to make, just that their thinking is often narrow, at best. Focusing almost exclusively on the short term for immediate shareholder gain, they do so at the expense of the 'long-term health' of countless organisations. The negative impacts, Duff McDonald argues, are soon felt further afield – from employees and the wider community, to a nation's best interests.[28] It's this same bias that encourages industry giants to minimise, if not avoid, their tax obligations by moving their profits offshore; to degrade the environment; and to employ third-world workers on low wages in substandard working conditions.

'One of the critical shortcomings of these [MBA] courses is that few graduates appear to have any real understanding of earth's biophysical systems ... Ecological literacy and what a sustainable future means for the economy and jobs should be an integral part of all business training.'
Erika[29]

Since the 2008 global financial crisis, business schools have had a major rethink, claims Walter Baets, director of the University of Cape Town's Graduate School of Business. Yet, he admits, more is still needed on the 'management and leadership' fronts. Today's workplace, Baets believes, needs 'more than just the skills to administer', it needs the 'knowledge and wisdom to administer with a purpose'.[30] In *Rethinking the MBA*, the authors touch on further weaknesses in current business courses, including a lack of 'heightened cultural awareness' and personal introspection, along with the ever-present 'emphasis on greed'.[31]

A Better Way Forward

So where does this leave MBA managers, and our MBA-led workplace? It appears there'll be fewer MBAs in the future. Given the fast pace and complexities of our globalised world, organisations need more than a 'one size fits all' approach. Companies need a diversity of backgrounds, individuals not limited by MBA groupthink.[32] In 2015, Ernst & Young (EY) abandoned its academic qualification threshold for employees, stating that such qualifications didn't guarantee 'business success'. A great deal, EY believes, can also be learned on the job, rather than in a classroom.[33] Stanford psychology professor Carol Dweck suggests that alongside intelligence and emotional intelligence, the workplace needs people with 'growth mindsets', who have the potential to adapt.[34]

Los Angeles-based entrepreneur, podcaster and career coach Ashley Stahl suggests the future workplace will focus on 'soft skills more than technical ones: communication, emotional intelligence and resilience to name a few'. Such skills, she believes, 'are better honed in the actual workforce than in an MBA program'. So while some 'corporate tracks' such as management consulting require an MBA, 'true entrepreneurs will go out and start a business regardless'.

Sydney Finkelstein goes further, stressing the importance of creativity, curiosity and critical thinking – a willingness to have your ideas and approaches taken apart – to ensure your organisation finds the best way forward.[35] This more inclusive and emotionally intelligent approach is a much better fit for these fluid times.

The 2016 World Economic Forum report on the Fourth Industrial Revolution talks of incentivising lifelong learning, as well as cross-industry and public–private collaboration. And with the likelihood of increasing disruptions and resource constraints, social skills such as persuasion, emotional intelligence and teaching others will be in higher demand than narrow technical skills.[36]

When work isn't working, when we feel undervalued, ignored or oppressed, it can be a desperately lonely space. And, for many, it's been this way for too long, adding to a whole range of issues as people struggle to cope. As we've noted, emerging from the pandemic we have the chance to do things differently and better. These wider winds of change offer us a once-in-a-lifetime opportunity to recalibrate in ways that, up until recently, we'd never thought possible, inspiring us towards more holistic, sustainable workplaces.

WHEN GREED BECAME GOOD

No discussion around loneliness and isolation is complete without examining the burgeoning cracks in our economic system. There has been a lot of talk about greed lately, sparked by concern about the growing gap between those on massive salaries with plenty of means, and a rise in poverty and homelessness. What happens to our social fabric when so many are left out in the cold?

At the same time, we've become more than a little entranced by celebrities and their over-the-top lifestyles. Constantly tuning in to catch up on the latest instalment of the Kardashians, the Real Housewives series and others, some now see wealth as the most significant of life achievements. Not everyone who is wealthy, or aspires to be wealthy, is greedy. Bill and Melinda Gates are testament to that. Yet too many have become so focused on 'getting', on out-of-control shopping and brand slavery, that all other considerations, including generosity, kindness and fair play, disappear from view. Try to have a debate about creating more equality in these quarters, and you'll be met with plenty of lip service, but very little action.

Greed Rules

How is greed playing out in our relationships, and how is it making us feel increasingly out on a limb? 'In a world in which economic factors are given priority over ethical considerations in decision-making,' suggests professor of philosophy Laura Rediehs, in a Carnegie Council for Ethics paper, 'humans lose their dignity.'[37] How is this loss of dignity and the resulting isolation playing out? A good place to start is to examine the remuneration people are getting at work. Here we see that, in 1980, CEOs were paid around 50 times more than the average worker. By 2017, this had risen to 361 times what average employees earn in the United States.[38] While the figures differ from country to country, the overall trend is the same. Running a company is demanding, no-one doubts that, but it's hard to see how such payouts can be justified. John Paul Rollert of the Booth School of Business in Chicago describes greed as the 'hobgoblin of capitalism', and this particular hobgoblin, it seems, is currently alive and well in the workplace.[39]

As we've seen, there was a time when organisations operated in a more benign fashion – when profit was leavened with a strong desire for integrity, too. Then, in the seventies, new challenges arose. After generating incredible prosperity after the Second World War, the American economy began to flag – drained, in part, by overseas conflicts and threats of conflict, with the ongoing war in Vietnam and the roller-coaster Cold War with Russia. The question the country faced was how to stimulate the economy. How do you keep people spending, when they are facing a squeeze? Credit cards were made readily available for mums and dads. After having always saved money for items before purchasing them, suddenly everyday consumers were given the opportunity to buy now and pay later. For the millions of households offered credit, a whole new world opened up. Suddenly their dream holiday, new wardrobe or car were immediately within reach. Saving up before purchasing became a thing of the past.

Shareholder Value Is King

At this time international markets were also opening up and new technologies were emerging. Successful American companies were now feeling the pressure of more competition. The question was, then, how to stimulate more growth. Nobel laureate Eugene Fama suggested that a company's stock price was the best indication of how a company was travelling. As this idea gained traction, it was thought that too much of management's time and energy, not to mention shareholder income, was wasted on customers, employees and the wider community. Organisations, it was felt, needed to be more focused. It made sense to tie the interests of managers to that of shareholders, to measure management performance by the share price, and so the concept of shareholder value was born.

There was plenty of excitement at this new approach. Chicago economist Milton Friedman and others of his ilk insisted that the single 'social responsibility of business' was to 'increase profits', and so that's where companies headed.[40] With the rise of shareholder value as a company's single goal, the previous goal that companies held of making a 'decent profit' evaporated. Short-term gain was now the aim. To maximimise company profits, thus keeping shareholders happy, resources were diverted away from investment and innovation – in building for a sustainable business future. Slowly but surely this weakened the capacity of organisations, and by extension the economy, to be revitalised. To make up the shortfall, companies were bought and sold, their assets stripped. Suddenly staff members were being referred to as human capital, as a way of reflecting their value and/or cost to an organisation. Now employees were simply another resource, along with financial and other resources, available to an organisation.

With people viewed simply as assets, it's no surprise that unconscionable work practices followed where, for example, companies became unwilling to let go of workers, aka *their* human resources. Some of the worst employment practices in the developed world are in America, where it's estimated that over 30 million workers have been subjected to 'non-compete agreements', which means they can't work for a competitor, or start their own small business in the same field. Initially such agreements were for highly technical and senior management professionals on serious salaries. Now, though, they also impact countless low-income employees, from hairdressers and housecleaners, to people working in warehouses and fast food outlets, who find themselves with few choices, other than to remain where they are.[41]

> 'The most disturbing change that I have seen [in recent years] is first the social acceptance of greed, and then its transformation into a virtue by the shadow play of economic theory … We need moral imperatives in our society for it to function properly, and we have discarded a key component … compassion.'
> *Alex*

Feeding Frenzy

The focus on shareholder value was hailed as brilliant, but not everyone sees it that way. Harvard professors Lynn S. Paine and Joseph L. Bower regard the single-minded pursuit of profit (i.e. shareholder value) in recent decades as 'the error at the heart of corporate leadership'. This approach, they state, has encouraged poor conduct, from questionable accounting practices and high debt, to poorly thought-out takeovers and a frenzy of share buybacks.[42]

Needing to squeeze every last cent out of the company on behalf of the shareholder, organisations have become leaner and meaner, with an emphasis, Professor Henry Mintzberg notes, on mean, creating what he calls a 'syndrome of selfishness'.[43] This drive to cut costs led to millions of clerical, customer service and manufacturing jobs being lost, as companies moved these positions offshore to low-paid workers in third-world countries with few benefits or rights.

It's this same drive for profits that encouraged the explosion of subprime loans, the granting of mortgages to those who were financially vulnerable. As more and more subprime loans were issued, investment banks took to packaging up solid investments with these questionable assets, then selling them to unsuspecting investors, until the real estate bubble burst, sparking the global financial crisis. The result for most was catastrophic. What followed was the decimation of millions of people's lives – people who had trusted men and women in suits, only to lose their homes and life savings. Amongst others, Lehman Brothers, one of the world's biggest investment banks, filed for bankruptcy, the largest bankruptcy in American history. For the privileged few, including the bank's CEO Richard Fuld, the fallout was far less painful. According to a *New York Times* piece, Fuld had earned around US$45 million in the year before the Lehman Brothers' collapse.[44]

'We have learned from decades of corruption and cheating in the financial sector that the rewards far outweigh the fears of being caught and punished.'
Les[45]

MBA Fingers in the Pie

During this crisis, notes journalist Phillip Delves Broughton, Harvard Business School (HBS) graduates were in key positions across America as CEOs of banks and senior partners in investment companies. HBS graduate George W. Bush was President of the United States, with HBS graduate Henry Paulson as Treasury secretary, and HBS graduate Charles Christopher Cox heading up the Securities and Exchange Commission.[46]

Looking back at this dark moment in time, Mark Carney, former Governor of the Bank of England, refers to the ten years after the global financial crisis as the 'lost decade'.[47] It was a time, reflects Ian Harper, director of Access Economics, of greed, of 'seeking individual financial gain in ways that did not respect the common good'.[48] Kevin Hassett, formerly of the American Enterprise Institute, also slammed this event as narcissistic, as one of 'reckless brilliance' that very nearly destroyed Wall Street.[49]

Greed, notes Oxford philosopher Neel Burton, is 'an imperfect force', because it keeps us in a place of lack, a feeling of never having enough, which, he believes, aligns perfectly with 'our dumbed down consumer culture'.[50] 'Enough' is the key word here, and something we need to think carefully about as we face the financial realities of a post-pandemic world. What does enough look like for you and for me? What is this 'enough-ness' likely to deliver? Is there room in this pursuit for others, or have we fallen victim to rampant consumerism, or worse?

Clawing Our Way Back

The global financial crisis took a massive injection of public funds to save the world's financial system from complete disaster, and yet a handful of years later it's hard to see that much has changed. One of the arguments in support of our current market economy is the trickle-down or 'all boats rise' theory, where, as wealth increases, the benefits flow through to society as a whole. However, this has proved not to be the case. Too many, including those who are working in essential services, are feeling increasingly isolated, struggling to find affordable accommodation and to make ends meet.

These are the people who faithfully saw us through the worst of the pandemic. They deserve better.

During the 2008 global financial crisis, 42.5 per cent of the planet's wealth was held by one per cent of the population. According to Credit Suisse's 2017 report into global wealth, this one per cent now owns half the world's wealth.[51] This increase in wealth has occurred over just a handful of years, during a period when an everyday person's wages remained at an all-time low and when an increasing number of households are spending everything they earn just to get by. As the COVID-19 virus began to bite, it exposed many ugly realities about 'the haves and have-nots' in society, and about the bleeding of funds away from essential services, especially in America – a move that left too many dangerously vulnerable.

What's Wrong with a Little Self-Interest?

We need to move forward with our eyes open. Psychotherapist Jon Shore reminds us that 'the greedy have no boundaries they are not willing to cross. They function in our world with no moral compass. Their sole purpose is to amass the largest pile of assets no matter what the cost.' Knowing this, we cannot afford those who chase profit above all else to continue to dominate the agenda, regardless of the social and environmental effects. Wealth, we're told, benefits everyone in the end. But, as we've seen, this is patently untrue.

In seeking to move beyond this isolated and isolating way of living, we need to be aware of how we, too, may be contributing to this unhelpful trend. The language of rampant selfishness, of never having enough, can so easily skew how we regard our assets. Until recently, people saved for retirement, putting aside money to take care of their financial and medical needs as they aged, so as not to be a burden on society. Now people are told they're in the business of 'wealth creation'. The focus has shifted from being a responsible family and community member, by saving over your working life, to wanting to maximise every single thing you own, without taking too close a look at how you earn your money, or where it is invested. This also means our homes are no longer simply a place to retreat to with loved ones, so much as assets to be traded.

To be clear, saving for retirement is a good thing, and investing wisely makes good sense. But when we become so focused on profit to the exclusion of all else, we fall into the trap of knowing the price of everything, yet never truly valuing anything beyond its monetary worth or returns. In seeking a better way forward, we need to be clear about where we stand, and what impacts our stance has on us and others. Does our approach to our assets enhance our lives, along with our communities and nation or, in chasing profit, have we come adrift from the social fabric?

Criticise greed in certain quarters and you're likely to be labelled anti-progressive or even a socialist, responses that are simplistic, if not deliberately misleading. Capitalism has served most of us well. We have benefited from the entrepreneurs in our midst, and hope to continue to do so. But the ability to make large or small amounts of money must never be above scrutiny. When we chase profit to the exclusion of all else, we let go of our wider responsibility to each other, and to helping create a better world.

American author and philosopher Ayn Rand has had a huge influence on many attitudes to greed. She famously said that capitalism is the only financial approach in which 'exceptional men' are not 'held down by the majority'.[52] Emerging from the turmoil of the Russian Revolution and the lead-up to Stalin's

Russia, Rand arrived in America aged 20, later stating that 'man exists for his own sake, that the pursuit of his own happiness is his highest moral purpose'.[53] One of the problems with this argument is that, yet again, we see a muddying of the waters, where questionable forms of self-interest are excused as simply a desire for self-improvement.

What Does Enterprising Mean?

Nobel prize-winning economist Milton Friedman, one of many to state that greed is a natural part of life, insisted that the goal is not to stamp out greed, but to put mechanisms in place to ensure it does the least harm. The problem with this argument is that these mechanisms continue to fail us. We mustn't forget that the drive for profit has dealt the world some serious blows – economically, socially and environmentally. We saw this during the global financial crisis, and before this with the collapse of Enron and other companies in the early 2000s, as well as in the real estate bubble that devastated Japan's economy in the late nineties.

> 'A syndrome of selfishness has taken hold of our corporations and our societies, as well as our minds.'
> *Henry Mintzberg, Professor of Management Studies, McGill University*[54]

More recently, we've witnessed astonishing levels of greed in the findings of Australia's Banking Royal Commission, where banks were taking money from deceased estates, charging people for financial advice they never received, and involved in bribes to pass questionable loans based on misleading documents. In addition, some bank employees forged customer signatures and sold 'worthless' insurance products.

'In almost every case,' noted commissioner Kenneth Hayne, 'the conduct in issue was driven not only by the relevant entity's pursuit of profit but also by individuals' pursuit of gain.' These were cultures that actively rewarded misconduct. A lot of time and effort was put into incentive, bonus and commission schemes throughout the financial services industry. Sales and profits were meticulously measured. Yet, noted Hayne, these companies failed to comply 'with the law and proper standards'.[55]

Every decade has its dark moments. This, it seems, was one of ours. Then we had COVID-19, and groundbreaking decisions were made. People began purchasing what they could from businesses they *valued* – not to chase bargains or prestige, but to help these beloved, often local, businesses through. On a wider scale, as whole economies were placed in hibernation, banks across the globe worked with governments to give borrowers who had lost their jobs a break from their mortgages and credit card repayments. This was an unprecedented move, and in seeking a better way forward we encourage them to continue to do the right thing.

Stuck in a Less Than Ideal Space

There was a time when greed was seen as distasteful, morally suspect. Perhaps it will be so again. Richard Eskow, senior fellow for the Campaign for America's Future, could well be onto something when he talks of greed as 'an expression of pain and fear'.[56] In seeking to move beyond this mindset, we need to better understand it. In a fascinating article in *Psychology Today*, philosopher Neel Burton examines greed in terms of Maslow's pyramid of human needs. On the lower levels of Maslow's pyramid are a person's basic physical and psychological needs – for safety, love and a sense of belonging, and of self-esteem. Once these needs are met, people can move beyond neediness to a place of genuine self-fulfilment.

When we progress past the lower levels of need, we have the chance to realise our potential. We're now motivated by values *beyond* our personal needs. 'The problem with greed,' Burton reminds us, 'is that it grounds us on one of the lower levels of the pyramid.' Put simply, individuals and organisations become stuck in a place of neediness.[57] Personal neediness is a lonely place to be, especially when we already have plenty. During the pandemic, suddenly our focus widened. We needed to work together, to cooperate, to come through. Now as we emerge from this 'moment', it's important that we're clear about what needs fixing, not just for our own individual sake, but for everyone's sake.

In a 2002 paper written shortly after a series of corporate scandals including Enron, Henry Mintzberg, professor of management studies at McGill University, questioned the assumption that the sole purpose of business is economic activity, thus leaving governments to take care of the social interests of a nation. It's this very disconnect between economic and social needs, this shattering of social accountability within and beyond the workplace, that led us into a very tenuous space, and one I suspect we'd prefer not to return to.

A Lot Yet to Learn

So what do we need to be mindful of? Economists, reflects Ian Harper, still have 'a very primitive understanding of the world'. He likens their practices to previous generations of doctors who used bloodletting as a medical cure-all.[58] There's still a lot, it seems, for us to understand about economies. Certainly the world has seen a surprising number of banking failures in living memory. The International Monetary Fund figures suggest there have been around 147 banking crises, large and small, around the world between 1970 and 2011.[59]

Where has this left the everyday person? There's little doubt that the shortcuts taken to shore up company profits in recent decades were bleeding the world's economy dry, with what London fund manager Alberto Gallo calls 'a self-reinforcing cycle of lower productivity, lower interest rates, higher debt levels and even higher inequality'.[60] It's a scenario where in almost a decade from 2005, the wages and income of between 65 and 70 per cent of households across 25 'advanced economies' remained the same or fell. Yet in the two decades before 2005, only two per cent of people were in this situation, where their wages and income had stalled or fallen.[61] The end result is that the gap between the haves and have-nots is growing, and doing so rapidly. It's now estimated that less than 50 per cent of today's millennials are likely to end up financially better off than their parents.[62] Add to this the challenges the pandemic has left us with, and we start to get a sense of the challenge we're facing.

The Way Forward

The responsibility for future change doesn't lie solely with the big corporations. Mums and dads, and other everyday investors across the planet, need to play their part. They need to pay closer attention to where the funds for their pension or superannuation are placed. As multibillionaire business magnate Warren Buffett points out, 'People start being interested in something because it's going up, not because they understand it.'[63]

It's essential that each of us gets a better fix on the detail of our investments, and on the wider economic landscape too, as most of us know precious little about economic history. As Paul Tucker, past deputy governor of the Bank of England, notes, 'People actually have got fairly good short-term specific memories [but] they just haven't got good long-term memories.'[64] Investment bubbles have happened before and will happen again. Alongside this, the environmental impact of each and every company needs closer scrutiny, as does the social impact companies have in their own workplace and on the wider world.

CEO of the American Whole Foods organic emporiums, John Mackey, recently rounded on companies that focused solely on 'profit maximization', treating 'all participants in the system as a means to that end'.[65] As co-founder of the conscious capitalism movement, Mackey, along with others, is issuing in a new approach to business that has 'a higher socially beneficial purpose in mind'. These are businesses that seek to benefit *all* those involved in that company, from customers and team members, investors and suppliers, to the community and environment. Still with an eye to making a profit and criticised for their role in gentrification, Whole Foods does work actively to promote a more holistic work culture based on trust, accountability, caring, transparency, integrity, loyalty and egalitarianism.

Finding Ways to Keep Jobs

If we want to turn around the current shortcomings in our economy, which are leaving an increasing number of people isolated and out in the cold, government and business need to work together. Remarkably, after the global financial crisis, Sweden's government worked with unions to reduce work hours for a while. This way people got to keep their jobs and companies got the chance to recover. At the same time, the government created temporary positions in the public service, reduced the payroll tax, and created tax incentives for companies to employ young workers and those who had been out of work for a while.[66] We saw such solid, more egalitarian initiatives again during the worst of our COVID-19 days, when people took pay cuts, working fewer hours, so that as many people as possible stayed employed.

This kind of expanded thinking takes so many more people with it. The same applies to our choice of investments. Good investments, we are learning, need to be about more than just financial returns, although they are also important. In his 2019 New Year letter to CEOs, Laurence Fink, who heads up BlackRock, one of the globe's largest money-management firms, talked of the 'wrenching political dysfunction' we're currently seeing in some of the world's leading democracies, and the important role companies can play in helping take nations, and the world, forward.

'Society,' Fink notes, 'is increasingly looking to companies, both public and private, to address pressing social and economic issues', which range from 'protecting the environment to retirement to gender and racial inequality', and helping 'workers navigate retirement', amongst other challenges.[67] When there's a higher purpose to what we do in business, we elevate what capitalism can achieve. As we emerge into our 'new normal', we're being given an opportunity for a bigger, much more inclusive vision, which has the capacity to transform our communities and nation, by daring to reach out and take others with us, and to help make the growing isolation that too many are facing a thing of the past.

Robert Shiller sums up the amazing potential of a more mature form of capitalism in his 2013 Nobel speech. '... We need to democratize and humanize finance,' he suggested, by 'making financial institutions work better for real people, dealing with the risks that are most important to them individually, and providing opportunities for inspiration and personal development.' This means financial institutions 'interact well with actual human behavior' and respond to 'how people really think and act'.[68] It's a grand vision, but without a vision we'll only end up with more of the same.

Generosity Mindset

There's no better way to banish the kind of greed we've been victim to than honing our generosity – finding valued-added ways of operating that benefit others, too. Generosity is a gift that keeps on giving, as we get to enjoy the feel-good chemicals that flood our systems.

- Take a close look at your investments/superannuation. Are your investments part of the problem or the solution? How might these be fine-tuned?

- Does your workplace have an active charity or charities it supports? If so, how can you expand the benefit you bring to others? If not, where can you start?

- Think about ways you and/or your workplace might give back through mentoring.

- What's needed in your community? How can you help bring this about? Are there elderly people needing shopping or help with the garden, or who would benefit from being included in neighbourly get-togethers?

- What if what we're earning isn't just about accumulating 'stuff' – how else can we spend our money?

- Reward the companies that are giving back – make them a priority. Let them know how much you like what they're doing, and approach companies that could be more generous, encouraging them to do so.

- What does 'enough' look like right now – how can you work on that? What do you have in your home that someone else could make better use of? When you travel, how much luggage do you take? If you were to travel lighter, how might this enhance the experience?

Humanising the Workplace

When workplaces are focused purely on the bottom line, they become stark, one-dimensional places, often lacking the wide-ranging structures to be genuinely sustainable. The way out of this dynamic is to take good care of an organisation's resources, most notably its human resources. To achieve this it's important to:

- Set clear and reasonable expectations. Understand the nuances of what a person does, and what can sensibly be asked of them, while maintaining high standards at all times.

- Never treat others as inferiors – at work you're on a journey together, and everyone, regardless of where they are on the organisational chart, has something to contribute.

- Be generous with praise, thanking people individually and collectively. Make time to celebrate individual and group wins. A culture of celebration helps infuse an organisation with positive energy.

- Don't wait for formal reviews to address less than ideal behaviour or work – it's crushing to put a lot of energy into a project only to have it taken apart in a performance review six months down the track.

- Encourage regular feedback – it's an excellent way to build up genuine momentum, and take others with you as you move forward.

- Feedback is a two-way process. People need to give leaders feedback, too, if you are to create a healthy transparent culture.

- Create a collaborative environment focused on ways to improve and/ or fine-tune your work culture and processes.

- Take an interest in people's lives at and beyond work – a thoughtful comment, a brief exchange, an opportunity to pause and have a laugh builds loyalty and trust.

- Support a solutions-based approach to challenges. When things go wrong, don't resort to blame, as it's simply another manifestation of fear.

- Cultures that thrive acknowledge that people will make mistakes, but that in freely admitting to them, swift remedies can be sought and everyone can move on.

14

Workspace Challenges

Time to Be More Open

Working from Home

Hot-desking

Lonely at Work

TIME TO BE MORE OPEN

Having looked at our overall experience of work, along with our changing work cultures and how we approach profit, it's intriguing to see what role our workspace plays in our job satisfaction. Office space design has undergone a number of changes in recent years. Yet sometimes, in the bid to achieve maximum efficiencies, we lose sight of the human factor. 'Is an office with enough space to stow my purse, hang my coat, and dry an opened umbrella on a rainy day too much to ask for?' asks Michelle. 'Without partitions to block noise and visual distractions, I spend a lot of time planning where to gaze to avoid inviting unwanted conversations, keeping my earphones in to maintain concentration, and my line on mute except to talk for conference calls ... The workplace is no longer comfortable or conducive to getting work done.'[1]

How did we arrive at this place, where there's so much to navigate now in our working environment? In the fifties, most offices were large open spaces, filled with endless rows of desks. Wanting a more organic feel to workspaces, the Germans came up with *Bürolandschaft* – the use of filing cabinets, plants and curved screens to give workers more privacy. The sixties saw the introduction of the cubicle, also designed for privacy and wellbeing. By the nineties, there was a new take on open plan, promising greater communication and innovation, and businesses such as Goldman Sachs and American Express were quick to get on board. Now most offices are open plan.

Delivering on Promises

As with most innovations, there is open-plan heaven, and then there are the offices the rest of us work in. 'Google spends more on their workplace than almost any company I know,' tells Matt.

'Googlers enjoy quiet huddle rooms, conference rooms, shared enclosed offices, multiple cafes, great food, games rooms, libraries and a host of other amenities as part of their basic work environment. Most importantly they have access to a dedicated service team who do nothing but go around and ensure that your workplace is working for you! (Can you imagine?!)'[2] For most of us, this is a distant dream. Far from enhancing communication, open-plan layouts appear to discourage face-to-face interactions. In one three-year study of workers transitioning to open plan, the amount of time staff talked face to face fell by a staggering 70 per cent. Once in their new open-plan spaces, employees resorted to sending each other emails instead.[3]

The more open a space, it seems, the more workers want to withdraw. 'People try not to talk in the open quiet area,' Sammy tells of his workplace, reporting that the open-plan layout at his company has caused 'more isolation and less collaboration'.[4] This observation is backed up by research. In an extensive review of research into open-plan offices, 90 per cent of studies came up with negative findings, highlighting a raft of issues from elevated stress levels and high blood pressure, to constant staff turnover.[5] Instead of encouraging people to collaborate, the additional pressures that come with open-plan layouts leave workers often 'indifferent' to each other.[6] Marco concurs: 'Collaboration is not a full-time activity – stop designing principally for that! ... I cannot code software collaboratively. It is an internal mental activity and I need to be left alone and have quiet.'[7]

Would Everyone Please Be Quiet?

What is it about open-plan layouts that doesn't work? Noise is a big factor, making it difficult, if not impossible, to get work done. In one study, a group was subjected to the same level of noise typically found in open-plan offices, while another group was given a quiet workspace. Both groups were given unsolvable puzzles to work on in their respective spaces. The group in the 'noisy' space gave up on the puzzles long before the 'quiet' group, and also experienced heightened levels of adrenaline, thus increased stress.[8] Faced with so much ambient noise at work, some resort to playing music through earbuds, but this, psychologist Nick Perham has found, is also a distraction and can impair our thought processes. We do need quiet, it seems, to work effectively.[9]

> 'The open office concept is a trend-following, cost-cutting, personal-autonomy-and-privacy-destroying one-size-fits-all measure that's at best counterproductive and frequently disastrous.'
> Scott[10]

Leave Me Alone!

Another big challenge in open-plan workspaces is the number of interruptions people have to deal with. When professor of informatics Gloria Mark looked at the on-the-job behaviour of information workers in high-tech companies, she found that their days were full of interruptions. Half of these interruptions were 'self' interruptions, where workers became distracted. Of the remaining interruptions, some were easy to handle, such as a quick request for a signature. But when people were asked about a completely different topic, it took, on average, 23 minutes to get back on track. Mark found that when employees are continually interrupted their stress levels rise and their thinking becomes 'more superficial'. Interruptions, she states, are also 'really bad for innovation'.[11]

'As an architectural/interior photographer, I periodically photograph "open work spaces". The absence of partitions or walls makes the craft of image-making much easier. At the same time, the harm caused by the total lack of privacy isn't hard to miss.'

Dave[12]

Some Privacy, Please

Another complaint about open-plan space is the feeling of being constantly monitored. Back in the fifties, sociologist Erving Goffman suggested we all have front-of-stage and backstage behaviour. Front of stage, we're in full view and more aware of how others regard us, and of their expectations. Backstage, we're more able to be ourselves and to relax a bit. It's here that we prepare and rehearse for our time front of stage. To thrive, Goffman states, we need access to both spaces, as we can't always be 'on'.

The difficulty with open-plan spaces is that people are always 'on', as they lack privacy. They feel exposed, which impacts their behaviour. One open-plan worker admitted to finding 'private/judgement free' areas where he could communicate comfortably with others. Dealing with coughs and sneezes, and the minutiae of other people's jobs and lives, can be challenging. 'The open office space is exhausting and causes mental drain,' admits Stephen, who's worked in three open-plan offices.[13]

'We want organizations that breathe life into what we do rather than sucking the life out of us,' states Harvard associate professor Ethan Bernstein, who recently looked at the behaviour of workers in open-plan factories in China. Participating students working undercover were taught how to do their factory job when they were being watched, and how to operate when they weren't. The big surprise was that the 'working in private' approach was more productive than the official way of working. Large curtains were then set up on some production lines, giving workers privacy. The result? The production lines working *behind* the curtains were ten to 15 per cent more productive than those working in full view.[14]

One of the issues with open plan, states Bernstein, is that when redesigning office space, cost factors tend to come first. Having studied the impact of increasingly transparent workplaces on behaviour and productivity, he says the 'open office space "revolution" has gone too far'.[15] We need partitions, he believes, to help with overload and distraction.[16] Psychologist Dr Max Blumberg agrees. 'Our brains are not designed for the level of stimuli' experienced in open-plan spaces, leaving workers with a 'fight or flight' survival mode response.

Natalya, a biomedical engineer, had a difference experience:

> We went the opposite way. From open and semi-open environment to private offices with windows. I was shocked to realize how much my productivity went up. A report that used to take a week now takes 3 days. [I] hardly ever need breaks. In my new office I stay focused much longer. [I] work longer hours and leave less tired. This change was equivalent to my company hiring a half-time assistant for me. I would never agree to go back to open space and not accept a job with open-space environment.[17]

No Personal Items, Please

It's not just issues with noise and distractions that challenge people at work. A growing number of employers are insisting desks be cleared of personal items. 'It's hell,' admits Des, whose company recently implemented a 'no personalisation' policy. 'It has the feel of sterility, and not the "creativity" they were hoping for.' Bryan agrees, describing his clear desk environment as 'suffocating'.

These complaints may be justified, as personalising space can bring many benefits. It gives us the opportunity to express ourselves at work and to nurture ourselves. Personalised space also helps us feel we belong, that we're part of a wider team at work – a member of the sales and marketing team, as well as the after-hours work basketball team. Personalised touches can also hint at an in-joke shared with co-workers.[18]

The Benefits of Personalised Workspaces

One study of London office workers revealed that those who decorated their workspace were almost a third more productive than those who didn't.[19] Perhaps this insight helps explain why 'clear desk' policies create a lot of emotion. 'If the professionalism of my desk ever becomes more important than my effectiveness,' admits Martin, 'it will be résumé blasting time!' Having a few personal items around can add to the comfort level of many at work. Rex keeps a picture of his daughter on his desk. 'I find it helps focus my attention on my goals,' he tells. 'This little person is relying on me to provide a good life. That means enough money, healthcare, and most of all my time.'

No-one wants their workplace to look like a dump, but could we be throwing out the proverbial baby with the bathwater by insisting on totally clutter-free spaces? Personalised space has many nuances, explains Melissa Marsh, who runs the socially led New York design company Plastarc:

> It's comforting for people to have pictures of nature, the family or a pet. Then there's the need to store practical items at work – a toothbrush or cereal to snack on. Some people do go over the top with personalisation. This can be passive resistance,

or a cry for help. For some personal items are a way of not disappearing, of being remembered even when they're not in the office. For others it's 'this way you know me, you can see I'm a whole person'.

Most people, it seems, have a strong psychological desire to personalise their workspace.[20] According to noted cognitive scientist Daniel C. Dennett, stamping our mark on our environment lessens the load on our memory, and helps us take in new information. Remove these personal touches and our brains are under increased pressure, and more likely to feel overloaded. Imposing a desk free of personal items creates what cutting-edge workspace design company Haworth's global director of design, Jeff Reuschel, calls 'environmental lobotomies', spaces with zero meaning.[21] Or, as Justin puts it, 'We're an open office with a clean desk policy ... the entire place looks like an empty office to rent.'

One powerful way for organisations to re-humanise work and push back against any feelings of isolation is to allow more room for personal expression. Carla, a human resources professional with a major bank, tells of how everyone has their own locker at work with a chalkboard on the front. 'So you can make your locker personal,' she tells, 'and bring [more of] yourself to work.'

One reason given for getting rid of personal items is to create a less cluttered workplace. But as the Knowledge and Research team at Haworth points out, space is more nuanced than we might imagine. One person's disorganised pile may well be another person's 'intricate filing system'.[22] What comes across when talking to people about workspace is that, first and foremost, they want to do their job, in an environment that supports them to do what they do well. Take this away and they feel left out on a limb.

WORKING FROM HOME

With so many distractions at work, many are finding that home is the best place to get things done, though perhaps less so during the pandemic, when people were feeling more isolated. Working from home is a boon for those with long commutes, or those juggling work and family. Some just enjoy the solitude, the chance to get on with the job. 'I do financial management for a large consulting firm,' Pierre tells. 'People knock me for working from home most of the time, but I tell you, I do a damned sight more work than these guys. I spend less time just chatting with people, or going to get a cup of coffee, I just crack on with my work.' Grateful to escape the challenges of working open plan, Alex has worked at home for three years, and doesn't mind the arrangement, as his wife is out at work during the day and his kids have left home.[23]

As the cost of office rental is considerable for most businesses, there's a growing expectation that more employees will work from home a couple of days or more a week. Not everyone welcomes this move. A great deal depends on the physical and emotional comfort of their homes, and on the strength of their wider social networks – lesser-known considerations that came to the fore during the intensity of our COVID-19 lockdown. 'It's all right,' says Alex, a software engineer, 'but it [working at home] does get lonely.' Marshall agrees. 'I work from home, and yes, it can get pretty depressing sometimes. Luckily,' he adds, 'my roommate has a dog.' Some also find it difficult to motivate themselves away from the office. 'The hardest part for me was getting in a routine and treating it like a job rather than a paying hobby,' tells Sean. 'Setting and maintaining a good work schedule and routines, and always fighting the mentality of "Yeah, but I work at home, I can let this slide a little".'

I Just Can't Do It

Not all home environments are conducive to work, so some people head to cafes or libraries to get the job done. 'You actually have to have a home which is big enough for you to be able to work from home,' Penny reflects. 'Otherwise, there is no differentiation between what is your work space and what is the shared space of those with whom you live. If you live alone, working from home can be even more debilitating in that there is no easy way for you to carve out time for yourself which is not work time.'[24]

For some, the prospect of working from home is just too lonely. 'I've been approached to work from home,' Monique explains, 'but I don't want to, as I can go whole weekends without seeing anybody.' For others the isolation has become a habit. 'It's really easy to stay home,' one remote worker admits, 'to say no to opportunities to get out.' Aware of her growing isolation, she says she's now trying to connect face to face with at least one person every day.

Either way, good communication is essential if flexible work arrangements are to work. 'My company hasn't had an "office" for workers in 16 years or so,' Bert explains. 'We have a morning conference call every day, we chat constantly about projects and always pick each other's brains, just like we were across the hall from each other.' Getting the balance right is essential. 'I work from home one day a week, and am often away for work,' Shelley says, admitting, 'to go back to the office for a bit of routine is quite comforting.'

'Being onsite is a big deal,' admits Maurie, who works in systems admin. 'There's a ton of unspoken IT issues that aren't brought up unless you are right there in their face. If you're always remote, then you're not fixing all problems. So I try to have a good mix of remote and onsite.'

Every situation is different and needs consideration. 'One of my team members travels two hours each way every day,' says Carla, a human resources manager, 'so we're trialling her working from home three days a week. It's only been happening for a couple of months. When I checked in with her she did say, "I'm not sure how I'm going to go," because she is lonely. When we organised the office move … I was part of that change group where we said, "You just have a Skype meeting instead of a face-to-face meeting," but I don't know that it's turning out as well as everybody thought.'

Working Harder and Longer

Those working from home can struggle with keeping their work and private lives separate. Studies show that people are generally more productive working from home. Time is definitely saved not having to travel in to the office. It's even been calculated that workers in New York City working at home full-time save around 343 hours a year. However, the commute time saved doesn't necessarily translate into more leisure time. Studies suggest that workers who tend to work these additional hours, as well as answering emails at night and weekends, continue working when sick and are reluctant to take holidays.[25] The more freedom we're given, it seems, the more we tend to work, leaving people feeling pressured and constrained by their work.[26]

The blurring work–life boundaries can also ramp up stress levels. It's that feeling of never leaving work behind, which can make it harder to sleep. One United Nations study indicated that over 40 per cent of those working from home or multiple locations were more prone to insomnia than those who go to a regular workplace. Those who work from home are also more prone to increased work–family conflict, stress and sleep issues.[27]

> 'If you're not sitting next to a person, you're not hearing their conversations. If you're trying to pick up their work, or you're working remotely and you're only both in on Wednesdays, that's a challenge to keeping up to date as a manager.'
> *Carla*

'Working at home for a couple of days a week is great,' admits Shelley. 'More than that and it gets hard, especially if you're not visiting clients.' According to Dan Schawbel of Future Workplace, two-thirds of remote workers are disengaged.[28] His research with Virgin found that employees who work remotely are less likely to want a long-term career at their companies. Only five per cent of remote workers *always* or *very often* see themselves working at their company for their entire career, compared to 28 per cent who never work remotely.[29]

Keeping Up to Date

Informal on-the-job learning does take a hit if people are working part of the week at home, as they're less able to take part in informal conversations, or to note how someone else is handling a difficult client or issue. It's hard to gauge how much informal learning and networking is lost with remote working, but it was enough for Marissa Mayer, former CEO of Yahoo, to put a stop to her staff working from home early in 2013. To 'become the absolute best place to work, communication and collaboration will be important,' she said, 'so we need to be working side-by-side'. At the time, one Yahoo memo stated that 'some of the best decisions' come from informal chats in the hall and cafeteria. 'Speed and quality are often sacrificed when we work from home.'[30]

Working from home relies on good communication skills and the ability to take initiative. Shelley, who's in market intelligence, works from home a couple of days a week:

> Everything at work is set up through Gmail and Google drive, to have cross-market communication. We have loads of video calls with other markets. My consulting team is all around Asia, and we videoconference every day. I believe you have a better connection with someone if you can see them. Some people are a bit reluctant, but I feel it's really important, even if it's just at the start of a conversation, putting a face to a name when you're talking to clients. So even if clients don't put their video on, I put mine on and say hello, then turn the video off and continue. It makes a big difference.

As we emerge from the pandemic, it's essential that we're aware of these nuances. For some, working from home has been a dream come true, for others, a nightmare. Going forward, we need to take in the full spectrum of opportunities and challenges.

It's hard to gauge where the working-from-home trend will go. What we are seeing from some early adopters is a back-to-the-office trend, with a number of companies, from the Bank of America to IBM, banning working from home. Yet for those setting up their own business, or working at distance from head office, co-working can prove the perfect solution. Co-working spaces allow individuals to join a shared workspace with others who also need somewhere to work. This helps save on costs and provides shared equipment such as photocopiers and printers. Co-workers also benefit from the buzz and cross-fertilisation of ideas that come while working around others busy with their own projects. The first ever global co-working survey, conducted in 2011, found that three-quarters of those involved in co-working saw their productivity rise. Nine out of ten of these respondents also saw an increase in their social network, with eight out of ten extending their business network. Most also felt far less isolated.[31] With co-working growing in Australia alone by over 300 per cent between 2013 and 2018, this trend is set to continue.

Women-only co-working spaces are taking root, such as the Wing in the United States, offering childcare, 'beauty rooms' and 'lactation spaces'. While these spaces are committed to 'the advancement of women through community', men are welcome to visit and in some cases also work in them, as the business owners do also employ men.[32] Business benefits when such holistic services are offered, allowing for greater flexibility, and a more organic form of networking and support. These are powerful initiatives to help us push past any loneliness and get the job done. As we move beyond the restrictions placed on us during the COVID-19 lockdown, we have the chance to create far more nuanced workplaces and spaces, to better support our work.

HOT-DESKING

Most controversial of the recent trends in office layouts is 'hot-desking' or 'hotelling', where no-one has a dedicated workspace. Often the reason given for hot-desking is the opportunity for increased flexibility and collaboration. Employers are less forthcoming about how this can significantly reduce office workspace and thus office rental costs. 'There is a financial benefit to the organisation having only 80 per cent of desks,' one middle manager tells. 'So there are people sitting at breakout spaces and people everywhere, because there are not enough desks.' Where does this leave workers? 'I think the biggest difference between successful and unsuccessful agile working projects is whether you are doing it to save costs or whether you are doing it to make a better workplace,' states Melissa Marsh.

> '[Hot-desking is] a case of squeezing more people into less space.'
> Stephen McNabb, CBRE[33]

'We're living in a tech-enabled world, getting cheaper, faster access to things like video-conferencing, being able to video chat on our personal devices in an instant, being able to tap in to that when it's helpful to do so,' reflects Tyler Schofield, a professional at the cutting edge of transformational change programs in London and now Sydney. 'It's about having good structures and solid discussions with team members, with our superiors and colleagues, making sure that flexible working interweaves into this. This means rethinking the way work needs to be done and how relationships need to be built and maintained.'

Smarter companies have been relatively deft in their approach to hot-desking, allowing people to book a desk or workspace ahead of time. For those lucky enough to work at Deloitte Amsterdam, the building even matches a person's schedule with the best space available for them on the day. As with most things at work, when your needs are well catered for, you feel happy and productive. 'I work in a small team of twelve, and we have around twenty desks,' says Shelley. 'Some desks are a bit out of the way, designed for when you need time to focus. At other times it's about collaboration and sitting together. It depends on how much interaction you want,' she adds, admitting, 'I am a bit of a stickler for routine, so I generally end up staying at the same desk. There is a comfort factor with this, especially as my job is quite dynamic.'

Homeless at Work

'Technology doesn't provide a pure replacement [for previous ways of working],' Tyler Schofield cautions. 'You still need to upskill and inform people about what can be done and how best to do that, to create strong teamwork. You also need to work out how you deal with sensitive discussions, such as someone feeling overburdened, when you're geographically dispersed.'

In speaking with hot-deskers, there seems to be a divide between more senior members of an organisation and/or those who travel a lot for work (and who already enjoy a lot of freedom at work), and those who are 'office bound'. It's tiring, many complain, to trudge around the office day after day trying to find somewhere to work, not to mention the ongoing feeling of being 'homeless' that many experience with hotelling. Then there's having to pack up at the end of each day, regardless of whether you're in the middle of a project. 'It's easy to lose "small things" like pens, locks and your computer mouse as well,' Gibson says. 'If the expectation is that I would work at home otherwise, I would only go to my office for meetings, as it's impossible to get any actual work done there anyway.'[34]

For Andy, a product engineer, hot-desking was an even more intense experience. 'I have never felt more under-appreciated than I did when I was part of a shift to an open office environment,' he confesses. 'I was not important enough to have a dedicated desk. I have since left this company and am infinitely happier to be back in a cube – a space I can call my own and treat as such. At least I have one thing I know will be constant when I come in to work in the morning – the sense of home base in a hectic environment.'[35]

What Am I Meant to Do with My Stuff?

Often it's the little details that irritate most. There's nowhere to 'keep your things in one place', reports journalist Rebecca Reid, or to enjoy the 'comfort of something incredible like A DRAWER'.[36] 'Hot-desking is one of those things that seems logical in theory (and there are lots of good reasons why it is a good idea), but completely ignores human nature,' reflects Ingrid. Jost agrees: 'Why bother to go into work at all … The idea seems to be to break up and distribute the team so that you can never locate the person you need to talk to.'[37]

There's a wider exhaustion that sets in with hot-desking. One observer describes feeling constantly like an outsider, as if every day is their 'first day at work'.[38] 'Been there done that,' Trevor tells. 'Our team ended up working regularly 2–3 floors apart. We scheduled meetings just to discuss something for 5 mins. Lugging stuff from my locker to another floor, setting up, packing up and lugging my stuff back to my locker took about three-quarters of an hour a day. Complete waste of time and energy.'[39]

> 'I knew the move and change in work practices was going to be big, but I didn't realise it was going to take up so much of my time.'
>
> *Carla, human resources manager*

Practicalities of the Job

Is this just an overreaction to change, or is something more fundamental happening with hot-desking? 'I'm a technical officer,' states Grahame, talking of the additional difficulties hot-desking has brought. 'I have a shelf full of books, manuals and reference charts pinned on the wall I use on a daily basis – while doing my job.'[40] Now in a hot-desking environment, he struggles. It's interesting that the anxiety so many people feel about hot-desking is, first and foremost, at not being able to do as good a job. Priscilla agrees: 'I'm an adult, so give me a chair, desk and computer and I'll just get on with it. I've got my own phone so don't worry about that.'[41]

> 'Well, you have no clutter [with hot-desking], you get to choose, every day, where you would like to sit. You get to meet people you work with you may not have known before. Great for collaborating.'
> *Bea*[42]

For those in the office three or more days, hot-desking is often less than ideal. One executive found the experience so stretching, he bought a Vespa so he could spend as much time possible visiting clients. 'There is nothing good about this system, from the perspective of those who have to use it,' says Dev. 'It's dehumanizing, humiliating, and hugely inconvenient.' Dane agrees: 'Basically, the company had unwittingly rolled out the unwelcome mat ... Stuff got weird,' he adds, telling how some co-workers stopped showing up to work as it was harder to be monitored, while others began 'squatting' in conference rooms and on lounges.

Settlers and Vagrants

After studying one company's transition to hot-desking, UK ethnographer Alison Hirst described the dynamic as a mix of 'settlers' (those able to grab a good desk early) and 'vagrants' (who, due to a variety of factors, from family responsibilities to long commutes, can't get in to work extra early). The settlers, Alison Hirst noted, bag all the best spots, while the vagrants take what they can.[43] Pattie tells of a workplace where those who got in early were 'winners', while the 'losers' ended up all sharing two or three desks. 'If you come in at 9.30 am, which I do, there are no desks left in our neighbourhood,' says Carla. 'Some people then feel really anxious sitting in another neighbourhood. That creates a lot of anxiety for people, as they don't want to be the only person from their team going and sitting somewhere else.'

Working Harder Not to Disturb Others

Hot-desking also brings greater sensitivities to space. '[Our team had] been sitting next to each other for a few years and tossing ideas across the table, but now you have to go to someone and physically interrupt them,' explains Carla, 'and then you go and try and find a breakout space, so you're not interrupting the people around you.' This heightened sensitivity to noise can add to workplace stress, leading people to isolate themselves even more. 'Pretty much everyone in our office has noise-cancelling headphones,' says Shelley, 'and it's almost like a signal to the rest of the office to say, "I need to get work done."'

The new groupthink is that creativity and productivity are sparked by all the chance encounters and conversations hot-desking brings. However, according to Susan Cain, author of the bestselling book *Quiet*, which looks at the powerful contribution introverts can make, this concept has been taken too far. 'We leave very little place for deep thought and for focus and a work space where you can't be interrupted. And that's what's missing because solitude is equally a crucial ingredient of creativity. So we really need both, we need the solitude and the chance encounters.'[44] 'I agree 100 per cent that hot-desking is set up for extroverts,' says Carla, who works in human resources. '... So I find myself giving my desk up and saying [to an introverted team member] I'll come with you today to a different neighbourhood, to make it easier.'

Management Issues

'When we moved offices everybody became inwardly focused,' Carla reflects. 'I definitely feel we've lost that sense of team and personal connectedness. You really have to make an effort. Every day the first thing I do is talk to each person in my team individually and ask them how they're going or what they're doing, or if they're working remotely I send them a message. So [to sum up] I feel across the team we'd be feeling disconnected personally.' Office space is expensive, but so too is a disaffected workforce and, right now, workers seem to be struggling on several levels – additionally so, after the stresses of the pandemic lockdown, then emerging into a less secure job market. Productivity and attention to detail suffer, as do company loyalty and staff retention, when workers feel displaced. There are better ways forward.

LONELY AT WORK

Everyone needs a solid social base if they are to work independently, but for many this isn't a reality. The resulting sense of isolation for some is acute, as for Finlay:

> I am considered part of the 'international team'; a few people dotted around the world to assist with global coverage. The problem is that I have never felt so isolated in my life … In the end it seems that no-one really cares if I am in the office … and I just feel pretty lonely about it … This means if I don't go in for any reason – WFH [working from home], ill – I just stay home and that's that. But yeah, for example, I have literally worked

two weeks ... from home this month, and no-one has said anything during or even upon my return. I get up late on these days, but I always do my work. Still. I could have been dead!

As the work environment becomes ever more complex – with increased workloads, changing job specs and staff, and flexible work schedules – it's more difficult to stay connected. 'The workplace is in "massive social transition",' reflects Tyler Schofield. 'And [individual] loneliness is one of the big risks. So it's important to work out ways to lift people into the fabric.'

With longer working hours, people are exhausted and twice as likely to admit to exhaustion as two decades ago. 'The more people are exhausted,' notes social scientist Emma Seppälä, 'the lonelier they feel.'[45] This makes sense, as it's harder to stay connected with people at work when you're tired and stretched – harder still with work now encroaching on evenings and weekends, and even on holidays.

The blurring of work and home life with flexi-work can further add to what has been described as an 'epidemic of loneliness' around work. Also, the leaner companies have become, the more work remaining staff have to take on. 'With people so exhausted, by the end of the working day,' says Sandy Smith, global content leader with Intelex Technologies, 'they just want to go home.'

Is Loneliness a Real Issue?

'Sometimes the data on loneliness in the workplace is over-emphasised,' cautions Sydney psychologist Stephanie Thompson, adding, 'though culturally everything is so work-focused, and with such mobile populations, work has greater importance for many – a hope that relationships will be built out of work.'

What we do know is that you don't have to be working on your own to feel isolated. As we've seen with open-plan workspaces, there's a tendency to hide behind emails and to work with headphones on, limiting the chance for one-on-one connections. Global loneliness expert John Cacioppo stressed that loneliness is less about how loneliness might look, than how a person feels, as you can feel desperately lonely while surrounded by people.[46]

Fabian recently joined a big multinational firm, giving him an insight into how hard it can be for those struggling with loneliness at work:

> While I frickin' love my work here, I had to move a long way from the place where I grew up and where my parents were. But that's not the problem. I am shy and introverted so I usually have difficulties 'breaking the ice' at new places. In this new bustling city, I haven't casually chatted with anyone face to face since I came here which was about three weeks ago. It's not like I don't like the culture here as well. I love everything about my job and the place … I never had to deal with loneliness in spite of being shy and introverted. Now I sit in our cafe, eating my meal silently and by myself with nobody to talk to … It's becoming very painful for me to bear this. My friends or family often call me after work hours … But after that this becomes more painful as I recall that tomorrow I have to spend the entire day having no-one to talk to.

'We don't have "work families" any more.'
Dr Pauline Rennie-Peyton, psychotherapist[47]

How's Your Work Culture?

Until the change in management style in the eighties, most organisations would pause for 15 minutes midmorning, and again midafternoon, for a coffee break. People would sit together and have a brief chat, creating a genuine sense of family. Other workplaces had a tea lady, who'd come around with a trolley offering tea or coffee, and a biscuit. They'd serve your tea or coffee just how you like it, along with a brief chat. These interactions warmed the day, and tea ladies were often the most beloved members of staff. Now, though, some struggle to find one or two people they can connect with at work. We all know that workplaces aren't set up for people to make friends, but friendships can play an important part in how committed people are to an organisation. One Gallup study found a strong link between having a best friend at work and enjoying your job.[48]

Please Don't Ask Me to Do Flexi-work

It's easy to underestimate what it's like for those with few or no friends at work, until you listen to their stories. 'I've never been a social person but somehow managed for people to like me,' Ruby tells. 'I am down to just one "friend" at work and I'm terrified of what my job will be like without anyone who talks to me. I've been offered the option of working from home but as hard as it is sometimes I know that if I work from home I won't have any human contact at all and that scares me even more.'

Flexi-work has added another layer of complexity to the growing feeling of loneliness at work, with companies employing remote workers who may only come in to the office once or twice a week, or rarely, if at all. It takes even more effort on the part of employers to help flexi-workers feel connected and engaged, notes Sandy Smith, the former content director for the US-based magazine *EHS Today*, which focuses on the best work environment, health and safety management practices.

If you have an isolated life outside of work, then your workplace relationships become even more important to you. 'The workplace is the only source of community for many people,' reflects Dr Tim Baker, a thought leader in organisational change. 'People don't know their neighbours, let alone the person serving them in the corner store. So it is not just that people are lonely at work; they crave companionship at work because it is the only place they are likely to find it.'

Chitchat Helps

It's essential that employees are given the chance to connect while working. People need some 'small talk' at work, insists Dr Michelle Lim, Australia's expert on loneliness, as it helps build trust and connectivity. Don't wait for others to connect, advises psychologist Dr Pauline Rennie-Peyton. Take the plunge and ask someone to lunch. Make them a cup of tea. Bring in some biscuits to work to share, as such gestures encourage people to open up.[49] Small talk is a safe way for people to connect without ruffling feathers.

And while these interactions may seem so simple as not to be worth considering, given the fractured nature of work right now, many organisations are beginning to realise they need to work harder at bringing employees together to improve communication and connection.

Loneliness Impacts Performance

Only now are we learning the health impacts of loneliness – as mentioned previously, it can be as harmful to the body as smoking 15 cigarettes a day. Loneliness can also have a greater negative effect on us than obesity, and can impact our on-the-job performance and creativity. Chronic loneliness can even make us more vulnerable to an early death.[50]

With loneliness comes a feeling of being invisible, that who you are and what you care about don't count. The toughening up of workplaces hasn't helped people feel visible, let alone valued. 'Many companies used to sponsor company-wide events – holiday parties, corporate meetings etc.,' reflects Sandy Smith, 'that allowed co-workers to meet each other, to interact, to even meet each other's families', but cost-cutting has changed all that.

Poor treatment of employees has also left many out on a limb, as Jesinta tells:

My mom worked at [a global accounting company] for almost thirty years. It once was a fun working atmosphere, office parties, office sponsored footraces and volleyball etc. She would work all-nighters to get projects in with her staff, and as hard as it was, it was a blast. Over time, all the extras, all the amenities got whittled away. Even as profits soared office outings disappeared, then office parties, then bonuses and raises got smaller. The workers stopped caring as much, and rightfully so.

The Challenges of Emotional Work

There's another little-discussed aspect of loneliness in the workplace, described as 'emotional work', which impacts teachers, nurses and flight attendants, and all those expected to remain calm and upbeat regardless. Sociologist Arlie Hochschild was first to highlight how hard and lonely the always-on, mustn't-ever-get-cross performance of emotional work can be for these workers.

What makes this work so difficult is having to suppress personal hurts or frustration in favour of smiles and sympathetic expressions, even when dealing with impossible children, rude clients, angry passengers or abusive patients.[51] Such roles, where professionalism overrides a person's wellbeing to a high level, can exact a huge price. It's not uncommon for these workers to end up emotionally burnt out, or with unbearable stress levels. Some describe the pressure as being so great that they feel like they're 'crying inside', or in a life-and-death situation.

We know that those with strong emotional intelligence fare better in these kinds of roles. Good emotional skills do help workers who daily face endless tricky work situations, making them better able to see a client's point of view.[52] Only now, though, are we realising just how lonely these roles can be, unless these workers are in supportive work cultures. It's essential that workplaces understand the pressure these employees are under, and that they regularly check in with them to ensure they're fine.

Most people are reluctant to admit to their loneliness at work, given the 'winners and losers' work cultures so prevalent now. Added to this, employers often regard loneliness as a personal problem. The 'time is money' attitude in many workplaces isn't helpful either. 'Even though we spend half our waking hours at work, some companies frown on employees turning work into a social occasion,' says Sandy Smith, who has spent years promoting best work environment, health and safety management practices. 'Even a small amount of networking or talking is now frowned upon,' she reflects.

Loneliness Breeds Disengagement

We now know that loneliness does impact our work, making us more defensive and less engaged, and less willing to share our ideas and expertise. Former US Surgeon General Vivek Murthy blames the 'always on' work culture for our growing sense of isolation at work, which in turn impacts our performance – from our creativity to our ability to make good decisions. 'I sometimes worry that we have lost sight of the fundamental need that each of us have for human connection,' Murthy admits, stressing that it's essential to 'protect time with family and friends'. People, he states, need to work in a culture that values kindness and encourages genuine connection, as 'individuals cannot be truly fulfilled or successful without each other'.[53]

Professor John Cacioppo agrees, insisting that people need *meaningful* connections.[54] In the workplace this might include encouraging individual staff members more. 'Work cultures need to make time for impromptu moments of appreciation,' suggests Dan Schawbel, research director of Future Workplace. Gestures that make people 'feel special' can yield huge rewards. Managers need to get more creative, and to realise that office drinks aren't enough to create a genuine sense of belonging. True connection, Schawbel suggests, is about being appreciated for who you are. It's also about being seen as a whole person, being encouraged to bring your 'full self to work'.[55]

What might this 'full self' look like? Tyler Schofield gives us some possibilities:

> In my current project, I have ten different bodies [organisations] coming into one building, and there's a real fear [about this]. Oftentimes it's about a loss of identity. So, I'm working with human resources to encourage a greater belonging, as work isn't just about your work. It's also about 'I'm training for the marathon and you are too, so perhaps we should go running together.' So we're looking at such activities as a yoga afternoon, a knitting circle, a book club, social activities that get people across organisations together.

We're also currently identifying 'diversity champions' within the organisation to be there for new and established members of staff so people can go to that individual and know it's a safe space. It's about helping people feel they have a connection, someone to confide in, without them having to be a natural extrovert, or having the social skills to do these things.

Loneliness expert Professor John Cacioppo also stresses the importance of feeling useful, which he describes as being able to 'step out of your pain long enough to "feed" another'.[56] Workplace charities can be excellent in helping join the dots here, as can getting involved in social justice causes, such as Australian publishing's push to assist indigenous literacy, made possible through the Indigenous Literacy Foundation.

Loneliness isn't to be confused with being an introvert, someone who often enjoys working on their own, and simply needs some peace and quiet to recharge. Loneliness bites deep. It's that feeling of being utterly alone, set adrift. While a lot of effort is being put into workplaces and spaces, we're often missing the mark. Sometimes the best solutions are surprisingly simple. One industrial design team from Delft University of Technology found that when an office coffee space was screened off with tables and chairs, there was *more* conversation between staff than in an open area with no seating. The payoff? Eighty per cent of conversations were about work.[57]

As we move forward, we need to take greater care of our workplace ecosystem, to ensure workers feel connected, supported, valued and inspired to give of their best.

15

Opportunities for More Benign Design

Connecting with Nature

Socially Led Design

CONNECTING WITH NATURE

Workspace design does matter. Though most organisations still haven't got their working spaces right, effective solutions may lie closer than we think. We've been aware for some time of nature's ability to clear our heads and inspire, and now we're getting a sense of how this can enhance our workplaces. A recent study into sustained attention revealed that all that was needed was a 40-second glimpse of nature to help people focus at work. In this study, participants were given a task to concentrate on, then were split into two groups. One group was allowed to glimpse a concrete roof for 40 seconds. The second group glimpsed a rooftop meadow. When the results were analysed, the latter group was found to make fewer errors and to work more consistently on their allotted task,[1] suggesting nature's capacity to help our overloaded brains.

In addition, we're now discovering that connecting with nature helps lower our blood pressure and improve our sense of wellbeing. A nearly decade-long study as to whether nature can impact a patient's recovery after surgery also came up with some intriguing results. Recuperating patients who were given a hospital room overlooking nature recovered more quickly and needed fewer painkillers than patients without a nature outlook.[2] So what can we do with these findings?

Ready Access to Nature

A few decades ago we started to find powerful ways to work with nature in the workplace. In the late eighties, the Reno Post Office was housed in a modern warehouse with high ceilings and black floors. The postal sorting machines were noisy, and the downlighting was harsh. A decision was made to lower the ceilings and install softer, more energy-efficient lighting. Once the renovations were finished, productivity rose by eight per cent, enough to pay for the alterations within a year. Sorting errors fell, as did lighting costs, and the space was so pleasant that workers would often stay back after work and chat.[3] While these were relatively straightforward alterations, it's interesting how much they impacted costs and productivity, and transformed how the workers felt about their workspace.

A few years later, Walmart decided to build an energy-efficient eco-mart in Kansas. Working with designers, they made great use of the available daylight. Once the new building was finished, it delivered on the promised energy savings, and had a surprising effect on sales. As all Walmart's cash registers connected back to headquarters, sales could be monitored in real time. Eager to see how the new store was performing, Walmart's senior managers tracked the sales and were astonished to see that the sale of goods in the day-lit part of the store were significantly higher than those in the rest of the mart. Shop-floor workers also spoke of how keen they were to work in the day-lit section of the store.[4]

Though many of us live divorced from nature, our ancient connections to 'nature's forms, processes and patterns' remain, explains environmental psychologist Judith Heerwagen.[5] How do these connections play out? Aware that recovering cancer patients often find it hard to get back into their routine and maintain a much-needed self-care regime, one study split recovering patients into two groups. The control group was given a variety of self-care regimes to choose from, while the experimental group focused largely on nature-based self-care activities – walking in nature and gardening. This latter group were soon showing a clear and continued improvement in their attention. They were also more likely to be back at work, including full-time work, and to get on with cherished goals, whereas the control group were not. Remarkably, the nature-based self-care program only involved about 20 minutes, three times a week.[6]

'Just as we need healthy food and regular exercise to flourish, we need ongoing connections with the natural world.'
Judith Heerwagen, winner of the 2014 Design for Humanity Award[7]

Green Buildings Assist Productivity

Since these studies, the green building movement has taken off, and is now impacting workplaces in remarkable ways, as the link between improved environmental quality and work productivity is seen over and over. This nature-based approach to design, known as biophilic design, makes good use of natural features, patterns and colours, along with indoor plants and, where possible, views of nature. One study comparing green and minimalist workspaces found that those in green offices enjoyed improved concentration and a 15 per cent rise in productivity. The green office employees also found their work environment enriching, and reported a noticeable improvement in air quality.[8]

We now know that green environments improve concentration, but how exactly does this work? Basically, we have two types of attention: focused attention, which we use during the hours spent in front of a screen; and effortless attention, which allows for more relaxed observation. Focused attention helps us perform a wide range of important tasks. Without it, little would get done. The difficulty is, however, that focused attention requires considerable effort, and soon exhausts us. And when we're fatigued, we're more easily distracted and more likely to make mistakes. No-one wants to be exhausted at work – it's not in anyone's interests for us to be tired. Interestingly, it's now thought that a whole raft of workplace accidents that were previously considered to be caused by human error, were in fact due to mental fatigue.

Our ability to focus, we're learning, is precious and fragile. Anything that can help refresh and refocus us is good for us – for the quality of our work and our safety, too. As we've seen, in recent decades people have been under a great deal of stress due to heavy workloads, volatile workplaces, repressive management, noise and other factors. Access to natural environments, we're finding, helps balance out workplace stressors, helping restore our focus and making us more resilient.[9]

Nature Outlooks Can Support Us

So how can we help people to refresh and regroup at work? Even subtle changes in the working environment can make a dramatic difference. One of the reasons nature is so uplifting is that it provides us with plenty of sensory input. Knowing this, we're now seeing the benefit of being in surroundings that stimulate our senses. Added to this, when we connect with nature, it has a way of engaging us without exhausting us.[10] One study of office workers found that those with a window looking out onto nature bounced back from low-level stress much faster than those facing a blank wall. And the longer people looked out at nature, the faster their heart rate was likely to drop.[11]

SOCIALLY LED DESIGN

Melissa Marsh, founder of New York-based, socially led design company Plastarc, believes good design is about how we occupy buildings, and how buildings support us. Too often, though, design features don't taken into account the full breadth of human needs in a given space. Successful design, Marsh states, combines the social, digital and physical aspects of a workspace. She sees Plastarc's mission as bringing all these aspects together to create spaces that support workers at a whole new level.[12] 'When we enter a workspace our senses take in a flood of information,' Marsh explains. This in turn impacts our mood and behaviour, and our wellbeing. 'We take in the colours and textures, the lighting, the air.' The best of these new design approaches, she suggests, 'combine the comfort of home with workplace needs'.

Taking Note of Our Senses

For Marsh, there are many layers to socially led design. One important factor is access to natural light, to help support the body's natural rhythms. 'This,' she tells, 'is best used alongside circadian lighting, with the possibility of additional effects such as dappled light projected onto walls.' For Plastarc, the choice of furniture also upholds this wider aim of design-led wellbeing. Marsh's team might, for example, use reclaimed wood in such office furniture as conference tabletops, providing immediate tactile stimulation for all those using those tables. And, in keeping with differing needs across the working day, Marsh encourages a mix of hard and soft furniture. To further boost wellbeing, she stresses the importance of having 'decent coffee' and healthy snacks, along with opportunities for the enjoyment of shared food, rituals around meals and snacks, and pleasant soaps and fragrances in restrooms.

As sensory beings, we need to engage our senses of sight, taste, touch, smell and hearing. That's why sensory experiences inspire us, and offer a tangible sense of wellbeing. One of the many reasons nature works for us is that it provides sensory opportunities in abundance.[13] Only now are we beginning to understand the importance of engaging our senses at work – varying light, sounds and temperature to keep people inspired and uplifted – because without stimulation people lose focus, and become tired and bored.[14] Non-visual nature cues in a workspace can add further interesting sensory layers, providing smells and textures that bring the senses to life. Even sounds of nature can be helpful. Studies show that after experiencing stress, such sounds can help restore around 37 per cent of a person's equilibrium.[15]

Good Lighting Is Essential

One of the powerful aspects of the green-led biophilic design is in promoting better lighting at work. Most of us are aware of the importance of the body's circadian rhythm – its sleep–wake cycle – and of nature's combination of daylight and darkness in supporting this rhythm. What we're less aware of is that sunlight is yellow in the morning, blue at midday, turning to red during the afternoon and evening. The bluer the light, the more of the feel-good chemical serotonin our bodies produce. And, where there's an absence of blue in our environment, melatonin, our sleep hormone, is manufactured. It's essential that we balance our serotonin and melatonin, as together they help promote wellness, supporting our immune system and our ability to focus, and later to sleep well.[16]

So how can lighting help at work? Unlike broad daylight, office lighting lacks the spectrum of colour found in nature, thus impacting our ability to sleep. A study into the effect of natural lighting at work, staged during winter at a company in upstate New York, showed that those working in 'windowed' offices with access to winter light – the time of year with least natural light – proved to be more focused than those in the company's interior office spaces.[17] Psychiatrist Baba Pendse has done a lot of work into the effects of lighting on mental health, and sums up this process as 'the better the lighting, the more information I can gather'.[18]

Lighting technology is now moving apace with colour-tunable LEDs, whose colour temperature ranges from yellow through to blue, and which can be synced to shift tones depending on whether it's day or night. There's increasing evidence that biologically friendly lighting delivers on many fronts. One two-year study of students found that, under full-spectrum lighting at school, they were happier and healthier, and had fewer days off school. These students also had nine times less dental decay and grew 2.1 centimetres (about ¾ inch) taller than students in schools with average lighting.[19] In another study at Boston-based Genzyme biotech corporation, three out of four workers felt more connected to their co-workers after settling in to their new headquarters, with its soaring atrium flooding 90 per cent of the building with natural light, along with abundant greenery and a high use of recycled materials.[20]

Keep Moving

Regular movement, we're now learning, is also good for us. 'Nature is always on the move,' notes Judith Heerwagen, as seen in the 'sun, clouds, water, tree leaves, grasses'.[21] When we move, almost all of the regions of our brains light up, assisting our creativity and problem-solving. How can this help us at work? With sitting now seen as the 'new smoking', putting us at greater risk of heart issues, obesity, type 2 diabetes, anxiety and depression, an increasing number of workplaces are moving to sit–stand desks, enabling people to vary their way of working during the day. Embracing the need to move around and to stimulate the senses, Airbnb's San Francisco headquarters provides tented and art-deco-inspired meeting spaces, a green wall and large atrium bathing the building with light, large exterior windows providing fresh air and ventilation, and a Mumbai-styled cafe.[22]

When global crowdfunding company Kickstarter repurposed a former Brooklyn pencil factory, they discovered that its location was on the pathway of migrating Atlantic birds, so the roof was planted with flora to support these birds and butterflies, and an outdoor area was created for staff. Inside is a mix of 'refuge' spaces for those needing to concentrate, along with 'prospect' spaces to help minimise stress, boredom and feeling tired.[23] Similarly Pasona Group, one of Japan's leading recruitment companies, uses light wood and good lighting in its Tokyo headquarters, and encourages staff to grow their own food, using passionfruit vines and lemon trees for partitions between desks. In addition, they grow salad leaves in raised beds in seminar rooms, creating a funky, light-saturated urban farm.[24]

There are so many ways to create the kind of workspaces where people can thrive and, stresses UK green architect Oliver Heath, it doesn't require a big budget. Simple changes to the work culture, such as encouraging people to get out of the building for lunch breaks, making the most of natural views, and creating the opportunity to eat together all help, as do such initiatives as having pets visit now and then.[25] And, suggests Mehmet Atesoglu, digital marketing manager for Formaspace, if you're hoping to attract millennials (soon to be the largest demographic in the workplace), then biophilic workspaces are the go.[26]

After all the angst experienced at work and with the pandemic, we now have the opportunity to reconnect, to share a bigger vision of what work can deliver. And, with such innovations at our fingertips, perhaps the solutions are now within reach.

16

Transforming
Our Cities

Changing Cityscapes

What Do Hipsters Have to Offer?

CHANGING CITYSCAPES

During the last hundred or more years, our cities have struggled to house and transport increasing numbers of people. Cities, as we now know them, have been made possible partly due to the creation of plate glass, cast iron and reinforced concrete that enabled high-rise structures to be built. These new structures have been linked by ever-larger, more complex freeways to transport a growing population and to keep goods moving. Cities have continued to expand, as have tower blocks and motorways, until just after the turn of the new millennium, for the first time ever, the majority of people are now living in cities.

When we think of large cities, we tend to think of the traffic and crush of people, the noise, the loneliness, and perhaps even the soullessness. Yet there are many other facets to cities, too. Some of these are captured brilliantly in Olivia Laing's musings on her own loneliness after arriving in New York, in her award-winning *The Lonely City*.[1] And cities are also changing. We're beginning to see how they can be more intimate, safe and stimulating spaces, giving our lives far more texture, and helping us connect in meaningful ways. 'What I love most of all is how endless the city is,' New Yorker Huon reflects. 'It changes before my eyes, whether I am moving through it or not. It is endlessly amusing, fascinating, trying, perplexing, grimy and beautiful. People put on a show, for others or for themselves. People dress up, or they slouch along. It lifts you up or it tears you down. But it's never boring.' If planned well, cities have many layers to offer. What, then, is needed to help city-dwellers thrive?

Cities Have Their Own Ecosystems

Several decades ago Canadian–American writer Jane Jacobs saw cities as living ecosystems that flourished when there was a rich mix of uses on offer and good urban planning, which takes in the needs of the people there. Jacobs' activism helped preserve cherished parts of Manhattan and other cities, where well-established communities were under threat from planners who showed little interest in local residents.

Earning the title of the 'mother of urban design', Jacobs spent years pondering the qualities that made cities beautiful or unattractive. High-rise buildings with the odd park, she argued, weren't the answer. Urban planning needed to be a whole lot more intricate than that. Jacobs believed that cities worked well where there was room for old and new buildings, and for smaller blocks, so areas were easier to navigate, thus promoting neighbourly exchanges. How much green space, she pondered, was needed for each residential acre, to give people a sense of freedom? Which kinds of park enhanced a neighbourhood, and which attracted crime? Density, she believed, also had its uses, as it has a way of bringing people together, and came with the added benefit of plenty of 'eyes on the street'.[2]

Too often, though, urban planning 'damaged' city life, noted Jacobs, as she watched whole neighbourhoods ripped apart and their ecosystems destroyed to build freeways and low-income housing.[3] 'There is no logic that can be superimposed on the city,' she claimed. 'People make it, and it is to them, not buildings, that we must fit our plans.'[4] While she wasn't opposed to gentrification, Jacobs could see how often it nudged aside simple households, shops and small-scale businesses – dwellings that were the heart of that community.[5]

Meanwhile, in sixties Europe, Danish architect Jan Gehl began his professional life as cities were being defined by large concrete buildings and streets built for cars. Here, all too soon, streets were clogged with traffic. Yet in love with all things new, modernist architects were busy sweeping the past aside.

Old buildings were demolished to make way for tower blocks that were crammed in together, with little thought to how their placement and design impacted people's lives.

Pondering this disconnect, Gehl came to see that how a building 'lands' in a cityscape is important, as it helps shape the life of the city and its inhabitants. Travelling across Europe, he began to get a better sense of the elements needed to create more amenable public spaces. Venice was a city that helped point the way. With 'small, personal, and intimate' public areas, and streets around three metres wide, he saw how easy the space felt, and how effortless it was to walk the city. All this was in sharp contrast to the growing numbers of concrete monoliths found in most urban areas, creating wind tunnels and sunless locations, which gave people no reason to pause and nowhere to sit. Instead people could be seen speeding up and hurrying past these uninspiring, often uncomfortable locations. Added to this were a growing number of busy freeways, which further fractured the flow of pedestrians attempting to cross their city.

> 'Cities have the capability of providing something for everybody, only because, and only when, they are created by everybody.'
> Jane Jacobs, The Death and Life of Great American Cities[6]

Human Scale

The great challenge for cities, Gehl saw, was to achieve high density that also took into account the human needs there. The way forward, he believed, was to work on a way to enhance a city's quality of life, to create a real sense of wellbeing and vitality. This meant, in part, planning intimate spaces for overlapping generations and allowing for a shared economy.

These and other findings formed part of what Gehl would call the 'human scale' – a scale where we can comfortably take in our environment, be inspired and feel part of what's going on around us, regardless of the size of the city.

As Gehl's ideas began to take shape, he started to look even more closely at how humans interact with their environment, realising there's a 'social field of vision' at work in the spaces we move through. At distances from 100 to about 25 metres out from a specific location, we're not close enough to take in much detail. But from there on in there's a 'richness of detail' available to us that, Gehl explains, intensifies 'dramatically' metre by metre. So, by the time we get to between seven and zero metres of our destination, all of our senses are engaged, as we're able to take in every detail.[7]

One of Gehl's biggest challenges in introducing his human-scale concept was to get people out of their cars. With everyone used to driving the freeways, people couldn't imagine life without their vehicles. Then change started to happen. In 1989, when the San Francisco earthquake decimated whole sections of the city, the Embarcadero Freeway collapsed and, to everyone's surprise, the city coped. Now that space is filled with trolley cars, trees and pleasant places to walk, inspiring the city to continue to transform its freeways into inviting streets for pedestrians.

Perhaps one of the most recent dramatic transformations of a city space is at Cheonggyecheon in Seoul, where a choked eight-lane highway was removed to open up an underground waterway, which was then bordered with trees. Hugely popular with locals and visitors, this waterway, with its stepping stones and tree-lined walkways, has boosted local businesses and transport, attracting back wildlife that had vanished from the city. Remarkably, the temperature of the city centre has also fallen by several degrees.[8]

Protection, Safety, Delight

For cities to work, Gehl believes they need to offer protection from the weather, traffic, noise and crime. It's also essential that planners take into account the comfort factor – creating places where people can walk, sit and play, have interesting views by day and good lighting at night. Another aspect of human scale is the way it actively engages the senses with the addition of trees, plants and water features. Green mobility is another cornerstone of the human-scale approach, enabling people to cycle or walk effortlessly through their city. All these details help give people a sense of connection and delight – one or more good reasons to linger in city streets, rather than rushing off home.[9]

While cities continue to evolve, not everyone enjoys urban spaces, often because they seem overwhelming. Yet, increasingly, we're understanding the elements that help create a sense of intimacy, even as visitors to a city. Susan, aged 63, tells of how she enjoys holidaying in big cities. Choosing to rent an apartment rather than stay in a hotel, she looks forward to 'living like a local' while visiting a city and immersing herself in the buzz. 'When I lived in New York, many years ago, I felt I was living in the beating heart of the universe,' she explains. 'That's what city life in a great city feels like to me. There is nothing like it.'

Copenhagen began its urban transformation almost 50 years ago when Strøget, in the heart of the old city, was given over to pedestrian traffic. Initially, locals were less than enthusiastic about the move. But in the first year alone, foot traffic grew by over a third, and the street flourished. Copenhagen wanted to be a city not just for shoppers and tourists, but for everyone, so planners went on to create a safe network of small city streets crossing larger streets without interruption. The greater the pedestrian and bike safety a city offers, urban designers came to see, the more the city is available to a wide cross-section of residents. Now children in Copenhagen can be seen out on bikes with their parents from the age of five. By seven, children are able to walk to school on their own, and by ten they can be seen cycling across the city by themselves. When a city works for young and old, Gehl states, then it's likely to work for everyone.[10]

Walking Works

Part of Gehl's human-scale concept is the 'life between buildings', which allows for a range of options as you traverse city streets – from walking or shopping, and opportunities for exercise, dance or play, to pausing to enjoy street entertainment and take in other moments of interest. Walking, Gehl insists, is the starting point. In lively, safe, sustainable city spaces there need to be 'good walking opportunities', allowing for 'direct contact between people and the surrounding community, fresh air, time outdoors, the free pleasures of life, experiences and information'. This allows people to choose their level of engagement at any one time – to be in their own space, while feeling part of street life, or fully entering into the sights and activities there. Such 'moments' in a human-scale city create a real sense of intimacy on the street, which in turn allows for chance encounters and brief conversations, where 'acquaintanceships can sprout'.[11]

Bringing Cities to Life

Comfort and connection are essential in good city design, and can happen on a number of levels. During the seventies and eighties, people moved out and away from cities to the suburbs in search of a more fulfilling life. With the transformation of our city spaces, this trend is reversing (though in recent times, regional areas are being revitalised, too). Wanting to make the city more people-friendly, Melbourne has worked hard on its human-scale experience, including its 'life between buildings'. In just over a decade, the city's laneways were revived, enabling pedestrians to walk easily through the city. Now over three times more people reside in the city than in 2006.[12]

One of the key elements of Melbourne's transformation was Federation Square, built on the old Gas and Fuel Buildings site, which now offers a mix of cafes, bars, exhibition spaces and open areas. There's also an outdoor amphitheatre for live events. At other times, you can sit outside on deckchairs and take in the world, or engage with those around you. Linked by a series of interconnected laneways and stairs, this old industrial site is now a lively part of the city, helping make Melbourne a destination city. Invariably, those who visit comment on how much they love Melbourne's alleys and laneways.

Feelings of intimacy are important if we are to feel at home in a city. While visiting London on the 2017 Dulux Study Tour, participants got to see the city at ground level and from above, taking in the architectural wonders of 'The Gherkin', 'The Shard', 'The Walkie-Talkie' and 'The Cheesegrater'. Designed to foster the next generation of architects, this tour prompted some interesting responses. Imogene Tudor told of how the 'only authentic moments of connection' for her were where they experienced 'the human scale' of the city – in an historic church, inside a colourful atrium, when stepping into a courtyard defined by nature, and in pockets of open space where Londoners could be seen relaxing, drinking in pubs and bars. 'It's a relief to find the places of a scale we feel comfortable in,' reflected a fellow participant, Claire Scorpo.[13]

Opportunities for Delight

As urban design progresses, we're starting to pay attention to what experimental psychologist Professor Colin Ellard calls the desire lines and emotions of city space. This means being more aware of the visible and invisible layers of city life, and understanding how much the design – the complexity of a building's facade or 'skin' – can influence us. It's critical, Ellard insists, that cities guard against monotony, as spaces 'with no game' can lead to depression, addiction and stress.[14]

In one of Ellard's experiments, participants' alpha brain waves were monitored while they stood in front of a variety of buildings and in nature. Our alpha waves are those brain waves that enhance our creativity and help keep depression at bay. The study revealed that participants' alpha waves were highest in nature, and at their lowest when standing in front of dull facades. 'The holy grail in urban design is to produce some kind of novelty or change every few seconds,' Ellard says.[15] This is often best seen in parts of a city where there's a busy stretch of shops, cafes and restaurants, where there are tables and produce spilling onto the pavement.

> 'We are, as animals, programmed to respond to thrill.'
> *Former aerospace engineer Professor Brendan Walker,*
> *University of Nottingham*[16]

The Power of Awe

As we are sentient beings, the power of our feelings can't be underestimated. In one study, students were shown 60-second clips of whales, waterfalls or astronauts floating in space. After only a minute of virtual images, those who were awed by these images admitted to feeling less time pressure. In a second experiment, people were asked to recall 'an awe-inspiring' event, then respond to survey. Those recalling a moment of awe were found to be more likely to volunteer for a charity, compared to those who didn't. Participants were then given the hypothetical opportunity to 'purchase' an object or experience – a watch or a Broadway show, a jacket or a restaurant meal. Those who'd recently 'felt awe' tended to choose the experience over a physical possession, a choice that's linked with greater long-term satisfaction.[17] Awe, it was observed in this study, is a vast concept, which has the ability to alter our sense of the world. It 'makes us feel small, not larger than life, the way happiness can', notes Stanford professor of marketing Jennifer Aaker, when reflecting on this research.[18]

Charles Montgomery, the author of *Happy City*, also believes that good design shapes the 'emotional infrastructure' of a place. In 2014, his lab sent researchers out onto Seattle streets. Posing as lost tourists, they were stationed in areas with 'active facades', where there was plenty of visual interest, and along huge warehouse blocks with 'inactive' or nondescript facades. Results showed that pedestrians at 'active' sites were nearly five times more likely to offer help to the 'lost' tourists, than those at the inactive locations.[19]

Transforming Neglected Spaces

How, then, do we create 'active' locations, when so much of our towns and cities are already built? After decades of neglect, many New Yorkers wanted to see their derelict goods line torn down, until they discovered a wild garden had taken root there. Not wanting to see this extraordinary elevated green space destroyed, Robert Hammond and Joshua David founded Friends of the High Line, which spearheaded the transformation of this forgotten space. Now one of New York's most treasured parks, this elevated walkway was part of an old railroad that once served the factories and warehouses of Manhattan's West Side.

James Corner, the lead architect, who describes his job as 'place-making', believes part of the pleasure of such spaces is being able to 'just sit and watch the world go by', along with the sensory enjoyment of wild and more formal landscaping, with grasses and flowers, seats and trees, and art installations. 'I'm fascinated,' he tells, 'by the interplays between city and nature, between the garden and geography, between small scale and large scale, between art, imagination and something more tangible.'[20] The High Line is now home to over 200 species of perennials, grasses, shrubs and trees – all chosen for their varied textures and colours. Many of the grasses here were already growing on the abandoned goods line.

Described by one visitor as 'beautiful and astonishing', since opening the High Line has attracted well over 60,000 Tripadvisor reviews alone, most of which have the full five-star ranking. Sparking such banners as 'Tourist in My Own City', 'Genius Invention of an Old Railroad', 'Awesome Fun and Very, Very Clever Attraction', this 22 blocks of elevated walkways with gardens and outdoor art, delights numerous residents and tourists daily. 'We enjoyed the serenity and simplicity of the path … ' Ainslee says in her Tripadvisor review. 'Smells of cooking breakfasts wafted up from the nearby apartments further along the route, and the people we did pass seemed to be enjoying a leisurely morning too.' Lauren agrees, telling in her review of how, 'The lovingly restored and maintained section of abandoned rail line offers a calm, peaceful and different way to view Manhattan. Amongst the well-kept plants and gardens, there's art, seating, a few places to eat and relax and view the city from different angles.'

'WOW, look what they did [with the High Line]! Nice oasis in the concrete – every city should do something like this – amazing time in nature in the big city.'
Patricia H., on Tripadvisor

With such locations come endless additional opportunities for people to connect and create moments that inspire and delight. On a chilly January afternoon visit a couple of years back, when the High Line was covered in snow, I witnessed the remains of the park's first ever snow sculpt-off – one of hundreds of events the park now hosts. In one week alone, there's a guided tour of the medicinal and utilitarian plants in the park; an 18-person band; and a design tour that takes in 'notable architecture' along the walk, in addition to the regular High Line tours and Tuesday romantic evening walks.

Reclaiming Derelict Spaces

Space is always at a premium in a city, but there are often forgotten spaces ripe with possibilities. After the success of the High Line, New York's Design Trust for Public Space now has an even more ambitious goal – to restore additional El-Spaces in Manhattan. These street-level areas, currently seen as unsafe or undesirable, under roads and railways, cover a space estimated to be four times that of Central Park. One five-mile corridor under the Rockaway Freeway, for example, is thought to lend itself to a green space for cyclists and walkers, street artists and pop-up markets.[21] Meanwhile, in Jerusalem, the once-neglected Valero Square now boasts a series of huge 30-foot long-stemmed 'poppies', whose giant scarlet blooms open during the day and light the Square at night. These magnificent 'poppies' also respond to the presence of pedestrians or passing trams, playfully transforming this previously lacklustre space.[22]

Each city has the opportunity to work with its own nuances to create spaces where people can pause and relax, or actively engage. Sydney is a city of ten distinct villages, each with its own unique feel, along with its recently restored Goods Line. There has been a deliberate push to make these areas bike- and pedestrian-friendly, to support small local businesses, encourage public art, and preserve and enhance each area's vibe, cultural identity and heritage. Now pocket parks and pavement gardens flourish, amid an ever-widening network of bike paths. Within a few years, previously rundown parts of the city have become sought-after locations to visit, socialise and live in. Most cities need more work, which includes finding innovative ways to support live music and other 'after-dark' venues with street safety, and far greater attention to providing low-income housing, but significant strides are being made that feed a sense of intimacy, inspiration and belonging.

WHAT DO HIPSTERS HAVE TO OFFER?

Love hipsters or hate them, it's becoming abundantly clear that we can't ignore them, or some of the interesting things they've been up to. Whether or not you have a passion for checked shirts, rolled-up skinny jeans and well-tended beards, most of our lives, particularly in cities, have been impacted in some way by hipster culture. The simple truth is that where hipsters land, others follow. We see this in the way dilapidated, often dangerous parts of our cities are reborn – from Kreuzberg in Berlin, to Brooklyn in New York, where real estate prices now rival those seen in Manhattan's posh Upper East Side.

There are a number of theories as to how hipster culture emerged. The word 'hip' was first used to describe the trendies emerging from the forties jazz scene. More recently, some suggest, hipsterdom took root in Brooklyn, New York and Silver Lake, Los Angeles towards the end of the nineties. 'Those cities were extremely violent then, and the authorities introduced various measures to bring down the crime rate. But these efforts were deemed to have sterilised the cities and stripped the neighbourhoods of their street culture,' explains National University of Singapore sociologist, Joshua Kurz, creating what he describes as 'a pushback among youth to reclaim these spaces'.[23]

Too Hip for Their Own Good?

Whatever their origins, hipsters are, in part, a reaction against our globalised, homogenised lives. Hipsters don't care for most brands, preferring the eccentric and the bespoke. Regarding brand slavery as bad taste, they've helped redefine success as something quieter and more personal, with ostentation to be avoided at all costs. There's also a fashion element to hipsterdom – sometimes described as 'cool without labels', which is one of a number of reasons why hipsters attract much ire. Why all the effort and attention to detail? Why dare to be different, when we can consume as much as we can relatively cheaply, with an almost seductive ease?

Yet to write off hipsterdom as just another fashion trend is to underestimate its impact. 'I like to believe there's something smarter lurking within our romance with hip ... an idea of enlightenment and awareness,' muses *New York Times* reporter John Leland, author of *Hip: The History*, written more than a decade and a half ago.[24] So what more, if anything, is there to hipsters?

Pushing beyond the monotony of mass-produced goods, hipsters seek a life that's more intimate, where experiences are to be savoured, where we're encouraged to linger rather than swill, where we choose one precious thing over countless bags of stuff. The hipster approach encourages us to embrace pre-loved clothing, to treasure these pieces as much as, if not more than, new items. Hipsters invite us to delight in the fact that a garment already has a history and that, one day, we'll hand on our jacket, slacks or frock, but for now we'll take good care of this item of clothing, and lay down our own set of stories while wearing it. As we emerge from the pandemic, where we've been forced to slow down, to rediscover aspects of our homes and lives that we've neglected, I wonder if we are ready to embrace greater nuance in how we approach our choices.

> **'I guess it's [hipsterdom is] the belief that mass production has some inherent flaw which has tainted society, and that only by throwing off the shackles of conformity will they be able to truly live a meaningful life.'**
> *Ahmed*

Little, Local, Less

After decades of addiction to acquiring as much as we can, this new wave inspires us to think about fewer possessions that, wherever possible, are locally made – bespoke objects that have been crafted with care. Capturing what's precious from the past, hipsters also show a genius for repurposing objects. There's a romantic element here, too. The love, time and attention to detail hipsters bring to locations, and to handmade items and food, are immensely appealing in our increasingly impersonal, mass-produced world.

Hipsters are 'a millennial generation searching for authentic alternative lifestyles which they believe come from a seemingly more innocent past before the internet and mass manufacturing', suggests assistant professor of communication and information

Liew Kai Khiun of Nanyang Technological University in Singapore.[25] So what, if anything, can we take from hipsters?

While upcycled furniture, vinyl records and Indie bands aren't for everyone, the hipster ability to re-imagine unloved spaces has created more multilayered, inclusive communities – places where care is also taken over the sourcing of raw materials and the creation of products. Many are drawn to this immediate sense of intimacy, now apparent in countless locations across the globe, including Lisbon's LxFactory in Alcantara, where the vast Ler Devagar (Read Slowly) bookshop, with its cafes, bar and artworks, entrances all who visit. There's also a performance space in this bookshop and, on Sundays, this former thread and fabric factory hosts a vintage market.

Such re-imaginings are more than fads. They're opportunities to get out and be exposed to new ideas and experiences, alone or with friends. 'A real community has emerged [in Brooklyn], people who want to unplug from a hyper-connected, dehumanised world, artists and others who don't fit into the classic American definition of success,' explain Daniel and Brenna Lewis when talking to *The Guardian* of their business, Brooklyn Tailors, which had its beginnings in their apartment.[26]

As more and more people enjoy what hipsters offer, their take on life has rapidly become mainstream. Detractors like to write off hipsters as elitists – as middle-class kids with well-off parents to fall back on – but the hipster take on life is more complex and far-reaching than this. 'They demanded something better than the mass-market status quo,' insists Aleks Eror, a self-described 'purveyor of unpopular opinions'.[27]

Now, thanks to hipsters, we're far more aware of the importance of good food. Farmers' markets, with their strong emphasis on locally sourced, organic products, owe a great deal to hipster support. These days we're far more interested in where our food comes from and how livestock and producers are treated, with fair trade an important part of this equation. More than this, farmers' markets help create a powerful sense of community. 'One of the reasons given as to why farmers' markets resonate so strongly is that the connections made on market day, between stallholders, between shoppers and stallholders, and between shoppers – are real, purposeful and meaningful,' notes Jane Adams, founding chair of the Australian Farmers' Markets Association.

Creating with Passion

One of the places hipsters have left their mark has been in the revival of craft beer, as seen in the exponential growth in this sector. Who would have thought that a series of small businesses could take on the corporate giants? A decade ago, America had around 1600 craft breweries. By 2018, this had grown to 6300 breweries, producing in excess of 25 million barrels of beer, with ten per cent of this beer being sold directly to customers. 'Some people started tinkering around and the world changed around them – and they changed the world – but they never really intended to be revolutionaries,' reflects CEO of Craft Brew Alliance Andy Thomas, who runs a Seattle-based brewery offering a mix of beers and ciders.[28]

> 'While the monolithic industrial brewers have continued to get more monolithic, it's craft brewers that have been capturing the hearts and minds of the American public.'
> *Greg Koch, founder of Seattle's Stone Brewing*[29]

We have, of course, been here before with the arts and crafts movement, which emerged around the end of the nineteenth century. With its catchphrase 'By hammer and hand, do all arts stand', this earlier craft push also emphasised the importance of artisans and their beautiful handmade objects, often inspired by nature. Simplicity and fine workmanship were valued, in the face of the rapid encroachment of the Industrial Revolution. The impulse behind the craft movement lived on. It, too, was popularised, and its objects mass-produced, yet it also helped preserve artisanal skills, works and ideas.

Hipsters shy away from all tags, as individuality is essential to them, and that isn't necessarily a bad thing. Yet, like it or not, they do have a number of characteristics in common. 'Reasons people say that I'm a "hipster": I'm a vegan, I listen to alternative/ indie music, I wear big thick-rimmed glasses, my political views are more liberal than my peers (I'm a student at the University of Alabama … enough said),' Billie says. '[As for] my clothes, I like thrift stores, I'm obsessed with vinyl records, I own a MacBook, I like to garden and grow my own veggies. I don't think these things make me a hipster, but it's just what I like. Can't help it.'

Appearances Aside

Hipsters have impacted so many areas of life, including architecture and interiors, as seen in industrial and other repurposed fittings, exposed brickwork and warehouse conversions – trends that are now mainstream. Many precious buildings and the history they held would have been lost, were it not for hipsters. Those visiting inner-city suburbs cannot help but be charmed by how hipsters embrace locations that are peeling at the edges, or worse, and breathe new life into these neglected spaces.

One of the reasons there's an uneasiness around hipsters, though, is that often the arrival of hip cafes and artisan bakeries, brew bars and farmers' markets herald gentrification, making previously rundown parts of a city suddenly desirable. This is understandable, given that the very act of bringing a city location alive can and does displace the most vulnerable, along with locals and small businesses that have faithfully served a location for decades, as rents soar. Too often the passion and inclusiveness of revamped city areas is lost as costs rise, with this new vibe attracting competition and pretension, and those chasing profit, as the heart of that place fades, or is lost. But this is no reason to abandon the reviving and personalisation of city space. This surely needs to be addressed, for example with zoning regulations that insist on a proportion of low-income housing in neighbourhoods and that work harder to carefully preserve their integrity.

Street Art

Amongst the many delights of hipster suburbs is the plentiful street art, enlivening otherwise dull, often ugly, facades. Creating interest, energy and inspiration, street art helps make artworks more accessible, often challenging our ideas with their wide range of offerings. '[Street] art is about expression, creativity, freedom, asking and raising questions, protesting, analysing and even beautifying. A way to step beyond convention. There's freedom with putting work in the street,' reflects South African blogger Janaline Smalman.[30] The ready availability of street art also helps a community see itself afresh, bringing colour and a whole range of new ideas to neighbourhoods, creating more inviting spaces for visitors and residents – spaces where people can pause, get involved in chance conversations, and be inspired.

Hidden Places

Who doesn't want to see more texture in our communities? One of the delights of the hipster approach is the quiet reveal. They understand the joy of a secret location, as found in such places as Shoreditch's speakeasy bar Callooh Callay, with its Lewis Carroll-inspired interior, and a concealed room behind a Narnia-style wardrobe. The pure thrill is in the hidden. Yet unless you know about this London bar, you'd walk right past it. Elsewhere in Shoreditch, rooftop locations have been opened up so that people can now gather over a drink with friends while gazing out over the chimney tops at the city. While such locations are often pricy, these are ideas that can travel, and be adapted in more affordable formats.

Sydney's Newtown is a hipster haven, with a range of quirky businesses, including Jack the Clipper, which offers everything from a wet shave and skin fade, to a full suite of barber's services. Here customers are invited to 'enjoy a complimentary beer, with some swanky tunes in the background', while 'street style barbers' ply their trade. Client feedback is almost unreservedly positive – a testament to the reasonable prices and the barbers' skill. 'Absolute legend!' claims James, delighting that Jack 'gives a neat fade and is a master with the cut-throat'. But it's not just the skill and the passion that draw people in, it's also the environment, in which people feel free to express themselves. 'I requested an obscure, particular haircut,' Julian says, 'and they listened and respected what I wanted.'

Offering flush-mounted toe plates or recorking, Newtown's artisan cobbler, Nathan Baxter of Baxter & Black, tells of how his longstanding passion for shoes has taken him to England and Budapest to learn his trade. 'Shoe repair and shoemaking have provided countless hours of joy in my life,' he admits. 'I'm proud to now offer my services to the wider community and look forward to meeting you and your shoes.' Yet even with these and other offerings, Newtown is also changing as prices are rising, a salient reminder of how dynamic urban environments are, and how many factors need to be balanced to preserve and enhance local ecosystems.

Pondering these and other possibilities, is it possible hipsters could help point the way out of our current sense of estrangement? In a world where people feel increasingly isolated, where mass-produced goods and global franchises are the order of the day, we need to find new ways to connect, to simplify, to find joy in the precious skills of those who have come before us. There is a lot we can learn from hipsters to help lift us out of the fog of our constant distraction. As Linton Weeks, a national reporter for America's National Public Radio network, reflects, 'Hipsters, after all, know how to adapt: how to make the cheap chic, the disheveled dishy, the peripheral preferable. A shaky, shabby economy is the perfect breeding ground for hipsters.'[31] And given we're in more tenuous economic times, this may well be a sustainable way forward.

17

Belonging

What it Takes to Belong

Finding Our Way Back

WHAT IT TAKES TO BELONG

Much of what we've been pondering is a way back to belonging, which in itself is complex, and something we all crave from our earliest years. To create a genuine sense of belonging, we need to pay attention to the environment our kids are growing up in. Amid the dazzling tech possibilities available to them, we need to ensure we're not raising our children to be lonely, by habituating them to aloneness – by allowing them to spend hours on their own in their bedrooms on their devices. International resilience expert Michael Ungar sees this trend of kids spending so much time on their own with their devices as a real threat to the younger generation's ongoing wellbeing: 'Our children are putting themselves at risk for a lifetime of social isolation and the mental health problems that come with it,' he warns. When we don't interact with others, we end up less than comfortable around people, especially those we don't know, leaving us hyper-vigilant, 'overly sensitive to social cues', and struggling to deal with one-on-one conflict.[1]

A recent American study into 13- to 18-year-olds backed up these concerns, reporting that teens had experienced a marked increase in loneliness since 2011 – a finding that aligns with the increased use of devices. We already know that iGen teens are going out far less. The upside, of course, is they are involved in less risky behaviour than previous generations. Yet spending face-to-face time with peers is important. Take this away, and teens soon feel isolated. 'Adolescents low in in-person social interaction and high in social media use reported the most loneliness,' according to this study.[2]

It's concerning that loneliness is worse in younger generations, with iGen-ers and millennials reporting higher feelings of loneliness and isolation on the Loneliness Scale than older people. When publishing its latest Loneliness Index findings, Cigna in the United States reported that iGen scored a loneliness score of 48.3 out of 80, making them 'the loneliest generation'. What does this mean in real terms? More than half of iGen participants in this study identified with ten of the eleven feelings associated with loneliness, while around 60 per cent felt left out or isolated from others.[3]

Compatibility Isn't as Important as We Think

As we seek to reclaim a sense of belonging, we're being invited to expand on our vision of what this might mean. Living increasingly segmented lives, we've come to see connection as finding those with whom we have something in common. Yet genuine connection isn't necessarily about surrounding ourselves with like-minded people. In fact, states Rick Warren, the internationally bestselling author of *The Purpose Driven Life*, 'community has nothing to do with compatibility'.[4] It's about learning to work with what we have, to expand our humanity and creativity to interact positively with and be surprised, if not delighted, by others who may be very different from us. It's about building bridges, rather than seeing others who are different or problematic in some way as problems to solve or discard.

When We Don't Enjoy a Sense of Belonging

Whatever our point of difference – be it colour, creed, how mentally or physically able we are, or our sexual orientation – the simple truth is that none of us want to be sidelined or ignored. When we lived in villages, we interacted with a wide range of people with differing needs, fragilities and skills. Some navigated life better than others, but all of this happened in plain view. Now it's easy to shut ourselves away, or to carefully distance ourselves from someone who's different. But what does this do to our humanity?

Difference is challenging, until we learn to relax around each other and give people a go. No-one wins when we fail to take the first step, or when we retreat. 'Every straight male friend I've told about being gay, has thereafter subtly but swiftly decreased the amount of time we spent together,' Mal says, adding, 'I now have a solid "all or nothing" policy. Either they know from the beginning, or they never will.' How must it feel to experience a sudden cooling in a relationship without any explanation? What is it we fear that leads us to cut people off? Is it because we don't know what to do with our discomfort, or how to act or to deal with an awkward situation should it arise? Part of bridge-building is daring to admit that we're not sure how to react, while affirming that we want that person in our life anyway.

> 'When my best friend in the whole world came out in our
> tiny southern town, my heart hurt for him. Because no matter
> what he was, GAY overshadowed it all. Smart, funny, sweet,
> excellent musician, and now a lawyer. And still he is known
> almost exclusively as "Sherry's son. You know, the gay one".'
> *Leyton*

It takes time and patience to live comfortably with difference without feeling threatened by it. And it requires sensitivity, too. In seeking acceptance, a person doesn't necessarily want to wear their point of difference like a badge, as this too can be alienating. 'I feel like there is a huge difference between respecting each other, and seeing each other as an equal,' Toby says, reflecting on his life as a gay man. 'Even if people [respect] your orientation, on the moment they learn about it, suddenly it's the most interesting thing about you.'

'If you're straight, you'll never understand what it felt like to feel "less",' Julia says of being a lesbian woman, insisting she's not asking for more than anyone else – just to be treated as equal. Equal means a lot of things, including knowing the person you love will be looked after when you're gone. Marriage equality, we've come to see, was never just about marriage, so much as having the same rights as heterosexual couples, especially should something happen to one partner, thus leaving the person they love even more vulnerable.

The chance to finally get married has been a lifesaver, Randy says. 'When I married my beautiful wife, who happens to have been born with X and Y chromosomes and is therefore considered a transgender female, it was the fulfilment of nearly a decade of love of which we had previously been legally barred from gaining official recognition,' he reflects. Knowing his wife will be financially secure with access to his military pension when he's gone helps Randy know that, should he get sick, he'd be able to die in peace.

> '[Assumptions] get stressful sometimes. Like, really stressful. There's a reason, among the older crowd at least, that LGBT folks often form such tight communities. It's not that we don't love y'all. It's that we sometimes get tired.'
> *Marion*

As we seek to connect, we need to resist the temptation to pigeonhole people. 'There is no singular "black community",' Jay insists. While this may be so, that's how people tend to react to groups of people who are different from them, stereotyping them rather than seeing them as individuals. 'It is the expectation of pretty much everyone you meet, as a black person. And if you don't fit it, you are an aberration. To everyone,' Irving, an international teacher, tells. 'Even living here in Japan, everyone expects me to fit some component of this [black] template ... They are shocked when I tell them I'm a teacher.' Or as Fitz, a cable TV technician, complains, '[As a black person], people profile you ALL THE DAMN TIME.'

Australian-based real estate investor Yumi agrees, telling of 'random suspicious looks' he gets on his evening jog, and how he watches 'random strangers suddenly grasping onto their belongings with a tighter grip just because I chose to take a rest a metre or so away from them'. Then there's 'the "casual" yet very probing question' people ask him constantly: 'Where do you come from?' or 'Where do your parents come from?' And all this happens, Yumi adds, 'when I'm at work doing my level best to assist clients accomplish the main objectives that caused them to visit my office'. However, what saves the day for Yumi is when there's an honest desire to connect, even if a person's questions are clunky. 'Being "different",' he adds somewhat philosophically, 'has afforded me the ability to make strong connections with people ... I have made great friends through these awkward, at face value, interactions.' And now, given the issues the Black Lives Matter movement has raised, we are all being challenged to stop and understand what it's like to be in another's shoes, to get a sense of the weight of history, often deeply personal history, that shadows the experience of people of colour, and to bridge obvious and less obvious gaps.

> 'I am not black but I am of Hispanic descent.
> So I am brown ... EVERYONE THINKS I'M
> GOOD AT BASKETBALL!!! AND I SUCK AT
> F**KING BASKETBALL!!!!!'
> Sanchez

Every community, including the 'disabled', battles the attitudes and prejudices of others. 'Most spend their lives in isolation, being ignored and not acknowledged at all; therefore having contact with other people in society is considered a blessing,' Carlsson says. 'Just the simple gesture of being acknowledged means so much to those with disabilities. If the world would recognise the disability community and give us opportunities, then the world will become a better place.' Tina, who lives with dwarfism, adds, 'For me, it [an unhelpful assumption] has to be when people tell me that I'm "brave" or an "inspiration", or just assume that I'm some incredibly amazing person, before they have even learned my name. As flattering as it seems, they don't know me, and it just feels like they don't see me as a fully realised person with flaws and vices like anyone else.'

In Need of More 'Third Places'

Belonging is also about the spaces we occupy. Alongside our homes and work, urban sociologist Ray Oldenburg explains, are the all-important 'third places', which help us feel like we have an additional place where we can relax with others, where we can be ourselves. For many young people, the 'third place' is often cyberspace. Clubs, churches and mosques, and other organisations, religious or otherwise, also fill this space.

Part of the reason that inner-city communities thrive, suggests University of Queensland sociologist Peter Walters, is that they're filled with lively third places – clusters of bars, cafes and affordable restaurants where people can meet informally or be 'alone together', enjoying a sense of belonging. Further out from the city there are fewer opportunities for third places. Here small shopping centres are often not within walking distance, and huge malls offer little in the way of connection.[6]

However, these all-important third places are slowly starting to work their magic in outer suburbs and in regional centres, too. When we understand their importance, we can help push for them and bring them about.

For centuries, cafes have been much-loved third places. Australian entrepreneur Peter Baskerville, who has created and run a number of cafes and coffee shops, learned early that good cafes are not just about serving food and drinks. They're sanctuaries, spaces where people can work or just 'chill out', he says, with the added comfort of others knowing your name and how you like your coffee. Journalist Lauren Suval agrees. When her life was unravelling, she gravitated towards her local coffee shop for 'something, anything, to hold onto'. Here she met someone and got talking. This person listened, prompting Suval to keep returning to the cafe, making further connections that created a real sense of 'kinship' for her. 'I don't go for the tea,' she reflects. 'I don't go for the coffee. I don't go for the wi-fi. I go because it feels like home.'[7]

Time to Get Creative

If we're serious about creating more socially cohesive lives, we need to get more imaginative about the ways we connect. We're seeing a major pushback against political correctness, with some feeling they're not being heard. While it's important to legislate against abuses, we need more creative opportunities to reach out and simply celebrate what it means to be human. Connecting can be spontaneous and deeply fulfilling when the conditions are right.

In 2014, Palestinian brothers Ameer and Joey El Issa, along with their sister, Mouna Emsis, dreamed up the Bearded Bakers. Selling knafeh – a creamy, Middle Eastern dessert of sweet cheese and semolina, topped with crushed pistachios, soaked in rosewater sugar syrup – this 'skyrocketing business', which operates from a shipping container, has taken everyone, including its creators, by surprise.

In an experience described as 'part theatre stage and part travelling dance troupe', the Bearded Bakers dance amongst bonfires, inviting the crowd to dance with them. 'The beauty in what we do is in the simplicity,' Ameer tells. 'Unexpected places are always the best.' Like most ventures, they have had their issues. 'When you break the mould and challenge the boundaries you will always encounter setbacks and hurdles, but what we realised really early on was that each time something didn't seem to go our way, the changes we had to make opened up new doors.'[8] These new doors now include Bearded Bakers pop-up containers in Melbourne, New York and Beirut.

Tiny Homes Solving Homelessness

There are so many issues around belonging needing attention, some of which have soaked up huge amounts of funding without achieving the desired results. Sometimes the solutions are surprisingly simple, as seen in Melbourne's recent 'Tiny Homes' initiative. To overcome homelessness, the city has begun building relocatable, pet-friendly, small homes, rented out to those who were homeless. 'I'm learning how to be stable,' says one tiny homes resident, who's lived on the streets since she was a teenager.[9] 'I feel like someone took me from, basically hell,' admits Deborah, another resident, 'and put me on this cloud of puffy niceness.'[10] For Hayley, living on the street meant 'being in a trauma state and never feeling safe ... not being able to relax and constantly on guard.' She is now a Tiny Homes ambassador.[11]

Helping the Elderly

Another area in need of attention is the escalating isolation felt by our ageing population. In the UK in 2006, Hilary Cottam, formerly of the World Bank, got together with a dotcom entrepreneur, an innovation strategist and industrial designer to found Participle, an organisation dedicated to addressing social issues.[12] Bringing together social scientists, anthropologists, psychologists and economists, they spent nine months researching the lives of older people, discovering what the elderly most wanted was social contact, along with help with the 'little things', and a sense of purpose. Connecting through shared interests was also important, rather than just connecting with those of the same age, gender or cultural background.[13]

The following year, Circle was formed to support those people over 50, to build and maintain strong social networks and to take care of their practical needs. Starting with 250 older people and their families in Southwark, South London, this local enterprise employs five people and is led by a full-time director. Members pay an affordable annual subscription, which gives them access to a free local phone number, providing paid and free social events, such as reading groups and poetry evenings held in members' homes. Helper support includes anything from mowing a member's lawn and supporting a member's return home from hospital, to a sympathetic ear on the phone.

When people join, they're encouraged to buy £10 'tokens' in readiness for paid outings, or an hour's labour from neighbourhood helpers – anyone from students and housewives to the newly redundant.[14] Circle has created strong, independently reviewed social and health outcomes, including a reduction in social isolation. Seven out of ten members also reported more participation in social activities, an increased number of friendships, confidence and happiness. Circle has meant less reliance on public money, assisting people to keep living independently for longer.

There's a lot to be done to glue us together, but there are also some remarkable opportunities if we have the will and headspace to make them happen.

FINDING OUR WAY BACK

One of the themes that's emerging is the biting need to do things differently. In a few short years, we've become addicted to, then utterly exhausted by, our need for constant excitement and change. But as we contemplate life as 'liquid moderns', perhaps it's time to find a more sustainable way of living individually and as communities. To be a disrupter is immensely seductive, yet, as individuals and as a society, we need to ask whether we have the psychological resilience to sustain our current level of change, or if it will ultimately undo us, especially given the repair work now needing to be done as a result of the pandemic.

While disruption may seem 'sexy' and bold, more powerful still are opportunities for regeneration and reconnection in our homes and cities, in our relationships and at work, which are possibly more organic, more manageable, more 'human scale'. Already an array of possibilities are emerging in what previously felt like a hostile space.

In seeking to reconnect, first we need to be clear about where we're heading. We can only do this when we put aside our devices, push back against the endless wave of fearful narratives, reduce our need for wall-to-wall entertainment, and refuse to be satisfied at being fed only those views that match our own. This means a conscious widening of our lens, and spending more time thinking about the future – not just for ourselves, but for our communities, our nations and our world.

Building a Better Future

When we look back at the generation of builders – those courageous figures preceding the baby boomers – we see a generation focused on creating a better world. Living through two world wars and the Great Depression, the builders witnessed firsthand what happens when things drastically fall apart. They learned that the only way to survive, and then thrive, was to reach out and connect – to work together, to hold a vision for the future and, digging deep, to make that future possible. They had the character and commitment to achieve this, knowing that much of what they were building would most benefit those who came after them. And now, it's time for us to step up.

Everywhere we're encouraged to embrace competition and self-interest. For some decades now we've been told we can have it all and, in seeking to make true this vision, we've lost a deeper sense of meaning and wellbeing. In our determination to best those around us, we've sacrificed all the potential that comes with a genuinely deep sense of belonging.

Sharing Delivers Huge Benefits

Yet things are changing. As Rachel Botsman, a global expert on the collaborative economy, so aptly puts it, the currency of our new economy is trust. This 'confident relationship to the unknown', she reminds us, is essential for innovation and progression, and for building relationships, too. Once we lived in villages, where trust was experienced face to face. Then, as we moved to cities, our trust was transferred to institutions.[15]

Now through such platforms as Airbnb, strangers are trusting each other to share and to do the right thing – freeing up spaces, skills and possessions in ways and on a scale that we never thought possible. This 'collaborative consumption' uses the best of technology to build trust and connect people in meaningful ways, making the most of the resources we have, through dozens of platforms such as Etsy, eBay and Gumtree, where we have the ability to create and form personal relationships when buying items, making the moment memorable. Rewiring our world to share, swap, rent, barter or trade brings with it endless opportunities to connect – from pet-sharing and house-sitting, to recycling and upcycling thousands of items.

> **'The greatest tragedy is not death, but life without purpose.'**
> *Rick Warren,* The Purpose Driven Life[16]

'Instead of consuming to keep up with the Joneses,' Botsman suggests, in this new economy, we're 'consuming to get to know the Joneses'. The immense upside of a sharing economy is that it's helping to build trust. And not surprisingly, it's growing exponentially, as we're hungry for more meaningful ways to connect. We witnessed this again and again during the COVID-19 lockdown when local businesses rapidly reworked their offerings to help us all out with everything from hand sanitiser for the home, to much-needed masks and personal protection equipment for our health workers. These are exhilarating, life-enhancing opportunities.

On a practical level, it's an easier, more personal approach to buying, trading and swapping items and skills. Through such platforms as TaskRabbit, Upwork and more, we're making online connections that enable work to be done in the real world. In just two decades, we've evolved from trusting people to share information, then our credit card details. Now, Botsman notes, there's a 'third trust wave', connecting us with trustworthy strangers. So, just as we have a credit rating, now we're growing a reputation rating, which indicates how much someone can trust us, helping us get more jobs and impacting how much we can charge.[17]

Technology Must Serve Us

While we're benefiting from the many advances in technology – in our hospitals and homes, while travelling, when banking and shopping – we must remain vigilant to ensure technology serves us, and not the other way around. With the ever-narrowing 'use-by' dates of our appliances, we're constantly replacing or being persuaded to upgrade items, demanding more time and effort of us, where often the new functions on offer come at the expense of those that served us perfectly well. 'The net effect,' associate professor of philosophy at St. Lawrence University Laura Rediehs observes, 'is the strange inversion of technology dictating how we work and what we can do, rather than serving our needs and priorities.'[18]

As humans, we tend to be optimistic about innovation, which isn't a bad thing. It can, however, make us vulnerable, when we assume every new advancement is the road to the promised land. Presently we're seduced into thinking technology is the answer to our many issues – as is, by extension, artificial intelligence. Yet regardless of how scintillating our future tech prospects are, we can't allow them to come at the expense of our humanity and ability to genuinely connect. 'We need to understand how we can harness technology to increase our uniquely human capabilities – creativity, empathy, innovation, communication, connection – and the freedom to use them at work,' states a recent EY/Unilever report and debate, #HumanAtWork. 'Only by being more human can we deliver the growth and sustained economic value we, as a global economy, all seek.'[19] It's essential that we're wary of fixes offering greater ease – not to remain stuck in the past, but because 'easy' rarely comes without its own set of challenges.

While artificial intelligence is proving useful, we're already witnessing a drop in empathy, which is worrying, as empathy is one of the key factors in what makes us human. We need to ensure that those working hard in the artificial intelligence field take into account the importance of empathy, as we're already struggling with an increasingly mechanistic approach to life.

To achieve this, it's important that we take greater care in how we relate to others, and ensure we're not infected by the need for immediate gratification that social media offers – that instead, we're prepared to put in the time and effort to reach out and nurture our friendship groups and contribute in some way to a growing sense of community. These needn't be grand gestures. Sometimes connection is as simple as collecting a neighbour's mail or shopping, or reaching out over a coffee in a moment of need. What's essential is that we bring our whole selves to what we do in these moments, so we can reclaim the opportunity to be deeply listened to and understood.

18

A Vision for the Future

Along with the many stresses that are bearing down on us in the areas of loneliness and isolation, there are the issues of unemployment and a fragile economy resulting from the pandemic. If we're serious about turning around all the estrangement currently felt in our homes, workplaces and communities, it's time now to embrace some of the many opportunities for regeneration that are before us. For too long we've been locked into satisfying our own needs at the expense of our neighbourhoods; chasing what often proved to be transactional relationships, marked by unhealthy forms of competition at work and beyond; embracing every new piece of technology that comes our way; and feeling constantly drained and disconnected in the process. We've also delighted in the multiple disruptions the technosphere has delivered, as well as the endless mash-ups of ideas and products, turning everything from banking and supply chains, to the delivery of fashion and music, on its head. While this has brought us new ways of seeing and experiencing the world, there comes a point when, if we keep on fragmenting, we will fall into chaos.

If we wish to turn around our deepening sense of isolation, we need to focus on finding ways to meaningfully connect, to cohere. Isolation isn't just uncomfortable or heart-breaking, it's damaging to our health, and can catapult us towards shorter lifespans and earlier deaths.[1] Isolation is harmful more broadly, too, making societies fearful and inward-looking, distrustful of others and of innovation. In seeking to reconnect, we have the chance to breathe new life into our homes, our workplaces and our communities.

So how can we help make this happen? We need to recognise that no generation holds all the wisdom. While it's fashionable to knock other generations, to lay all our ills at their door, a house divided is never a productive place to be. Together, as seen in the response to COVID-19 and local disasters, we have the capacity to help each other through the darkest times. And the ordinary times. Together we can draw on a great deal of wisdom and experience, along with new approaches, to surmount the personal and wider issues we face.

Our Biology Helps Point the Way

One of the surprise findings on this journey is how big a part our biology plays in our wellbeing and sense of belonging. Living in our heads, as most of us do, we have forgotten that we're sensory beings, that we operate best when we occupy supportive spaces – at home and at work, and in our cities. Light, sound, texture and the whole feel of a space can actively contribute to our mood, calming and inspiring us, and making it easier to process complex information and to connect.

It's ironic that, at a time when we're facing a sometimes terrifying level of environmental degradation, science is demonstrating how much we're in need of the natural world, not just to recalibrate, but to thrive – how time outside helps our children focus and learn;[2] how natural features can help transform our cities and workspaces, reducing stress and brain fatigue, and helping to calm and inspire. Who would have thought that just a 40-second glance at a city roof garden after a spell of serious concentration can help refresh our brains, enabling us to make fewer mistakes and work more consistently?[3] Or that access to the sounds of nature at work can reduce our stress by more than a third?[4] There's never been a more compelling case for reconnecting with nature, and taking care of our environment.

Fighting Fear

As we seek to move beyond our isolation, we need to pay greater attention to the narratives that we are fed. It's easy to be dismayed by the news, and by the many challenges the planet faces. Yet if we hope to create a brighter tomorrow, we can't allow ourselves to get drawn into all the fear swirling about us, and what for many is a burgeoning sense of hopelessness. Fear is unproductive. It distances us from others, and can so easily paralyse, further causing us to hide away.

These times call for courage – the kind of courage that the builder generation displayed a century ago. While almost all of that generation is gone now, their legacy remains. They taught us just how resilient human beings can be – how to push past our fear and come together to create lives that deliver the purpose and connection we crave – to build for a future we mightn't personally benefit from.

Resourcing the Emerging Generation

We need to support our kids to a greater level than is currently the case. If these children continue to spend large slabs of time in their bedrooms on their devices, their loneliness will only increase. Now, more than ever, we need to ensure we're not raising our children to lead isolated lives.

If there's one thing research into the young generation has taught me, it's that we need to make the time to listen closely to what these children are aching to share, and to respond thoughtfully, showing nuance and empathy. 'A lot of times, the reason we aren't opening up to you is because we don't think you'll take the time to understand the situation and reflect upon it,' tells Jason. 'Instead you'll just jump to the first conclusion that comes up and even with your best intentions, we don't think you'll handle it in a healthy manner so we just end up keeping things to ourselves.'

Children also need practical life skills to face what may prove a bumpy future. We serve them best when we teach them to make and mend; when we surround them with a diverse, supportive village; when we encourage an intimate relationship with nature; and when we teach them how to be skilled face-to-face communicators. We also need to model what empowered, considered adults look like; to help them recognise when they need assistance; and when and how to help others. Such skills teach kids how to connect so that one day they can create their own healthy communities. It's also important that they realise they have a valuable contribution to make. We cannot allow our children to feel overly apprehensive about the future. We need to empower them to believe they will find answers that we can't dream of to current issues, and for them to sense how powerful and exciting their participation in the future can be.

A Healthier Relationship with Our Devices

If we're serious about tackling our growing isolation, we can't afford to let our lives slip past while we're glued to our devices, constantly and obsessively accessing the 24/7 information and entertainment on offer there. We can't afford to be so dazed and distracted that our lives pass in a blur, leaving us reliant on influencers and the number of likes we garner on social media. Our lives and communities are so much richer when we come together in the real world. Let's push back against all the time lost on devices so we can relate meaningfully to each other, and be truly present with those we love.

Now we know that the mere presence of a device suppresses in-depth conversation, let's stow our laptops and smartphones, and commit to fully present one-on-one time instead – so we genuinely get to see and hear those around us. And, if we have to lose ourselves in something, let's do so in the infinite textures, nuances and vibes to be enjoyed in everyday life – by sharing impromptu meals, enjoying time out in nature and scheduling regular device-free evenings. This is about inviting in more spontaneity, as well as creating effortless rituals – regular coffees, walks, meals and time for our passions – that we then share with those who intrigue, challenge and uplift us, and those we care for deeply.

Diving into the Detail

As 'liquid moderns', daily we struggle with a growing sense of restlessness, which has us forever changing plans, jobs and relationships in search of new experiences, forever on the run. Skimming and scrolling our way through the day, our reading has become ever more superficial, as has our take on the world, making it harder to see our way clear of our isolation. To progress we need to be more comfortable with detail, and not assume the first piece of information, or the first or most comfortable opinion we trip across is the best advice, or even that it's correct. This is not the time to so overload our working memory with trivia that we can't think straight, let alone see our way through. This is not the time to retreat and leave all the important decisions for others to work out.

We also need to tackle our often overwhelming exhaustion, which leaves us with no real time to reflect, let alone connect. We can't have an increasing number of individuals, be they 18 or 77 years old, unable to sit quietly for several minutes without using their phone. Or, as indicated in one study, to have people who have no time to relax or sit with their own thoughts, who'd rather self-administer a mild electric shock than sit still.[5]

Ours is an ever more complex world. To navigate it successfully we need to become more comfortable with people and opinions that may differ a little (or a lot) from our own. We need to be more skilled at reaching out, at growing our village, as connection is so much more than just mixing with those of like mind. True connection helps nudge us beyond the familiar. It expands our humanity, encouraging us to meaningfully engage with a diverse range of people, so we can work powerfully together, if need be, in moments of crisis, while enjoying the nuances of daily life that we share. As part of this connection process, we need to nudge our thoughts beyond ourselves and our own needs, to encompass those of others. And instead of spending our days complaining, which can be so isolating, we're far better served if we turn our attention to arriving at new ideas and solutions to the problems we face.

Letting Go of the Need for Perfection

Alongside connecting with those around us, we need to know ourselves more intimately – to be clear about who we are and what feeds us, beyond what others expect of us. Ritu Sharma, director of the US Global Center for Gender and Youth, warns of the insanity and monotony of endlessly seeking to be happy and perfect, encouraging us instead towards 'energy-begetting' choices, rather than those that consume us.[6]

This is a call for greater authenticity and spontaneity, for more courage and honesty. So perhaps this is the perfect time to let go of the need to style and curate every aspect of our lives, and embrace all the joy and messiness of real life. It's easy to get drawn into comparison and end up drowning in our inadequacies. Yet what if we were to take all the energy we waste in competition, and grow our curiosity instead? What if we were to awaken our inner *flâneur* and explore more, try out new passions, and be intrigued and inspired by the wide circle of people we come to meet?

To push beyond our isolation, we must also resist the urge to hide behind our busy lives. For too long we've equated busyness with importance, when in fact it's an exhausting, lonely way to live. It's the kind of lifestyle that catapults us into gaming and streaming, and other forms of non-stop entertainment, as we're simply too tired to do anything else. Instead of trying to grab at everything life sends our way, what if we were to choose less, and spend more time working on our friendships and community – to allow time for contemplation, so we have the space in our heads to envisage more enjoyable and manageable dreams?

Transforming Work

Right now, too many workplaces are in serious need of an overhaul. Having shareholder value as the chief benchmark of success doesn't help. The social and environmental impacts and achievements of organisations also matter. Sadly, too many companies are immersed in self-interest and spin, while often imposing impossible workloads on staff. Too many lack good leadership and stability, and offer little in the way of authentic communication, encouragement or dignity.

Many workspaces are also failing to provide the kind of environment where people can connect and concentrate, let alone thrive. There is a level of distress for a surprising number of people working in open-plan spaces, and far more so with hot-desking, further compromising already fragile work cultures. And while flexi-work is valued by some, we need to be sensitive to how isolating working at home and at odd hours can be for others.

Accustomed to the immediacy and 24/7 availability of technology, we must take care not to regard employees as little more than machines – as always on, endlessly amenable, easy-to-replace workhorses.[7] Workplace remuneration must also be reviewed. Hard questions need to be asked and new lines drawn, given that some CEOs are now paid up to 361 times that of the average employee.[8]

It's also time to turn our 'working late' culture on its head, enabling people to enjoy reasonable work hours, and to have their need for downtime respected. In countries such as Denmark, one of the world's happiest locations, there's a genuine focus on work–life balance, with a 37-hour working week. Not surprisingly, Danes report the highest work satisfaction in the European Union. In Denmark, those working long hours are seen as inefficient and compromising their health.[9]

A Call for a New Kind of Leadership

So much more is also needed from leaders right now – engaging leadership, devoid of spin and half-truths. We need leaders who can be trusted to make good decisions, to create cultures of dignity – capable, well-rounded individuals who are good listeners, and not simply the person giving orders and managing their careers. In this constantly changing landscape, leadership is also less about leaders having all the answers, and more about the ability to home in on relevant issues, and draw out the expertise and innovative solutions from those around them, to find more comprehensive, inclusive ways forward.

Change is challenging, and sometimes distressing. Good leaders hold space, reassure and provide a calm environment from which to move forward. These kinds of leaders are not afraid of conflict. They know that tension is simply a cue that something isn't working as well as it could and needs some remediation. Empowering leaders are consultative and well equipped to help deliver a better way forward.

Nurturing Cityscapes

Alongside our homes and workspaces, we need to take a more comprehensive view of urban space. For too long we have viewed cities as inhospitable places, not realising there are huge opportunities for connection here. With all we're learning about urban space, we now have some powerful tools to help make our cities more intimate – with an abundance of spaces that can soothe and uplift, and help draw us out of our loneliness. Who would have thought that unusual and intriguing, richly textured or nature-inspired urban facades encourage people to linger, to feel safer and be more willing to trust others?[10] Or that the addition of trees and water features, cafe tables and chairs and more, helps grow our sense of connection?

As we seek to extract ourselves from the maze, renowned Danish architect Jan Gehl points the way, showing us that when we choose to live at human scale, we create spaces for young and old, and everyone in between, to feel safe and nurtured, more connected and less stressed. In seeking to revitalise our broken workplaces and neighbourhoods, and reclaim our neglected town and city spaces, we need to pay more attention to the opportunities we have to introduce human scale – people-friendly streetscapes that encourage people to linger, to take part in chance conversations, to grow their sense of belonging.

One of the many surprises on this journey is discovering the number of practical, relatively easy-to-implement solutions there are to help us move beyond our current sense of estrangement. And the potential these new approaches may well have to achieve far more than simply satisfying our all-important need to connect.

I have the sense that if we pause our habits for a moment, and put more thought into the quality of our experiences in our homes, workplaces and communities, we can create environments that are far richer than we experience right now. That with a little will and imagination, these can become encounters and spaces to enjoy, where we and others feel nourished, supported and further inspired to find even more fruitful ways of coming together.

Then, maybe, supported by stronger, more intact communities, we'll find ourselves better placed to tackle the larger planetary issues that currently haunt us. First, though, we need a more nuanced sense of what reconnection can look like – and then to wholeheartedly embrace the power of human scale wherever we can. So never doubt that your choices matter.

'Never doubt that a small group of thoughtful, committed citizens can change the world. Indeed, it's the only thing that ever has.'
Margaret Mead[11]

References

Given there are over 650 references in this work, Murdoch Books invites readers to visit our online portal, which takes you directly to the relevant study, article, interview or book for each reference. Some of the books cited are listed below, but you can find the full list of references by visiting murdochbooks.com.au, searching for 'When We Become Strangers' and clicking on the references tab there.

Anderson, Max and Escher, Peter, *The MBA Oath: Setting a Higher Standard for Business Leaders*, Portfolio, New York, 2010

Balzer, David, *Curationism: How Curating Took Over the Art World and Everything Else*, Coach House Books, Toronto, 2014

Barthes, Roland, *Camera Lucida: Reflections on Photography*, trans. Richard Howard, Hill and Wang, New York, 1980

Cacioppo, John T. and Patrick, William, *Loneliness: Human Nature and the Need For Social Connection*, W. W. Norton & Company, New York, 2009

Cappelli, Peter, *The New Deal at Work: Managing the Market-Driven Workforce*, Harvard Business School Press, Boston, 1999

Carr, Nicholas, *The Shallows: What the Internet Is Doing to Our Brains*, W. W. Norton & Company, New York, 2010

Datar, Srikant M. et al., *Rethinking the MBA: Business Education at a Crossroads*, Harvard Business Press, Boston, 2010

De Pree, Max, *Leadership Is an Art*, Currency, New York, 1987

Gehl, Jan, *Cities for People*, Island Press, Washington DC, 2010

Hamilton, Maggie, *What's Happening to Our Girls? Too Much Too Soon, How Our Kids Are Overstimulated, Oversold and Oversexed*, Viking, Melbourne, 2009

Hochschild, Arlie Russell, *The Managed Heart: Commercialization of Human Feeling*, University of California Press, Berkeley, 1983

Hopper, Kenneth and Hopper, William, *The Puritan Gift: Triumph, Collapse and Revival of an American Dream Amidst Global Financial Chaos*, I.B. Tauris, New York, 2009

Kellert, Stephen R., *Birthright: People and Nature in the Modern World*, Yale University Press, New Haven, 2012

Keys, Donald, *Earth at Omega: Passage to Planetization*, Branden Press, Massachusetts, 1982

Khurana, Rakesh, *From Higher Aims to Hired Hands: The Social Transformation of American Business Schools and the Unfulfilled Promise of Management as a Profession*, Princeton University Press, Princeton, 2007

Lasch, Christopher, *The Culture of Narcissism: American Life in An Age of Diminishing Expectations*, W. W. Norton & Company, New York, 1979

Levitin, Daniel J., *The Organized Mind: Thinking Straight in the Age of Information Overload*, Penguin, London, 2015

Mackay, Hugh, *Reinventing Australia: The Mind and Mood of Australia in the 90s*, HarperCollins, Sydney, 1993

McDonald, Duff, *The Golden Passport: Harvard Business School, the Limits of Capitalism, and the Moral Failure of the MBA Elite*, Harper Business, New York, 2017

Putnam, Robert D., *Bowling Alone: The Collapse and Revival of American Community*, Simon & Schuster, New York, 2000

Schawbel, Dan, *Back to Human: How Great Leaders Create Connection in the Age of Isolation*, Perseus Books, New York, 2018

Twenge, Jean M., *iGen: Why Today's Super-Connected Kids Are Growing Up Less Rebellious, More Tolerant, Less Happy – and Completely Unprepared for Adulthood – and What That Means for the Rest of Us*, Simon & Schuster, New York, 2017

Warren, Rick, *The Purpose Driven Life: What on Earth Am I Here For?*, Zondervan, Grand Rapids, 2002

Wolf, Maryanne, *Reader, Come Home: The Reading Brain in a Digital World*, HarperCollins, New York, 2018

Sometimes when contemplating our isolation or loneliness, unwelcome thoughts and feelings arise that we can't shift on our own. At such times, it's a good idea to reach out to your local doctor, or call *Lifeline Australia* on 13 11 14 or *Beyond Blue* on 1300 22 4636 for some solid help. In the United Kingdom, call *Samaritans* on 116 123; in the United States call *Lifeline* on 1 800 273 8255; or in New Zealand call *Lifeline* on 0800 543 354.

Appreciation

This has been a huge project, and one that's taught me far more than I thought possible. *When We Become Strangers* would not have seen the light of day were it not for the kindness and encouragement of so many, and for the sometimes feisty, yet always insightful interrogations I received along the way. Huge thanks to all those who've lent their voices, opinions and expertise to these pages, enriching them immeasurably.

Thanks to Matt Hay, whose gift of Sasha Sagan's *For Small Creatures Such as We* inspired my new chapter with Murdoch Books. Thanks, too, to publishing director Lou Johnson for her immediate response to and interest in the subject.

I am so grateful for the wisdom, warmth and passion of my publisher Kelly Doust. Much appreciation, too, to Kristy Allen and Josh Durham for such a beautiful jacket and design; for the deft and insightful work of my editor Justine Harding, and that of editorial manager Justin Wolfers. Thanks, too, to head of marketing and communication Carol Warwick, whose encouragement and hard work is every writer's dream; and to Kaitlyn Smith, whose behind-the-scenes efforts helped keep the whole process on track.

Thanks, too, to my precious writer friends – Walter Mason and Rosamund Burton, Belinda Alexandra, Josephine Dee Barrett, Chris McCourt, Sarah Smith and Catherine Milne, who understand the joys and despair encountered during each writing journey. Much gratitude also to the many who have worked tirelessly on my former books, for their selfless support in helping me reach this place.

Limitless thanks to my beautiful soul sisters – my dearest friends – you know who you are. Thank you for your ongoing love and belief in me, in being there to listen and reassure, and for never failing me.

None of my writing would be possible without my beloved Derek. We've journeyed far through good times and those that stretch – thank you for your constancy and for being the wind beneath my wings. And my humblest thanks to the Great Spirit, who inspires me to continue to explore new horizons, and to find new ways to question and celebrate this mystery we call life.